PRINCIPLES AND PRACTICES OF GRADING, DRAINAGE AND ROAD ALIGNMENT

PRINCIPLES AND PRACTICES OF GRADING, DRAINAGE AND ROAD ALIGNMENT

AN ECOLOGIC APPROACH

RICHARD K. UNTERMANN

Associate Professor
College of Architecture and Urban Planning
Department of Landscape Architecture
University of Washington

RESTON PUBLISHING COMPANY, INC.
A Prentice-Hall Company
Reston, Virginia

Library of Congress Cataloging in Publication Data

Untermann, Richard K.
    Principles and practices of grading, drainage, and road alignment.
    Bibliography: p.
    Includes index.
    1. Road construction.   2. Road drainage.
I. Title.
TE145.U62   625.7'3   78-2939
ISBN 0-87909-641-1

© 1978 by
Reston Publishing Company, Inc.
A Prentice-Hall Company
Reston, Virginia 22090

10 9 8 7 6 5 4 3 2

Printed in the United States of America.

CONTENTS

CONTENTS

PREFACE

This text covers the basic principles of grading, drainage, and road alignment. Grading is simply the manipulation of ground form, and is in a sense the backbone of site design. Grading, drainage, and other construction courses are frightening for most design students, as they involve mathematics, technical skills and a special language. This document changes all that by presenting an easy-to-do, nontechnical approach to grading. In fact, 90 percent of the mathematics normally associated with engineering construction has been eliminated.

This book can be used as an introductory text, and is divided into ten sections, which conforms to most college quarter time schedules.

The text has been prepared for all designers—civil engineers, landscape architects, architects, construction engineers and horticulturalists. Our object is to help designers become fully versed in the principles of grading, drainage, and road alignment in order that they may be capable of manipulating ground form from a design and ecologic point of view. The term ecologic is used in its simplest sense—to better understand the relationship between grading and what happens to the environment. Man has literally changed the face of the earth, and in so doing has eliminated approximately one third of the vegetative material and created many ecological disbalances. The text explains common ecologic problems created by grading, and offers alternative approaches to minimizing disturbances.

There are many facets to grading, which we have narrowed into two categories:

1. *How to grade:* mastery of methods and techniques for manipulation of earth forms. This includes the use of *contours* and *sections* to study and express design molding of the ground form.

Figure A
This book emphasizes an ecological approach to grading, with a bias to reduce grading whenever possible. This bias should not be interpreted as anti-city, for cities provide stimulating places to live, and because of their density may reduce the need to grade elsewhere.

2. *When not to grade:* a perspective developed through practical experience, enabling the designer to judge which constraints should guide proper grading. These constraints include soil type, mechanical problems, cost problems, alternative design solutions, esthetic and ecological considerations, etc.

The first several chapters describe approaches to develop skill in graphic manipulation of ground form; the following chapters introduce different constraints and considerations to the design process (Fig. A).

The text is divided into ten chapters, each forming a weekly lesson. Each chapter covers a topic through an introductory level and includes, where appropriate, examples, practice exercises, field exercises and review questions. There are six major grading and drainage problems that will build technical as well as graphic skills, a glossary and several appendixes. Complex formulas for vertical curves or for sizing pipes or for determining the cross section of a drainage channel are not included, as they often blur the principles involved.

RICHARD K. UNTERMANN

PRINCIPLES AND PRACTICES OF GRADING, DRAINAGE AND ROAD ALIGNMENT

INTRODUCTION
TO GRADING

Grading is the act of remodeling the form of the land. It is one of the most important tasks in site design and construction and is performed to accomplish *three* main purposes:

1. To create a flat area to put something on (a house, car, playfield, commercial building, etc.; Figs. 1–1 and 1–4).
2. To create circulation ways flat enough to travel on (a roadway, foot path, loading ramp, train track, bicycle trail, etc.; Fig. 1–2).
3. To create special effects or solve technical problems (to save a tree; mound soil to hide a parking lot; achieve the maximum gradient, yet prevent erosion or landslide; allow a lawn to be mowed; reclaim mined land, etc.; Fig. 1–3).

Figure 1-1

Figure 1-2

Figure 1-3

Figure 1-4
This Grade-All is filling and leveling a slight valley for use as a playfield. This particular piece of equipment scrapes, loads, and carries earth to another location where it can be dumped.

Grading is done whenever anything is built, moved, or changed in our landscape. Usually, grading is carried on *without* consideration for the special problems, considerations, and potentials necessary to assure a proper job. Grading can be simply moving several wheelbarrows of earth with a rake and shovel, or a massive operation moving thousands of cubic yards of earth through difficult terrain for a new freeway.

DRAINAGE — Drainage is an absolutely integral part of any grading project and will be considered in the same manner, that is, first, to learn the mechanical methods to drain a site, and then to complicate the picture with "other considerations" that affect drainage.

GRADING — Grading is an integral part of the entire design process. From the first analytical step, to final construction, decisions on grading methods, amount of grading, cost, etc., all these can be valuable inputs for decision making. When a designer first sees a site and begins to *analyze* and *develop a program,* he should ask questions such as: are there any constraints to grading such as soil type, rock outcrop, trees, water table, drainage pattern, etc.? When *conceptualizing* a design approach, questions of character or function may suggest a grading relationship: i.e., should the land form flow in a natural manner, or be restrained in a precise engineered form? Do truck or handicapped access or special uses require minimum gradients or large level use areas which suggest a preferred access route or use area?

As the design is further developed, and reaches a *schematic* phase, a rough grading and drainage plan is usually prepared to assure that the proposal works. Further into *design development,* a cut/fill calculation may be made, and the previous grading plan refined. The final design phase — *contact drawings* — is where the exact landform is determined, all drainage structures described and details worked out. During actual construction, grading and drainage may be further adjusted to save a tree, minimize cutting into a bank, or prevent an undesirable drainage pattern which was not previously anticipated.

CONTOUR LINES

Contour lines are the primary two-dimensional graphic convention used to delineate three-dimensional ground form. Contour lines show landform and the relationships of landforms. Contour lines were first used by Cruquius, a Dutchman, in about 1730 to represent the bottom configuration of a river. Others, perhaps independently, seized upon the idea of representing dry land surface with a familiar type of line symbol; but it was not until relatively late in the nineteenth century that contours became the common method of depicting terrain on survey maps. *Hachures,* another technique to depict terrain utilizing shading, was developed in the late eighteenth century, but never gained prominence owing to the difficulty of manipulating them to indicate landform change.

A contour line is a line drawn on a plan that connects all points of equal elevation above or below a known or assumed reference point. Therefore, all points on the contour line have the same elevation in reference to a common base. Contour lines express surface modulation and changing them indicates a change of ground form. To "move" a contour line $\frac{1}{2}$ inch (in.) in reality may mean moving a ton of earth 50 feet (ft).

Contour lines are used (1) to study proposed changes in landform, and eventually (2) to guide and direct the work of earthmoving contractors in executing the grading project.

Contours show landforms (a hill, valley, ridge, hogback, etc.). They show the relationships of landforms—this hill to that valley, to this stream, and finally to the ocean. As contours are shown two dimensionally, the scaled distance between them is exactly the same as in the field.

All grading plans have a vertical contour interval that should remain the same over the entire drawing. This interval stands for the vertical distance between contours, and is always indicated somewhere on the plan. Typical contour intervals are 1, 2, 5, 10, 25, or 100 ft.

Proposed and existing contours are both shown on the same drawing, which makes it possible to understand the exact location of work to be performed and the exact amount of earth to be moved. *Existing contours* are shown by a light dashed line (usually $\frac{1}{4}$ in. long, spaced about $\frac{1}{16}$ in. apart). Every fifth contour is shown slightly darker for legibility. *Proposed contours* are shown as a solid light line. This solid line begins where you propose to make a grading change, and moves away from the existing (dashed) contour, returning to the existing (dashed) contour at the end of the proposed grading change. It is therefore possible to "read" the change by studying the area between proposed contours and existing contours.

Contour lines are labeled with the number on the *high* side of the contour. Each contour line corresponds to a selected vertical interval, which may be 1 ft, 2 ft, 10 ft, etc. Generally, all contour lines on a map indicate the same interval. Be sure to label the interval somewhere on the map (Fig. 1–5).

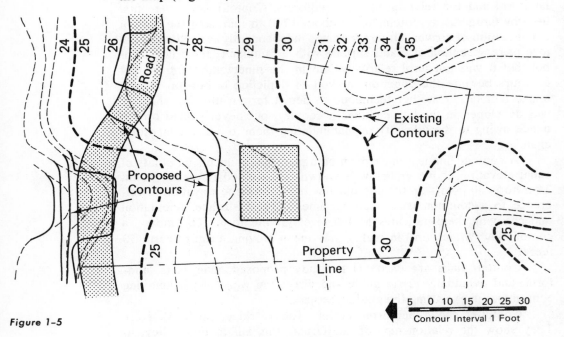

Figure 1–5

On generally flat sites where there is little vertical relief, the interval should be 1 or 2 ft, whereas in an area of marked relief the contour interval may be 5 or 10 ft, or even as large as 25 or 100 ft. If the relief changes from slight to marked within the limits of a map, intermediate contours can be dropped, or the contour interval changed from a small to a larger one for the marked relief.

"Reading" changes in contours is tricky, but can be mastered with practice. Basically, proposed grading changes either *add* earth (called *filling*) or *remove* earth (called *cutting*). A proposed contour that moves in the direction of a lower contour indicates adding earth (filling). For instance (see Fig. 1–6), proposed contour 7 moves in the direction of a lower contour 6 and indicates filling.

Conversely, a proposed contour that moves in the direction of a higher contour indicates removing earth (cutting). This can be seen where contour 8 moves in the direction of contour 9 and is removing earth (cutting). The amount of earth to be added or removed can be determined by comparing the proposed contour with the existing contours it crosses. Every contour crossed means cutting or filling an amount equal to that contour interval.

Profiles or cross sections can be easily constructed from contours and, conversely, contour locations can be determined from a profile. A freehand cross section is the best way to understand what the contours are doing. To construct a profile, draw a straight line through the contours and carefully measure the distance between each contour. Transfer these measurements to a piece of lined profile paper, and use the same scale to indicate horizontal and vertical scales. When all points have been located, connect the points with a freehand line and the profile should be accurate. (See Fig. 1–7.)

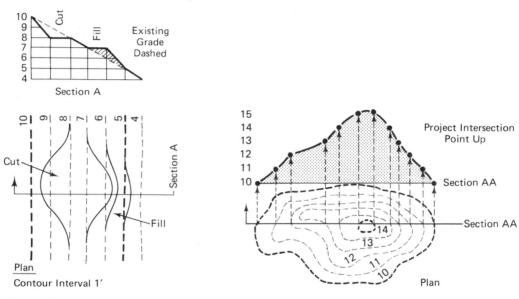

Figure 1-6

Figure 1-7

The most typical earth forms used in grading are described and illustrated next. Study each until you understand the connection between the contours and the actual form.

Valleys are represented by contours that point *uphill*. To construct the section, draw first the line where the section is to be taken (labeled line A); then project parallel lines up at each place a contour crosses line A. Somewhere above, draw lines parallel to A, and scaled the same as the contour interval. The point where both lines cross becomes the section line, and one has only to connect these points to complete the section (Fig. 1–8 a & b).

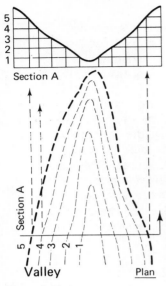

Section A

Section A

Valley

Plan

Figure 1–8(a)

Figure 1–8(b)   Valley with contours superimposed.

Summits are indicated by concentric, closed contours, plus adequate contour labeling to distinguish them from depressions. Depressions are often marked with hachures, and both should include spot elevations at the highest or lowest point. Summits drain well; depressions collect water (Figs. 1–9 through 1–11).

Spot elevations are additional number labels used to clarify the exact elevation that falls between two contours, such as 7.25, 6.75, or 21.93. Spot elevations are usually carried to the hundredth decimal point.

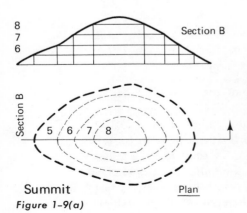

Section B

Section B

Summit

Plan

Figure 1–9(a)

Figure 1–9(b)   Summit with contours superimposed.

Figure 1-10
Grading a pond is really creating a depression, which is shown in plan form as concentric circles.

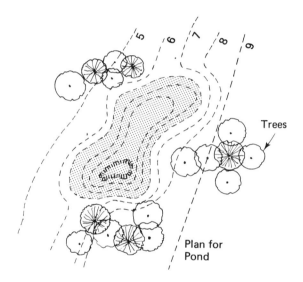

Trees

Plan for
Pond

Figure 1-11

Ridges look like a valley, but with the contours pointing *downhill* (note carefully the contour labeling, for this is the easiest way to determine if it is a ridge or valley). Ridges and valleys are often very wide, and may be difficult to distinguish on a large-scale map (Fig. 1–12).

Concave slopes are shown with parallel contours, each spaced further apart and with the closely spaced contours at the highest elevation (Fig. 1–13).

A convex slope is shown with parallel contours each spaced farther apart, but with the closely spaced contours at the lower elevations. Convex and concave landforms are the most common forms found in nature and should be well understood by designers. All transitions between flat and sloping land should be either a convex or concave slope (Fig. 1–14 a & b).

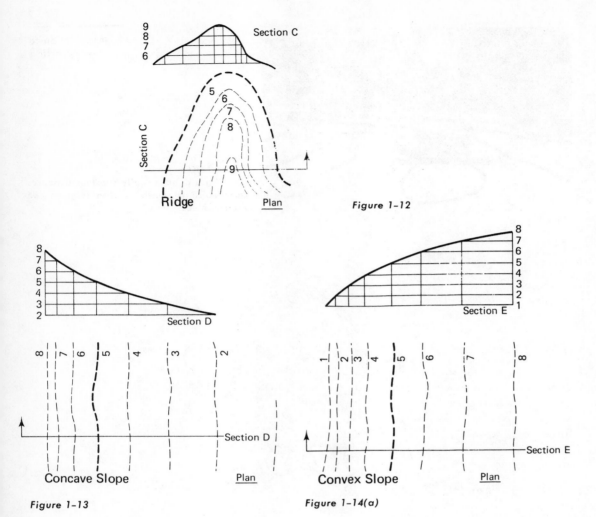

9
8
7
6
Section C

5
6
7
8
9
Section C
Ridge   Plan

Figure 1-12

8
7
6
5
4
3
2
Section D

8 7 6 5 4 3 2
Section D
Concave Slope   Plan

Figure 1-13

8
7
6
5
4
3
2
1
Section E

1 2 3 4 5 6 7 8
Section E
Convex Slope   Plan

Figure 1-14(a)

Figure 1-14(b)
Convex and concave slopes usually are found in pairs
in the landscape. Note the overpass that separates
pedestrians from auto traffic.

8

Two adjacent contours with the same numbers indicate either the top of a ridge or the bottom of a valley. Once again, the contour label indicates which it is, so check carefully (Fig. 1–15).

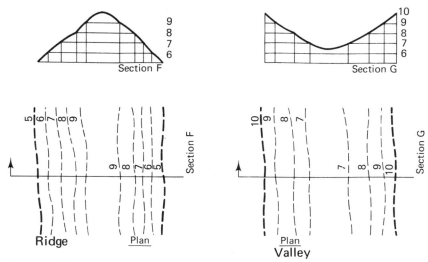

Figure 1–15

Drainage always occurs perpendicular *(at right angles)* to the contours. The perpendicular line is the shortest distance between contours, and hence the steepest route (see Fig. 1–16). Runoff naturally seeks the easiest (steepest) route as it travels downhill. Drainage landforms, such as channels, ditches, and valleys, are indicated by contours that point *uphill,* and are sometimes made more obvious by drawing an arrow in the direction of drainage or labeling it a swale (Figs. 1–17 and 1–18).

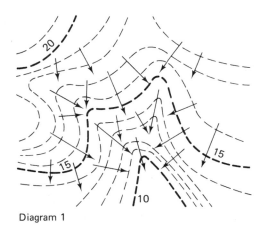

Diagram 1

Figure 1–16

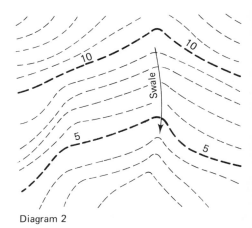

Diagram 2

Figure 1–17

Figure 1-18
Standing water is the result of a poorly designed grading plan. It is essential that every
grading plan be thoroughly checked to assure
adequate slope for drainage.

CHARACTERISTICS OF CONTOURS

See Figure 1-19 for clarification.

1. All points on a contour line have the same elevation. A contour line connects points of equal elevation.
2. Every contour closes on itself somewhere, either within or beyond the limits of the map. In the latter case, the contours will run to the edge of the page.
3. A contour that closes on itself within the limits of the drawing is either a *summit* or a *depression*. Depressions are usually indicated by a spot elevation at the lowest point, or by placing short hachure marks on the *low* side of the contour (see no. 3 for depression and no. 3a for summit).
4. Contour lines never cross other contours. The only exceptions are unusual landforms, such as a hanging cliff, natural bridge, or pierced or arched rock.
5. Contours that are equally spaced indicate a uniform sloping surface (see no. 5).
6. On a convex slope, contours are shown spaced at increasing intervals going up a hill; the higher contours are spaced farther apart than the lower contours (see no. 6).
7. On a concave slope, the contours are shown spaced at increasing intervals with the lower contour lines spaced further apart than the higher ones (see no. 7).
8. Valleys are indicated by contours pointing *uphill* (see no. 8). In crossing a valley, contour lines run up the valley on one side, turn and cross the stream, and run back the other side.
9. Contours that are close together indicate a *steep* slope (see no. 9).
10. Contours that are spaced far apart indicate a relatively level site or slight grade (see no. 10).
11. Contours never split in two; however, you will occasionally see two side-by-side contours numbered the same. This indicates

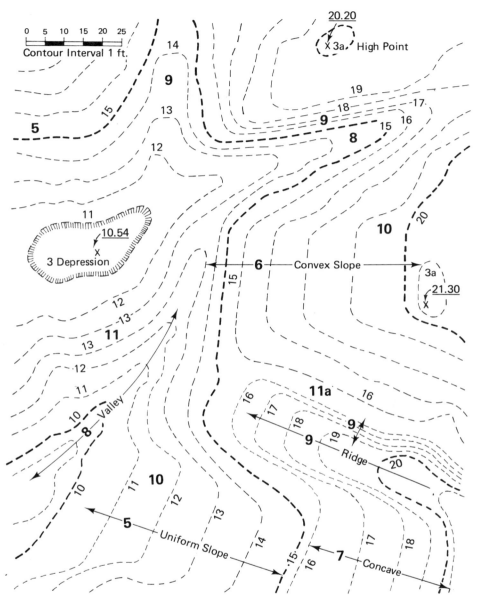

Figure 1-19

either a high or a low area. It will be high (see no. 11) if the numbers for both contours fall between the contours, or low (see no. 11a) if the numbers don't.

12. Contours are labeled on the high side—always.

Most topographic maps are made from aerial photographs by utilizing special stereo viewing equipment, which, by a means of a focusing device, scans the aerial map to determine a line of equal elevation. This line is, of course, a *contour line*. By locating established markers, the precise elevation can be determined, and all other contours will be accurate.

EXERCISE 1

TO HELP VISUALIZE CONTOURS, DRAW SOME FULL-SCALE CONTOUR LINES — Contour lines don't occur in the real landscape; they are imaginary lines used to depict landforms or plans. This makes visualizing them somewhat difficult. One method to overcome this is to draw imaginary contours on paved land. Find some heavy pieces of chalk, go outside, and start drawing contour lines on the land. Start first with a paved parking lot, but don't expect to draw exact contours. Begin somewhere at an assumed elevation, say the corner of the lot, and carefully eyeball *level* lines to see why contours take certain shapes.

This technique is particularly useful for visualizing what happens to contours at a curb, retaining wall, stairs, crowned road, or sloping sidewalk. Move from the parking lot into a roadway, patio, pedestrian walkway, or playground. The secret is to keep the contour lines approximately *level* at the same elevation.

OTHER METHODS OF DEPICTING TOPOGRAPHY AND GRADE CHANGE

Topographic relief can also be shown as follows:

By shading
With spot elevations
With profiles and sections
By a scale relief model
Through symbolic representations

SHADING

Shading is achieved by varying the line weight, or spacing lines different distances apart. Relief and topographic features are shown by shading the slopes in proportion to their degree of slope. Steep slopes are shaded darker than slight ones.

HACHURES

Hachures show relief by means of short disconnected lines drawn in the direction of drainage. The thickness and spacing of the hachures indicate the degree of slope. Make them heavy with closer spacing for steeper slopes and light with wider spacing for slight slopes. In effect, you draw approximate contour lines, and then fill them in with hachures (Fig. 1–20).

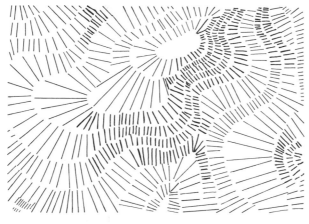

Figure 1–20

Before hachures can be drawn, it is necessary to draw approximate contours. The hachures are then drawn perpendicular to the two successive contours and spaced equal to one quarter of the distance between them. This rule for spacing contours is called the *quarter rule.* For extra clarity, make steep slope hachures thicker than those for shallow slopes.

CHARACTERISTICS OF HACHURES

A hachure is the shortest distance between two successive contours.

Hachures are always perpendicular to two successive contours.

Hachures show the direction of drainage down a slope.

When the hachures are heavy and close together, they show a steep slope; when they are light and far apart, a slight slope.

Flat surfaces, such as hilltops, plateaus, and river bottom lands, are shown by white spaces. Hilltops are identified by spot elevations and reference to other terrain features; valleys are identified by a stream line.

ADVANTAGES AND DISADVANTAGES OF HACHURING AND SHADING — Hachured maps are easier for most people to read than contour maps, but it is extremely difficult to determine precise elevations from them unless indicated by spot elevations. The range of hachuring is small. It is impossible to show many different degrees of slope, and determination of a precise degree of slope is somewhat difficult. It is very hard to show slight folds in the ground, and steep slopes can be shown only at the cost of obscuring other details of the map. Hachures are difficult to draw in the field. A large number of old maps have been made using this system of relief, but it is gradually falling into disuse; probably only very small-scale maps will be made using this system in the future.

SHOWING GRADE CHANGES WITH SPOT ELEVATIONS — Spot elevations are used in detail grading to indicate elevations that fall between contours. A spot elevation is simply a written number corresponding to the proposed elevation with an × marking the spot where critical grading or drainage elevations must be shown. Spot elevations are normally shown as a whole number plus decimals; for instance, 15.19 is designated by an × mark on the exact spot where the proposed elevation is located. Spot elevations can be used to indicate high points, low points, bottoms of walls, tops of curbs, breaks in direction of drainage, etc. Spot elevations can also be used between contours where specific or critical elevation must be indicated, for instance, the elevation of a tree to be saved (Fig. 1–21).

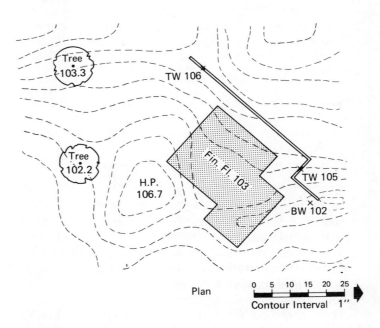

Figure 1–21

SHOWING PROPOSED GRADES USING PROFILES AND SEC-TIONS—Profiles and sections are often used to depict grades for circulation routes, although they can be used for all design areas. *Profiles* are usually taken along the length of the route, and show elevations of the center line and curb by outlining both the existing and proposed topography. Sections show existing and proposed grading through (at right angles to) the roadway, including shoulders, road surfaces, etc. Sections show proposed work as well as limits of cut, limits of fill, widths of road, sidewalks, curbs, etc. (for additional information, see Chapter 4) (Fig. 1–22).

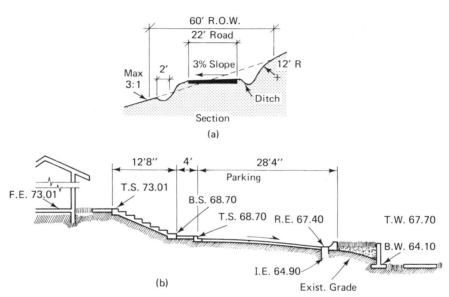

Figure 1–22   Vertical exaggeration is sometimes used to clarify or emphasize a point—be sure to note any exaggerations on the drawings. (e.g., 1" hor. = 2" vert.)

DEPICTING TOPOGRAPHY WITH A SCALED RELIEF MODEL— Contour plans can be transformed into a useful three-dimensional model by tracing the contours onto a layer of cardboard whose thickness approximates the contour interval and gluing the layers together. With elaborate model-making equipment, a topographic model can be carved from polystyrene, using the contour interval to show ground form. These models are normally expensive and not used in student work, but to help the public or a client visualize the project. The vertical elevation can be slightly exaggerated to make grade changes more obvious. (See Fig. 1–23.)

Figure 1-23
Complex urban development such as this cannot be adequately described with contours, and requires many spot elevations, sections, profiles, and possibly even a model.

SYMBOLIC RELIEF—Landforms also can be expressed symbolically with the degree of relationship not stated. For instance, a South Sea Islander's treasure chart, an Aztec map, a tourist guide to New York, a nautical chart, all use pictures to describe layout and elevation.

Converting contours from two to three dimensions is a useful variation of symbolic relief. These sketches help designers visualize landform and should be used at the conceptual design stage. (See Fig. 1–24.) They are really a refined doodle used to develop or design a desired landform.

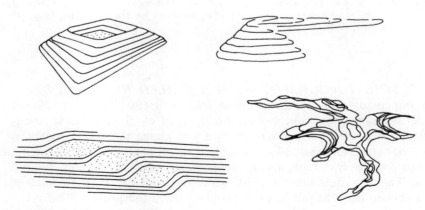

Figure 1-24 Conceptual landforms.

EXERCISE 2
THE HOLLOW CONTOUR MODEL

The following is a brief explanation describing simple techniques needed to construct a hollow contour model. We will use this type of model to help understand contour manipulations. However, this model construction method is worth mastering because of its ease of construction and fine finished appearance.

For this exercise, use two pieces of 8½- by 11-in. cardboard plus a piece for the base. Use any type of cardboard or wood to construct the model. Other materials needed will be glue (white glue is best), cardboard, carbon paper, matt knife, and pencil.

FIRST — Examine the contour maps carefully to make sure that you understand *all* the contours. Trace the contours on two pieces of board using the carbon paper until you have two exact copies of the contour map.

SECOND — From one of the boards cut out *every other* contour line. From the second board, cut the remaining contour lines.

THIRD — When all the contours are cut, glue them together by aligning the contour lines. Start from the lowest contour. You may put the contours on a base or make the model from only the landforms. Support the "edges" of the model as necessary. (See Fig. 1–25.)

When you have completed the first exercise, begin the second. Be neat! Align the contours carefully. Sand rough edges and wipe off excess glue before it dries.

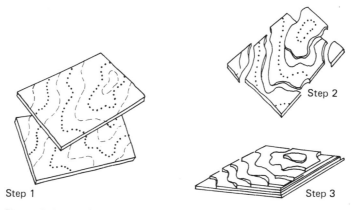

Step 1   Step 2   Step 3

Figure 1–25 Hollow core model.

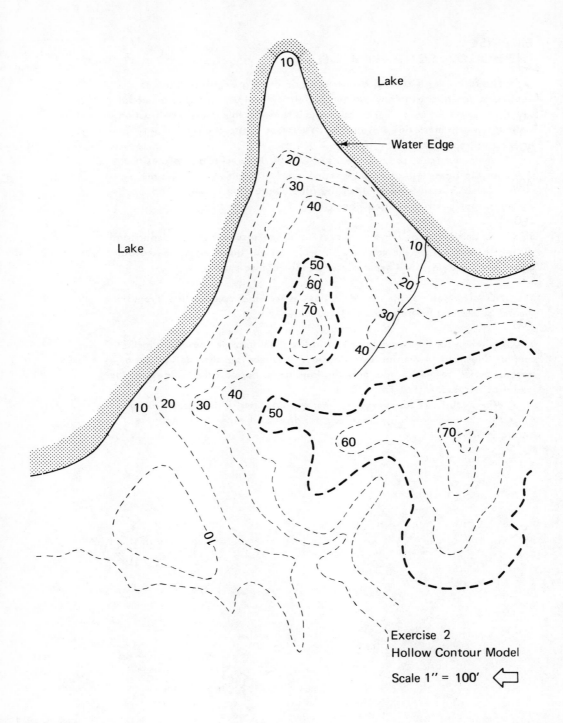

Lake

Water Edge

Lake

10

20

30

40

50
60
70

10

20

30

40

10   20   30   40

50

60

70

10

Exercise 2
Hollow Contour Model

Scale 1″ = 100′

18

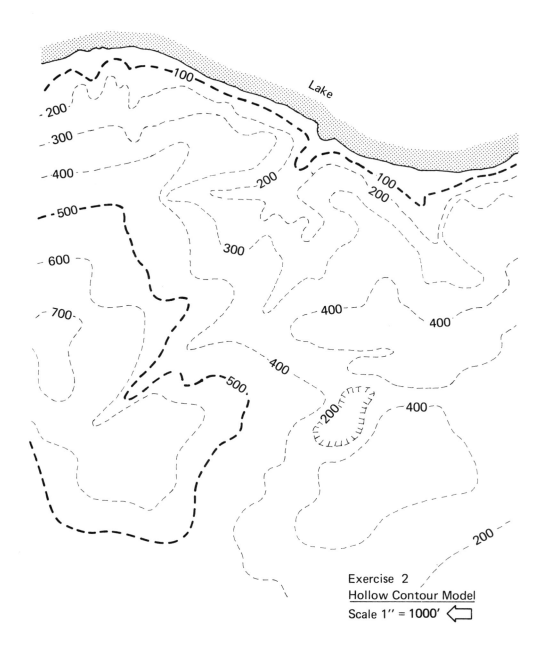

Lake

100

200

300

400

500

600

700

200

100

200

300

200

400

400

500

400

200

400

200

Exercise 2
Hollow Contour Model
Scale 1″ = 1000′

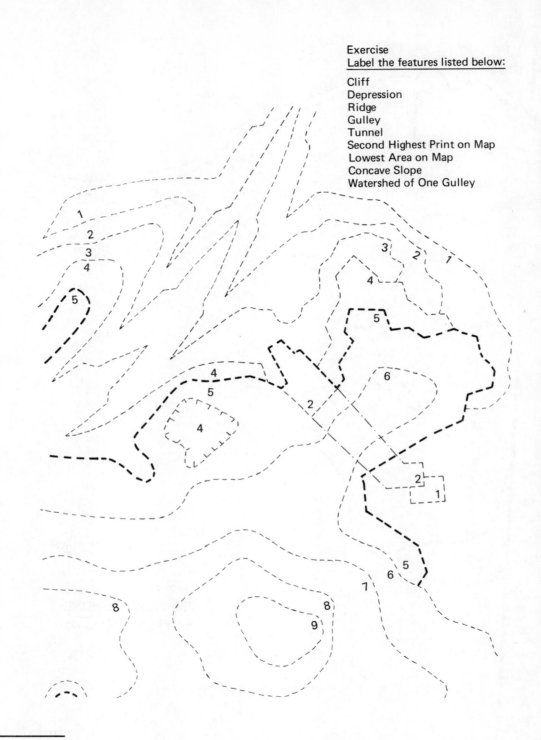

Exercise
Label the features listed below:

Cliff
Depression
Ridge
Gulley
Tunnel
Second Highest Print on Map
Lowest Area on Map
Concave Slope
Watershed of One Gulley

STUDY QUESTIONS

1. Grading is the act of remodeling the landform.
   (a) True   (b) False

2. Grading is performed to accomplish three main purposes. Which of the following is not one of these?
   (a) To create level areas for man's use.
   (b) To create circulation ways.
   (c) To create special effects and solve special problems.
   (d) To disturb existing vegetation.

3. A contour line
   (a) Connects points of different elevations above a known datum.
   (b) Connects points of the same elevation above a known datum.

4. A valley would be shown on a contour map with the contours pointing
   (a) Uphill.
   (b) Downhill.

5. A ridge would show on a contour map with the contours pointing
   (a) Uphill.
   (b) Downhill.

6. In topographic terms, a "hogback" is a form of valley.
   (a) True   (b) False

7. A depression is indicated on a plan by a series of concentric circular contour lines. The inner one is usually marked with hachures.
   (a) True   (b) False

8. Contour lines that are spaced equally indicate
   (a) A convex slope.
   (b) A concave slope.
   (c) A uniform slope.
   (d) None of the above.

9. On a convex slope, contours are spaced at increasing intervals going up the slope; the higher contours are spaced closer together than the lower ones.
   (a) Statement is entirely false.
   (b) First part of statement is wrong.
   (c) Second part of statement is wrong.
   (d) The entire statement is correct.
   (e) Let's forget the whole thing!

10. The steepest area on a slope runs parallel to the contours.
    (a) True   (b) False

11. The contour interval of a map is
    (a) The horizontal distance between contours.
    (b) The distance above mean sea level.
    (c) Equal to the vertical distance divided by the horizontal distance.
    (d) All the above.
    (e) None of the above.

GRADING FLAT AREAS

Buildings, parking areas, playfields—most elements we build require a fairly flat pad to sit on. We say fairly flat, for if they were dead level they would not drain and would be too wet or icy to use in winter. Therefore, these flat areas must slope slightly and be graded properly to assure adequate drainage.

Grading to make a flat area is accomplished in one of three ways:

1. By cutting into the slope (Fig. 2–1).
2. By filling out from the slope.
3. By a combination of cutting and filling (Fig. 2–2).

To clarify cutting and filling, grading consists of two basic operations:

Removing earth *(called cutting)*.
Adding earth *(called filling)*.

Figure 2–1
Grading by cutting into the slope. This steep slope was cut to create a flat pad for a building. Foundation and retaining walls will be constructed along the steep slope and new material used to fill the excavation following construction.

Figure 2-2
Grading by combination of cut and fill.
The various levels of this courtyard were
created by filling earth on a level site.
The soil was cut elsewhere on the site to
accommodate a parking garage.

A grading plan tells the contractor where to remove earth (cut) and where to add earth (fill).

GRADING PROCEDURE

The grading procedure is basically very simple, almost mechanical. The area to be graded flat is first located, approximate finish grades are established, the slope steepness for new banks is set, and the grading method (cut, fill, or combination) is determined. Contours can then be laid out in an almost mechanical process.

- The flat area should be large enough to accommodate the proposed use plus room for circulation around buildings.
- The finish grade can be set at any grade, but it will be easier if you use a grade 0.5 ft (½ ft) above or below the whole number you select (i.e., 7.5, 6.5, or 82.5). This simplifies the location of each contour, as you will see.
- The slope of new banks can be as steep as you want, limited only by soil type, erosion potential, and esthetics. Use of a 1:3 slope (1-ft rise per 3-ft horizontal distance) for cut banks and a 1:4 slope for fill banks is suggested. We will discuss how to choose the proper slope ratio in later chapters.

GRADING TO MAKE AN AREA FLAT BY CUTTING INTO THE BANK

This method creates a flat area surrounded by three sloping walls; the two side walls become higher toward the back, with the rear wall being the tallest. First, locate the proposed flat area on the topographic map. Determine the finish grade by locating the contour just *below* and outside the flat area and *raising it 0.5 ft* (½ ft). This grade will become the *finish grade* for the flat area. Move up to the next higher contour, and wrap it around behind (above) the flat area and back along the other side, connecting to the same contour. As this contour is *higher* than the proposed finish grade, it is located enough distance behind the level area to allow room for the slope up (2 ft back when using 1:3 slope ratio). Move to the next higher contour and wrap it around the flat area, maintaining the same distance between contours as before, and connecting back to the same existing contour. Continue up the bank until there are no more contours passing through the flat area or the adjusted contours. Draw proposed contours as a light, solid freehand line with a pencil (never use ink as it cannot be easily changed).

In Figure 2–3a, the area to be graded flat is shown with a dotted pattern. Contour 2 is the lowest contour not passing through this flat area and should be *raised 0.5 ft* to become the finish grade (at 2.5). Contour 3 is wrapped around behind the flat area and returned to join the *same* contour. (Note the use of *solid* lines to designate proposed contours.) Now do the same with contours 4 and 5. Existing contour 6 passes by without any interference and does not have to be adjusted. Keep each contour a scaled 3 ft apart to allow room for the 1:3 slope up between them. (See Fig. 2–3b.)

To explain the "slope up," if the contour interval is 1 ft, and you want to maintain a 1:3 slope (3 ft horizontal to 1 ft vertical), the contour must be 3 ft behind the flat area. If the contour interval is 5 ft, you must select a slope for the proposed banks that is *steeper* then the existing slope, or you will never be able to meet existing grade. *Meeting the grade* is jargon that describes the point at which proposed grading ends. One normally attempts to minimize grading by *meeting grade* as soon as possible.

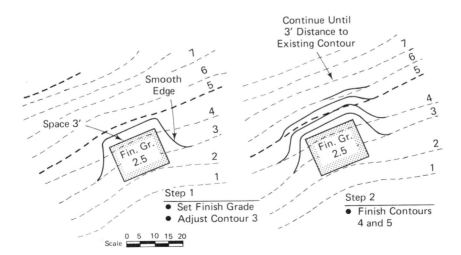

Figure 2–3(a)

Figure 2–3(b)
Flat area in cut with superimposed contours.

GRADING A FLAT AREA BY FILLING

This is essentially the opposite of the cut method just described. Rather than scooping out a section of the hill, you add fill to the hill, building up a flat area over existing contours. To begin, locate the area to be flat, set finish grade at 0.5 ft *below* the highest contour not passing through the proposed flat area. Now move down to the next lower contour, wrap it around the flat area toward the direction of the lower contours, and reconnect it to the same existing contour at the other side. Continue down the slope by wrapping contours around until all the affected contours have been completed. Space contours far enough apart to allow the slope down between contours.

EXAMPLE — As contour 5 (Fig. 2–4) is out of and above the flat area, 4:5 becomes the finish grade. Begin next with contour 4, wrap it around the flat area, and return to the *same* contour. Do the same with contour 2. Space each contour 3 ft apart to accommodate a 1:3 slope.

If we look carefully at the "flat" areas we have been grading in section, we find they are not really flat, but slope 1 ft (the contour in-

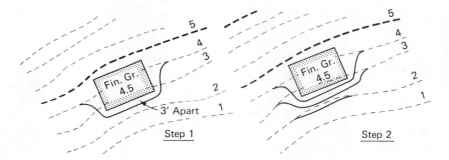

Figure 2–4
Grading by fill.

terval) over the distance. Although contours appear as a series of tiny terraces, in actuality all the contours are smoothed out. This slight slope may be desirable, for it will allow water to drain. If the area must be level, spot elevations or a section can be used to indicate that. Round the corners of contours to make them blend in with the surrounding landscape. Large arcs indicate smooth flowing land. Conversely, if each corner is angular, the landscape will appear architectonic or geometric in form. Angular corners are more efficient and disturb a smaller area of land. You can determine the total disturbed area by connecting with a light line the points where existing and proposed contours meet.

GRADING A FLAT AREA USING BOTH CUT AND FILL

This combination is the preferred method of preparing a flat area as it *balances* cut and fill. Balanced cut and fill means that there is an approximately equal amount of cut and fill, which reduces grading costs as you do not have to dispose of or import soil. Half of the flat area is created by cutting into the bank. This soil is then placed over the bank to create the remaining flat area by filling.

Begin by locating the area to be leveled on the topographic plan (see Fig. 2–5). Determine the finish grade by locating the *mid-grade* running through the flat area. There should be an equal number of contours above and below the flat you select as finish grade. In this case, contours 6 and 7 are the midpoint, so 6.5 becomes finish grade. Now wrap the contour below finish grade around the *lower* side of the flat area, and the next higher contour around the high side. Do this with the remaining contours until all the contours requiring manipulation have been adjusted.

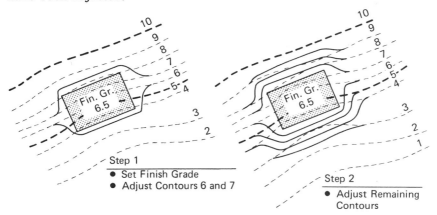

Figure 2–5
Grading by cut and fill.

A diagrammatic section through each of the preceding plans clarifies what we are talking about. Note the steep slopes and how one meets grade (Fig. 2–6).

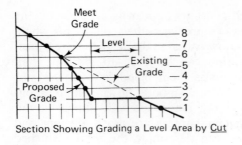

Section Showing Grading a Level Area by <u>Cut</u>

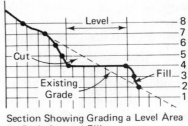

Section Showing Grading a Level Area
by Both <u>Cut and Fill</u>

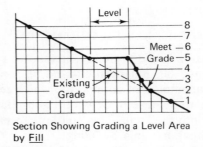

Section Showing Grading a Level Area
by <u>Fill</u>

Figure 2-6

manipulate all ground form. You must be completely familiar with their use, the way they look on plan, and manipulation skills necessary to achieve various results. As the text progresses we will learn ways to avoid slopes by using retaining walls, terraces, steps, pole construction, etc., but any substitute grading technique still relies on a complete understanding of these three basic grading methods.

Fractions are never used in grading and drainage and should be converted to *decimals*. Decimals permit rapid addition or subtraction and are easier to keep straight than fractions. Most grading computations carried to two places (hundredths) are adequate (e.g., 10.12 or 25.10). A familiarity with conversion equivalents between inches and decimals is essential and should include the following:

INCH TO DECIMAL	*INCH TO DECIMAL*
1 in. = 0.08 ft	7 in. = 0.58 ft
2 in. = 0.17 ft	8 in. = 0.67 ft
3 in. = 0.25 ft	9 in. = 0.75 ft
4 in. = 0.33 ft	10 in. = 0.83 ft
5 in. = 0.42 ft	11 in. = 0.92 ft
6 in. = 0.50 ft	12 in. = 1.00 ft

The proposed location of flat areas is a design decision that should be made quickly and then tested for grading problems. If grading doesn't work, is excessive, damages trees, etc., the flat area should be shifted and another grading scheme tested. This trial and error method indicates the close relationship between design and grading. Your speed in selecting the proper location with respect to grading problems will improve rapidly if you maintain a flexible trial and error approach.

Concave and convex surfaces should be used at the top and bottom of most slopes, and are usually graded by hand or with special small machinery after rough grading. To indicate them, draw a section, and note on the plan each area to be fine graded (Fig. 2–7).

Figure 2-7
The top of this steep bank should be graded back to create a smooth convex surface connecting with the top of the existing slope. The bottom portion of the bank is unfortunately too close to the sidewalk for a concave surface.

VARIATIONS IN SLOPE

In the preceding examples we discussed 1:2 and 1:3 slope ratios and described how to depict them using contours. Sloping land is a necessary by-product of grading, as it is not possible to pile earth vertically. The slope ratio is selected as 1:2, 1:3, 1:4, etc., slope (typically shown 1:3). A 1:3 slope means 3 ft of horizontal space is required for each 1 ft of vertical change in elevation. As contours are shown in plan view, to maintain a 1:3 slope the contours (assuming 1-ft contour interval) would have to be spaced 3 ft apart (see Fig. 2–8). (In Chapter 3 we will discuss how to determine what the maximum and minimum slope should be.)

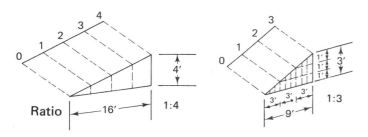

Figure 2-8

In addition to *ratio,* slope can be expressed as a *percentage* or as an angle. When expressed in percentages, a 1:3 slope becomes 33⅓ percent, a 1:4 becomes 25 percent, etc. Slope percentage is easiest to understand if you think of a 100-ft-long slope (measured horizontally). (Fig. 2–9). Then the vertical distance becomes the percent. To determine the percentage of any slope, divide the vertical distance by the horizontal distance. *Example:* What percent slope is a 17-ft change of grade (vertical distance) in 340 ft (horizontal distance)? Divide 17 by 340. $^{17}/_{340} = .05$ or 5 percent.

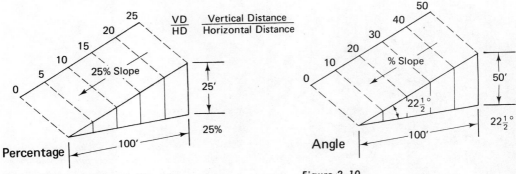

Figure 2–9

Figure 2–10

Angles are seldom used to describe slopes, as mathematical conversion of ratios or percent to angles is difficult. Angles can be measured with a protractor or converted directly from tables. To set the bounds, a 90° angle is straight up (1:0 ratio), a 45° angle is a 1:1 ratio, a 22½° angle is a 1:2 ratio (Fig. 2–10). The following table indicates conversion values between ratio, percent, and angle. You will note that percent is difficult to use for slopes steeper than 1:1.

	%	RATIO*	ANGLE°
Flat	0	0:1	0
	2	1:50	1
	5	1:20	3
	10	1:10	5
	20	1:5	11
	25	1:4	14
	33⅓	1:3	18
	50	1:2	26
	58	6:10	30
	100	1:1	45
	500	2:1	64
	1,000	10:1	84
	57,000		89.9
Straight up		1:0	90

* It is worth noting that ratio is sometimes expressed with the horizontal distance first; thereby, a slope designated 1:3 in this text would be designated 3:1. If the ratio seems excessive, check it to see if it is backwards.

- To convert slope to degrees, divide the rise by the run, and the tangent of that answer is the degrees.
- To convert ratio to percent, divide the rise by the run, and multiply the answer by 100.

FIELD EXERCISE

Becoming familiar with different gradients.

It is essential for designers to observe, experience and become totally familiar with different gradients—1, 2, 4, 10, 15 percent. Later, when preparing a grading plan, you will be able to draw on this familiarity and specify grades with which you are familiar.

EXERCISE: — Select a number of different uniform slopes that you walk through on a regular basis, and measure the gradient. Convert the measurement to percent or ratio, and think about it as you pass through the area. To measure the gradient, use two five-foot sticks marked in feet and tenths of feet. Level the horizontal stick with a carpenter's level and record the vertical height at the end (use a small triangle to plumb the vertical stick). To calculate the percent, divide the vertical height by the horizontal distance $\left(\dfrac{\text{vertical height}}{\text{horizontal distance}}\right)$. For example, if the vertical height is 1.10 feet (note the use of tenths rather than inches) and the horizontal length 5 feet, then 1.10 is divided by 5.0 equalling 0.22 or 22 percent. (See Fig. 2–11.) Repeat the exercises for steep, ratio slopes of 1:1, 2:1, 3:1, etc.

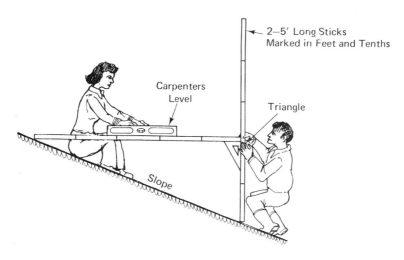

Figure 2-11 Determining gradients.

Observe the qualities of each gradient or ratio including the following:

How steep can an area be and still *appear* level?

At what gradient does water seem to puddle?

At what gradient does water seem to erode? with sand? with silt?

At what gradient is it difficult to travel on foot or bike? or noisy from passing cars?

How steep can a surface be and still work for basketball, tennis, football?

ADVANTAGES AND DISADVANTAGES OF EACH GRADING METHOD

You must eventually decide which grading method, cut, fill or combination, to use. There are no hard and fast rules, only general guidelines and experience, to consider in making the final decision.

GRADING BY CUT

The main advantage of creating a flat area by cutting into the bank is that the ground will be stable. Undisturbed earth is generally stable as it has had many years to settle and compact through natural forces. Depending on the type of existing soil, buildings, roadways, and other man-made projects can usually be constructed on cut areas without special, expensive foundations.

The main disadvantage of the cut is difficulty in disposing of the earth that you have cut away. Disposing of cut spoils usually means hauling it to another area, and often involves the use of dump trucks and paying a dump fee. In built-up areas, it is becoming almost impossible to find places to dump spoils—even adding more cost. When a site is available for dumping, it is often a marsh or swamp that has natural functions to perform and should *not* be filled.

There are other advantages; land is often too steep to place fill, and cutting may be the only method. If you want to disturb a minimum amount of land, cutting is the best way, as a steeper slope can be cut than filled. Grading by cut *minimizes* the possibility of erosion, although often the precious topsoil will be hauled away.

When extensive cut is required, excess earth may be used to create new topographical interest by berming. Equalizing cut and fill during construction is called balancing the grading plan (Figs. 2–12 and 2–13).

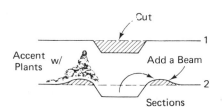

Figure 2-12   Balancing cut and fill.

Figure 2-13
Disposing of excess cut by creating a berm. This earth berm is used to separate a playfield from a play area, provide visual interest, as well as use up surplus earth. The toe of the bank needs additional hand grading to smooth it into the existing grade as a concave surface.

To summarize, grading by cut is advantageous when a stable building area is needed, on small sites where there is little room for fill slopes, and on steep sites where filling operations are difficult, if not impossible.

GRADING BY FILLING

The principal reason for grading by fill is to fill a low area to make it usable. This may be required to raise a low spot to reach grade or to level rolling terrain. (See Fig. 2–14.)

The disadvantages are similar to cutting; it is difficult (and expensive) to find fill earth when and where you want it. (One would expect that if it is difficult to dispose of fill, it should be easy to acquire it; but timing and the laws of supply and demand invariably get in the way.) As mentioned, newly filled areas are not stable enough for most construction projects without installing elaborate foundations or compacting with special equipment. Most foundations installed on fill must extend through the fill into solid undisturbed earth below. Compaction requires special equipment and creates problems in areas that you wish to plant later.

Filled areas and slopes can easily erode, as the soil particles are loose. Land slippage and slides can also occur, as there is little or no bondage between existing soil and new fill.

MAKING AN AREA LEVEL BY CUT AND FILL

This is the most popular grading method. If there is an approximate balance of cut and fill, expensive hauling and disposal fees are eliminated. It is most useful on large sites with minimum topography, where cut spoils can be disposed of without causing erosion or requiring elaborate building foundations. It is often possible to use excess fill material for parking areas or some other nonstructural purpose.

Regardless of the grading method used, all topsoil should be carefully stripped off, stockpiled (stored, so it can be reused), and replaced following grading so that planting and erosion control can follow.

This information is general, and biased to produce low grading costs. However, cost estimates must consider both short- and long-term effects. Often a specific design requires an operation that is uneconomic in immediate costs, but may be justified over the long term. Your design task is to develop a convincing argument. Justification for specific cases can only be made through a complete understanding of the total general condition.

EXERCISE 1
GRADING TO CREATE FLAT AREAS

PART 1 — Block grade the area first; that is, rough out the contours without regard to scale. Should you have a question regarding any grades, draw a section through the area to check it. Then carefully redraw your block

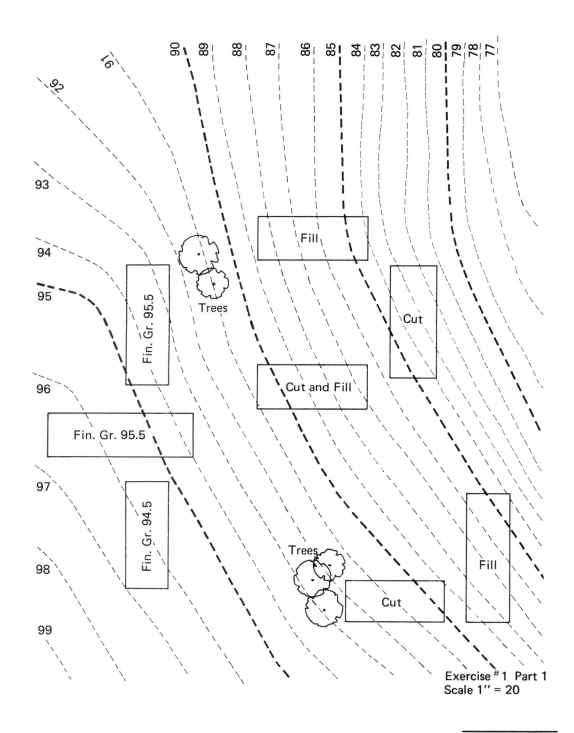

Exercise #1 Part 1
Scale 1" = 20

grading to scale. Use 1:3 slopes for *cut,* and 1:5 slopes for *fill* (i.e., your proposed contours in cut will be 3 ft apart, and your contours in fill will be 5 ft apart).

PART 2 — Grade the parking lots as follows: *Lot 1,* grade level in cut; *Lot 2,* grade in cut sloping uniformly to one corner at a slope of 3 percent (1:33); *Lot 3,* slope uniformly to the entrance at a grade of 2 percent (1:50). Block grade each lot first and then complete it to scale. Use 1:2 slope for the cut and 1:3 slope for the fill.

EXERCISE 2
GRADING A FLAT AREA

Prepare a grading plan for the housing development shown according to the following:

1:2 slopes for cut banks.
1:4 slopes for fill banks.
5-ft walk between building and banks.

Building-pad elevations:

Building A, 89.5	Building F, 94.5
Building B, 88.5	Building G, 90.5
Building C, 93.5	Building H, 87.5
Building D, 93.5	Building I, 89.5
Building E, 95.5	Building J, 90.5

Allow a 10-ft garden area at the same building-pad elevation for buildings B, C, D, E, F, H, I, J, and K. Gardens are opposite the parking lots.

PROCEDURE — Redraw and enlarge the plan on clearprint tracing paper. Draw it *freehand,* but be neat and careful. Use light guidelines drawn with T-square and triangle using 2H or H leads.

Grade parking areas with 3 percent slope (3 ft per 100 ft) in whatever manner *minimizes* grading.

Enlarge this drawing three times.

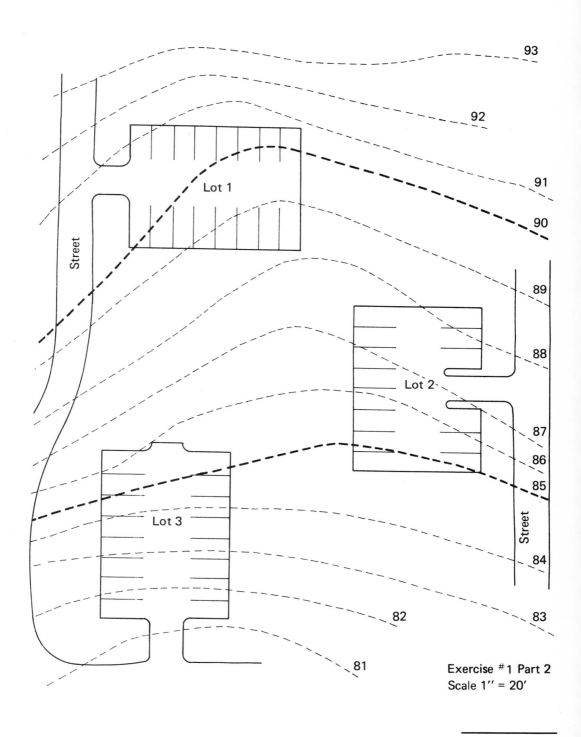

93

92

91

90

Street

Lot 1

89

88

Lot 2

87

86

85

Street

84

Lot 3

82

83

81

Exercise #1 Part 2
Scale 1" = 20'

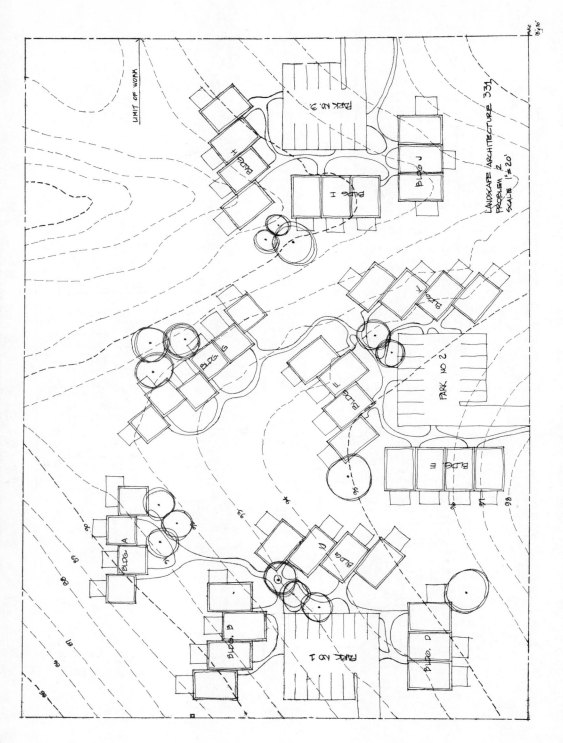

LIMIT OF WORK

PARK NO. 3

BLDG H

BLDG I

BLDG J

LANDSCAPE ARCHITECTURE 331
PROBLEM 2
SCALE 1"=20'

BLDG K

BLDG G

BLDG F

PARK NO 2

BLDG E

BLDG A

BLDG B

BLDG C

PARK NO 1

BLDG D

38

GRADING CIRCULATION ROUTES

People and vehicles move in two directions, *horizontally* and *vertically*. We move horizontally because we want to get somewhere, and vertically to get over something because we have to. This accounts for our first basic principle: *circulation routes should be as flat as possible.* This is a bit of an exaggeration, but will serve as a point of departure; for instance, people climb mountains and seek high places to enjoy views; but, in general, steep routes are tiring for people, bikes, and motorized vehicles.

If we think of a circulation route as a series of extended *flat areas,* we can use the same three grading methods we have just talked about. These methods, for review, are as follows:

Making a flat area by cut.

Making a flat area by fill.

Making a flat area by a combination of cut and fill.

We have devised two ways to travel vertically to get over difficult terrain:

1. We can gently slope the entire circulation route over a distance (Fig. 3–1).

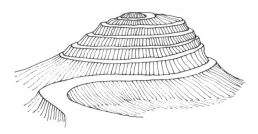

Figure 3–1

2. We can travel horizontally for a while on a flat area, then travel vertically for a short distance via a steep ramp or stairway (Fig. 3-2).

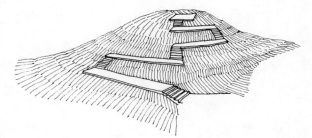

Figure 3-2

In designing a circulation route there are also two opposite locations the route can take:

1. Parallel to the contours—that is, almost parallel, but tilted slightly up to gain elevation. This route, although fairly flat, may require extensive grading to create a wide enough area to move on (Fig. 3-3).
2. Perpendicular to the contour requires the least amount of grading, but results in a steep trip (Fig. 3-4).

Figure 3-3   Perpendicular to Contours

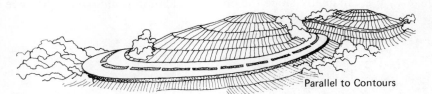

Parallel to Contours

Figure 3-4

Therefore, if you want to move over something by the quickest, shortest route, your design should move *perpendicular* to the contours. However, should you want to move gradually up or down or around a hill, your route should move parallel with the contours. The normal grading method is something between the two extremes, with roads and paths climbing and falling gently to allow a quick, effortless trip.

We can combine parallel and perpendicular alignments to develop a circulation route that will move any person or vehicle over a distance (Fig. 3-5). For example, to get from point A to point B we can ramp gradually over the distance, in which case our route would be between perpendicular to and parallel to the contours.

Or we can get there by terracing, in which case our route will be first flat (i.e., parallel to the contours) and then steep using steps or ramps (perpendicular to the contours) (Fig. 3-6). Once you have tested these two options (or any variations between), you can determine if the grading will take place in cut, in fill, or in a combination of cut and fill, and follow the grading methods learned in the last section.

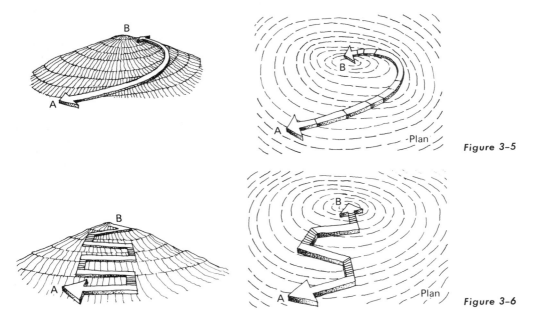

Figure 3-5

Figure 3-6

GRADING FOR CIRCULATION

Circulation routes constructed over flat country are relatively easy to grade; the technical skills are concerned with providing a *uniform surface* and assuring that the roadway *drains properly*.

1. A uniform surface means smoothing out the bumps by spacing contours evenly. Pedestrians can adjust to more variations in the path (and perhaps even enjoy it), but autos are forced to slow down to negotiate most adverse terrain and require smooth roadways.

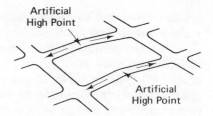

Figure 3–7
Create an artificial high point to drain level
road alignments.

2. Draining a flat road is sometimes a chore, as it requires creating artificial high and low points for water to flow from and to these high and low spots, as shown graphically with contours, spot elevations, and sections (Fig. 3–7).

Manipulation of circulation-route contours follows the same procedures as creating flat areas. Proposed contours leave the existing contours at the point of desired change, and move toward *lower contours* for fill and toward *higher contours* for cut. Proposed contours always rejoin the same existing contours at the end of the grading change. The point of connection is called the line of no cut/no fill.

1. *Grading in cut* To grade a road running parallel to the contours using *cut*, first locate the road on the topographic map in scale approximately where you propose to construct it. Next select the

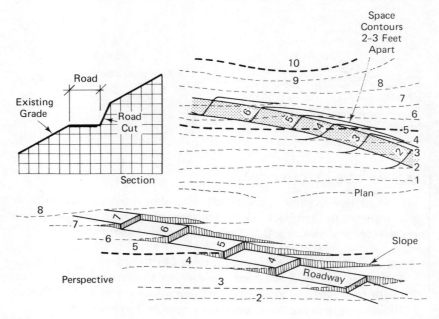

Figure 3–8

finish grade by finding the contour that is below the road but not crossing it (contour 2 in Fig. 3–8). This proposed contour should cross perpendicular to the road until it reaches the other side, then continue parallel and connect back to the existing contour. This creates a small bank on the uphill side. The process is continued with each successive contour, creating, in effect, *many* flat areas each vertically the contour interval apart. These diagrammatic forms will be smoothed out during actual grading operation. (See Fig. 3–9.) Remember, when grading by cut, begin with the *lowest contour* and work up. In the next example, grading by filling, the starting point is reversed, beginning with the top *contour* and working down. Contours are spaced according to the gradient or slope that you wish the route to assume, which is typically expressed in percentage. For a 10 percent slope, 1-ft contours would be spaced 10 ft apart. Roads are usually not very steep and seldom exceed 10 percent. It is common for most roads to be in the 2 to 6 percent range.

Figure 3-9
Road graded in cut with contours super-imposed. Note the swale for drainage between the road and bank, with contours pointing upward.

Note: The amount of bank created in grading any road usually seems excessive. However, as roads do not vary much from a uniform slope, it is difficult and expensive to avoid the bank. In design grading, the exact size, slope, and location of the bank become important. It may be possible to grade a shallow bank out over a long distance, to provide a sidewalk before the bank, to use retaining walls, to change the grade of the road, etc. (See Fig. 3–10 a and b.) Grading is a creative process with many possible variations, which will be discussed in later chapters.

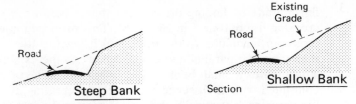

Figure 3-10(a)   Vary the steepness of slope during preliminary grading and
                 evaluate.

Figure 3-10(b)
This bank is a stable shale material, and
can be steeper than 1:1 without danger
of erosion or slippage.

2. *Grading by fill* Grading a road by fill works in the opposite way.
First, lay out the approximate road location to scale on the
topographic plan. Select the starting point finish grade by finding
the highest contour on the uphill side of the road. This proposed
contour should cross perpendicular to the road and run along the
other side until it reconnects to the same existing contour.
Remember, roads are uniform in slope, so contours must be
spaced equal distances apart (Fig. 3–11).

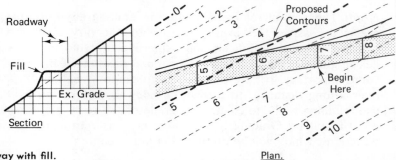

Figure 3-11   Grading roadway with fill.

3. *Grading using cut and fill* Grading a road using both cut and fill is the most common practice if the existing topography is *not* too steep. Typically, the uphill lane will be in cut and the downhill lane in fill. Begin with any contour, and draw it perpendicular to the road, crossing the existing contour in the middle of the road. This creates a cut bank *above* the uphill lane and a fill slope below the road. With care, cut and fill will balance, and there will be no need to import or export earth (Fig. 3–12).

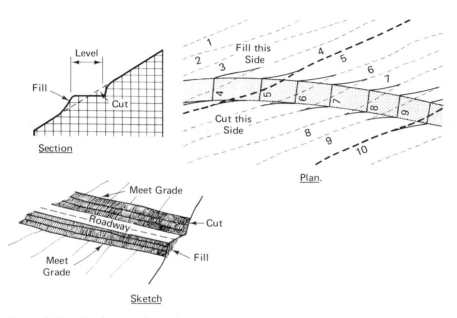

Figure 3-12 Grading roadways by cut and fill.

4. *Grading roads running perpendicular* to the contours is easier to understand than the methods just described, as the road runs right up the slope. Each contour appears as a giant step. Each contour is, in the abstract, a level surface, with an abrupt change at the next contour (Fig. 3–13a). Your task is to determine *how* steep the road can be, and then space the contours accordingly. In actual construction, the area between contours will be uniformly sloped and not a series of level areas (See Fig. 3–13b.) Once you have determined how steep the road can be (based on the vehicle and type of user—car, people, bike, wheelbarrow, etc.), space the proposed contours uniformly along the roadway and begin at the bottom, connecting each back to the correct contour.

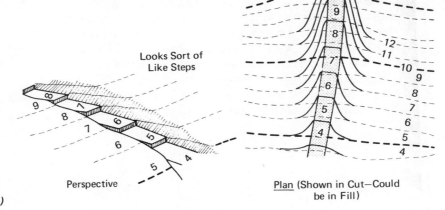

Looks Sort of
Like Steps

Perspective

Plan (Shown in Cut—Could
be in Fill)

Figure 3-13(a)

Figure 3-13(b)
Road graded perpendicular to contours,
with contours superimposed.

Connect the next proposed contour to its appropriate existing
contour, and on up until you reach the top. You will find that the
shallower the proposed roadway gradient, the taller the banks on
either side of the road become. These banks will be fairly uniform
on both sides of the road and you will feel that you are going
through a tunnel without a top (Figs. 3–14 and 3–15).

5. Roadways can also be aligned *parallel* to contours along the
length of the slope. However, these routes can become disruptive
if the roadway is wide or the slope steep, as cut or fill

Existing
Grade

Figure 3-14   Sections   **Shallow Bank**   **Steep Bank**

Figure 3-15
This pathway was cut down considerably to maintain a shallow gradient, creating the steep banks and enclosed space. The banks could have been graded off and planted in lawn, but a damaged sidewalk nearby provided material for the broken concrete retaining wall.

requirements become excessive. Grading in cut steepens the uphill bank; fill steepens the downhill bank.

SWITCHBACKS — A circulation route across steep banks (almost parallel to the contours) eventually has to double back on itself at a higher elevation. A switchback is used to turn the corner. It is formed by the convergence of the two routes, and is usually level for a short distance. The inside edge (narrowest portion) slopes wildly unless a retaining wall is used, whereas the outside edge moves around in a gentle level arc. To accommodate the width required for turning, extensive cut and fill are required. Switchbacks are useful for pedestrian circulation, but are difficult for auto use as autos require considerable room for turning (Figs. 3-16 and 3-17).

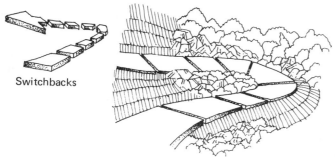

Switchbacks

Figure 3-16

Steps are used to move people up steep banks. They can be wood, concrete, rock, brick, etc., with details and design varying in width, length, stair tread and riser dimensions, etc. The exact proportions of stair riser to tread is often the subject of long discussions; however, for rough calculations we can assume a 12-in. (1-ft) tread and

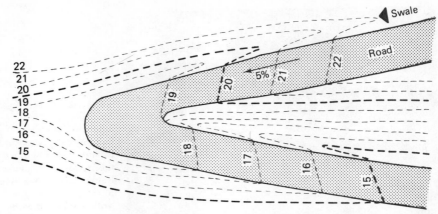

22
21
20
19
18
17
16
15

Figure 3-17(a) Grading for a switchback. Note the swales at the base of both banks, and the angled contour crossing the road to direct runoff to the swale.

Figure 3-17(b) A switchback. The bend of this switchback is very difficult for cars to negotiate and may require several back and forward passes to complete the turn. Note how steep the slope between the two roads becomes and the danger created by that steep cliff.

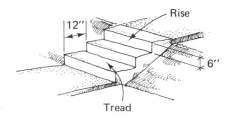

"Informal"

Figure 3–18

a 6-in. (0.5-ft) riser. This dimension works well outdoors, and additionally is convenient for calculating and dimensioning during grading design (Fig. 3–18).

Most stairs should be a minimum of 3 ft wide for single passage and 4 ft wide for double passage. Stairs should be grouped in a minimum of three risers to avoid accidently stumbling on an isolated step (Fig. 3–19).

Stairs are normally shown symbolically on the grading plan to indicate the number of treads with top and bottom spot elevations. Construction details on another plan minimize the need for extensive detail on the grading plan. Contours are drawn to the approximate stair, and away from the other side. (See Fig. 3–20).

Figure 3–19 Disappearing steps are sometimes difficult for older people and should be avoided unless there are at least six and can be easily seen. Note the handrail against the building.

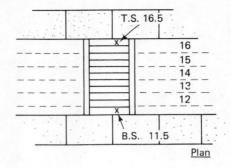

Plan

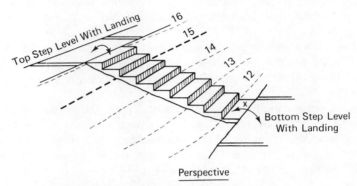

Perspective

Figure 3-20   Stairs fit comfortably into a 2:1 slope.

EXERCISE 1

This exercise will introduce you to the manipulation of contours for grading circulation routes.

1. Analyze the topography; where are the high points, the low points, ridges, valleys, etc.? Then *grade the road in cut.*

2. Grade the road to a minimum grade of 2 percent.

3. Grade the road to a maximum grade of 2 percent, but include a 6-in. crown.

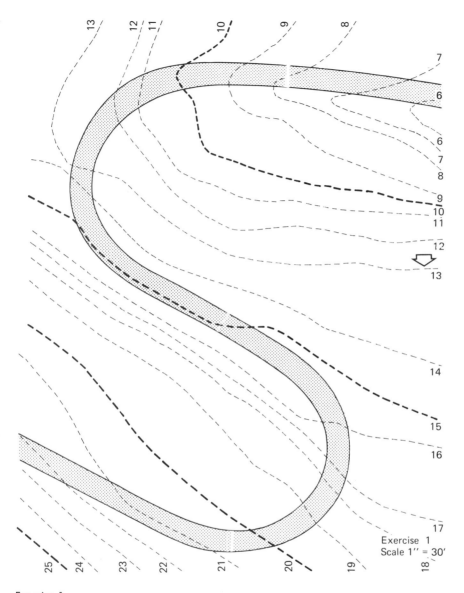

Exercise 1

Exercise 1
Scale 1'' = 30'

EXERCISE 2
GRADING FOR CIRCULATION

There are *two* parts, the top proposed route, and the blank topography on the bottom. You are to grade the given proposed route according to the criteria listed below, evaluate the solution, and *realign* the road as necessary on the topography below. You will end with a graded proposed route plus your suggested route, which will also be graded.

Criteria for proposed route:
Maximum 5 percent grade (5 ft of rise per 100 ft of horizontal distance).
No road crown.
Maximum 1:2 cut slopes; maximum 1:4 fill slopes.

Criteria for your route selection:
Maximum 5 percent grade.
6-in. crown.
Save all possible trees.
Minimize grading.
Maximum 1:2 cut; 1:3 fill.

PROCEDURE—Draw the base map on clearprint 1000H, enlarged three times. Grade the proposed route, analyze the problems, develop your own alternative alignment, and grade it. Remember, the contour interval is 2 ft. Be neat; use careful graphics. Draw freehand, but use guidelines first; watch your line weight.

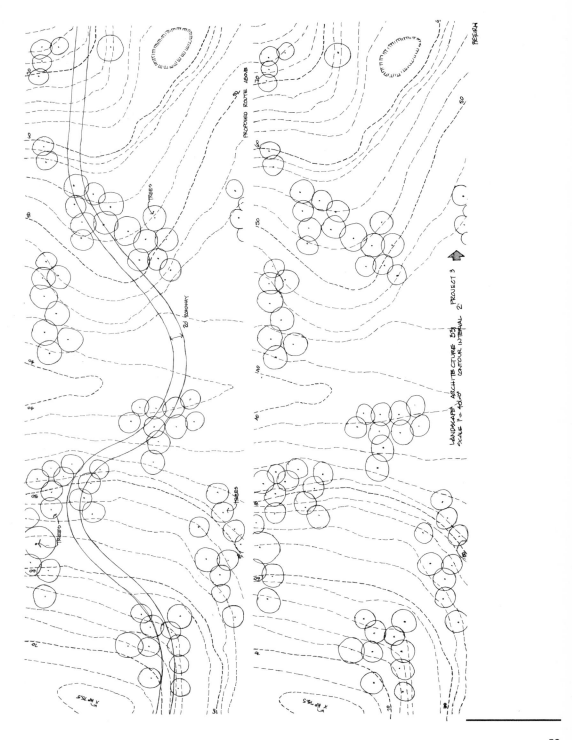

LANDSCAPE ARCHITECTURE 53   PROJECT 3
SCALE 1" = 40'-0"   CONTOUR INTERVAL 2'

RIGHT-OF-WAY — Although the paved portion of public streets may be as narrow as 20 or 25 ft, it is typical for the municipality to own additional land on each side of the street. This total width, called the right-of-way, accommodates sidewalks, planter strips, street trees, utilities, room for grading, and in snowbound communities, room for storage of plowed snow. A 50- or 60-ft right-of-way is typical for most residential streets, allowing for a 25-ft-wide paved road plus a 12- to 17-ft wide sidewalk area on each side (Fig. 3–21). In low-density neighborhoods one sidewalk may be sufficient. The roadway can be offset to allow more room on one side for a bikeway; for example, a 25-ft roadway might be placed 10 ft from one side of a 60-ft right-of-way, leaving 25 ft on the other side for a bikeway (Fig. 3–22).

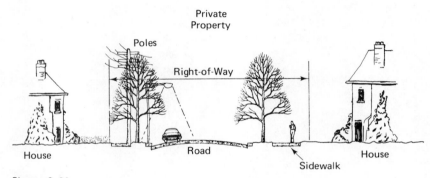

Figure 3–21

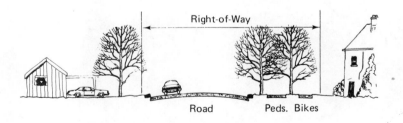

Off Set Right-of-Way to Allow for Bikes

Figure 3–22

Finally, it is often possible to select a circulation route that avoids steep areas; for instance, roads can be located in the valley or along the river rather than on the steeper areas. Roads can travel along the bottom of a steep bank on a level area to get around it.

SUMMARY

The two conceptual methods of traveling vertically, ramping gradually over a distance or traveling along the level and then ramping steeply, form the basis for all circulation networks. They will never change, so you must learn to manipulate them quickly and be able to test or combine both methods into the best possible route.

Two additional decisions must be made when designing circulation routes:

1. The maximum steepness (gradient) of the circulation route.
2. The proper width of the circulation route.

Gradient is normally expressed in percent and is determined by the type of vehicle and use of route. For instance, cars travel best on grades not exceeding 10 percent; people can travel for long distances at grades of 3 to 5 percent, and for shorter distances at steeper grades of 12 to 15 percent, or even 30 percent. Road grades are often determined by the public agencies that review the project; for instance, the Highway Department sets maximum grades for highways, and the Public Works Department sets grades for local roads and pedestrian ramps.

The width of the roadway is determined by many factors, including available land, efficiency and speed of travel, acceptable congestion and traffic volume, safety, and visual and ecological factors. In steep or difficult terrain or scenic landscapes, it is usually desirable to have a narrow route. The narrow road eliminates massive grading and reduces the environmental impact in steep topographic areas.

4

THE GRADING AND DRAINAGE PLAN

The grading and drainage plan is used to describe grading construction tasks for implementing a site design. It is also used for measuring required earthwork. The final grading plan generally shows the site boundary, existing topography (landform), existing site features, and proposed elements to be constructed. It is shown in two-dimensional form using contours, notes, and other symbols.

Grading and drainage specifications (called specs) are also a part of the grading plan. Specs describe in word form the acceptable standards of quality, methods of performing work, special requirements, etc., necessary to carry out the project. They form a written description of any grading contract and should include all special considerations and warnings that the designer feels are important.

The grading plan is usually one of two to five parts that form the site construction documents. Other parts may be layout, electrical, planting, irrigation, and lighting and utility plans. Because these other drawings are included, the grading plan is usually *not dimensioned,* but must be accurate for scaling if necessary, and must conform to all the other drawings.

The final grading plan is the last of four or five grading schemes that may be necessary for design of a project. Initially, *grading concepts* are roughed out on buff tracing paper; each concept indicates an acceptable approach with a list of advantages and disadvantages (concepts may include a cut solution, a balanced solution, an unbalanced solution, a solution using extensive retaining walls, a minimum grading solution, etc.). These concepts will usually be dated, numbered, and retained until the preferred concept is chosen. This concept procedure usually takes place during the preliminary design phase, and forms an important contribution to this design stage. Usually, proposed grading will be symbolically indicated on the preliminary landscape plan suggesting ground form, slopes, drainage, etc. Following approval of the plan, the grading and drainage proposals are reviewed and updated as needed, and work is begun on the final plan. The final plan should remain flexible until the end, being adjusted and refined as more information is obtained.

Your design process should progress in similar fashion, with several approaches being tested and adjusted with other findings. Work at the early stage should be done freehand and quickly, using different colored pencils to indicate various features. As the work progresses, portions may be hardlined (drawn mechanically with a straightedge and triangle), but contours are always drawn freehand (it is becoming common to draw all construction drawings freehand, which speeds up work and simplifies the task).

BLOCK GRADING

Block grading is the first step in roughing out a grading plan for a large piece of land or long roadway. It allows you to quickly test a variety of design solutions without completing the detail grading of each scheme. Once the preliminary landscape form is laid out, every *fifth* contour is manipulated, leaving those between untouched (Fig. 4–1). When all the fifth contours have been blocked out, you can quickly check percentage of grade, balance of cut and fill, difficult or problem areas, whether the project is in cut or fill, the number of trees to be removed, and obvious drainage problems before wasting time developing a final presentation (Fig. 4–2). If the plan doesn't work, it should be changed or modified where necessary, and another block grading test administered. When an acceptable solution is discovered, the in-between contours can be filled in using interpolation. To interpolate, divide the lineal distance between every fifth contour by five (the actual number of contour spaces between) and measure this distance from one end to locate each contour. The preliminary block grading of a roadway is shown in Figure 4–1. Block grading also allows you to "see" the form of the land and determine necessary changes without becoming involved in detailed manipulation of a great number of contours. The block-graded area can then be "filled" in to appear as in Figure 4–2.

OPTIONAL GRADING PLAN
INFORMATION DIAGRAMS

To fully understand a grading project, it may be desirable to prepare several special-analysis diagrams, including the following:

Slope-analysis diagram with several sections to distinguish between steep and shallow areas of the site. It can be done in colors (with bright colors indicating steepest areas) or using hachures. The slope is usually divided into percentage categories, 0 to 5, 6 to 15, 16 to 25, and 26 percent and up, or more refined

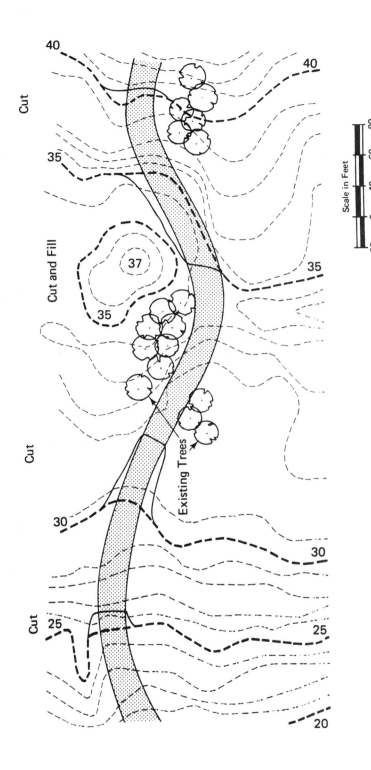

Figure 4-1 Block grading—step 1.

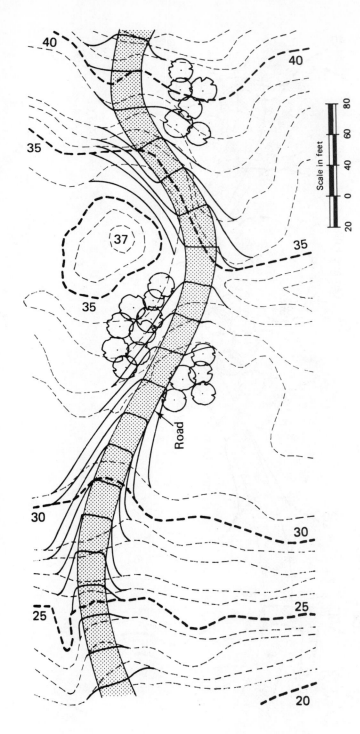

Figure 4-2   Block grading—step 2.

Figure 4-3
All grading must be carried out within your
property lines. This cut area is very close to the
property line, and will require a retaining wall
to protect the neighbor's property.

in shallow areas: 0 to 3, 4 to 7, 8 to 11, 12 to 16 percent, etc.

Drainage map seems obvious, but a map showing natural
and artificial drainage ways, areas of flooding, wet or boggy areas,
ground water levels, aquifer discharges, existing wells, off-site
flows, etc., may be important in determining a drainage concept.

Geologic map showing soil types, subsurface layering, rock
outcrops and base and surficial geology; helps indicate foundation
stability, drainage potential, slippage area, etc.

Vegetation map showing existing trees and large shrubs. Their size,
variety, and condition can be an important guide in determining
which trees will be saved, transplanted, moved, or removed (don't
be afraid to suggest transplanting a tree).

Cultural map showing all the man-made artifacts and needs:
roads, buildings, utility structures, easements, etc.

Extensive mapping of existing conditions can lead to the familiar
analysis—paralysis; or it can act as a guide to assure proper and
thoughtful decision making. As projects become larger and more complex, it is essential to have all information accurately recorded for convenient reference at any time. The size and complexity of a project will
indicate the amount of research necessary for any grading scheme.

WHAT'S ON A GRADING
AND DRAINAGE PLAN?

1. *Definition* A grading plan shows the proposed structures and
   configuration of the site and the relationship of existing and
   proposed contours to the land. The plan defines the vertical
   location of the land, landforms, and elements placed on the land
   in a two-dimensional form.

2. *Purpose* The grading plan directs the contractor in implementing

site design. It is a guide for construction and a means of measuring earthwork.

3. *Requirements*
   a. The grading plan shows *existing* site conditions that might affect construction either by their removal or permanence, including the following:
      (1) Topography.
      (2) Structures: buildings, roads, dams, paths, etc.
      (3) Vegetation: size, type, condition, action (save or remove).
      (4) Legal restrictions: property lines, easements, setback, etc.
      (5) Utility structures: catch basin, manhole, culvert, etc.
      (6) Utility lines: drainage, sewer, water, gas, electric.
      (7) Any unusual site conditions.
   b. Proposed site conditions (superimposed over existing conditions):
      (1) Proposed contours showing landform changes.
      (2) Proposed structures, roads, parking, etc.
      (3) Drainage structures and center line of proposed drain pipes.
   c. Coordination:
      (1) Relate to other construction drawings (layout plan, planting, etc.).
      (2) Key plan elements to other descriptive notes and plans.
      (3) Relate to details, sections, profiles.
   d. Abbreviations: keys, legends, symbols (see page 63).
   e. Storm sewer: plan location and profile; show rim and invert elevation, pipe size, and location. A profile and section is helpful on some plans.
   f. Details as required (catch basin, area drains, French drains, etc.).

4. *Graphics*
   a. Legible, clear, accurate.
   b. Pleasing compositions with measured line and tone weight.
   c. Legible printing.
   d. Scale bar, north arrow, legend, key, notes, and title blocks.

GRADING SYMBOLS AND ABBREVIATIONS

Symbols and abbreviations simplify your drafting task; if used carefully and consistently, they can clarify and aid in understanding the drawings. There is really no set of accepted symbols; however, the following have proved successful; as long as they are noted in the *legend*, you will have no trouble in using them.

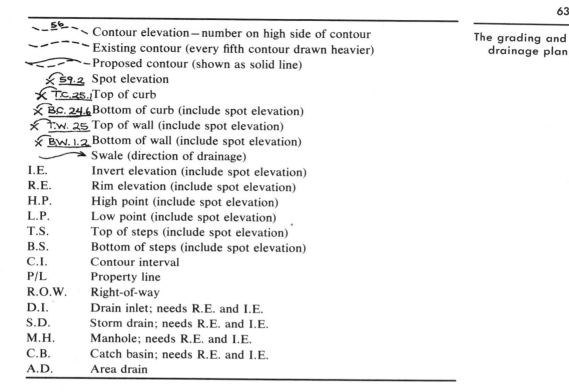

I.E.	Invert elevation (include spot elevation)
R.E.	Rim elevation (include spot elevation)
H.P.	High point (include spot elevation)
L.P.	Low point (include spot elevation)
T.S.	Top of steps (include spot elevation)
B.S.	Bottom of steps (include spot elevation)
C.I.	Contour interval
P/L	Property line
R.O.W.	Right-of-way
D.I.	Drain inlet; needs R.E. and I.E.
S.D.	Storm drain; needs R.E. and I.E.
M.H.	Manhole; needs R.E. and I.E.
C.B.	Catch basin; needs R.E. and I.E.
A.D.	Area drain

See Figure 4–4a through c.

DRAWING SECTIONS, ELEVATIONS, AND PROFILES

A *section* is a vertical cut through the subject area that exposes an end view of all the elements. Sections are the easiest way to explain in the third dimension what can only be expressed symbolically on a plan. Their location should be chosen so that as much desired information as possible can be presented economically, yet with clarity. Contour lines are normally *not* shown in a section; therefore, critical elevation points should be given to show absolute heights of the section. *Elevations* are more lifelike than sections, and show visible elements beyond the cut line. Elevations are often rendered with shadows, people, cars, benches, etc., and are meant to convey a feeling about the space, rather than just show vertical relationship. There are two broad types of sections:

1. *Architectural elevations* are important illustrations for lay people who have difficulty interpreting architectural plans in determining

Figure 4-4(a)
Grading plans for urban courtyards make extensive use of spot elevations. Steps and catch basins are often numbered so critical grading information can be listed elsewhere. This courtyard is raised using ramps and steps as shown on the accompanying plan.

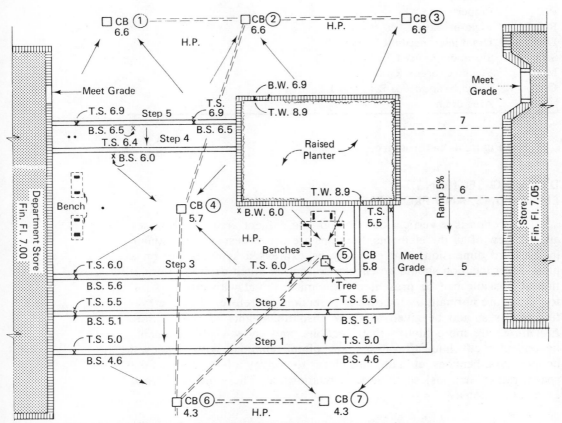

Figure 4-4(b) **Diagramatic grading plan for raised urban court shown in photo.**

64

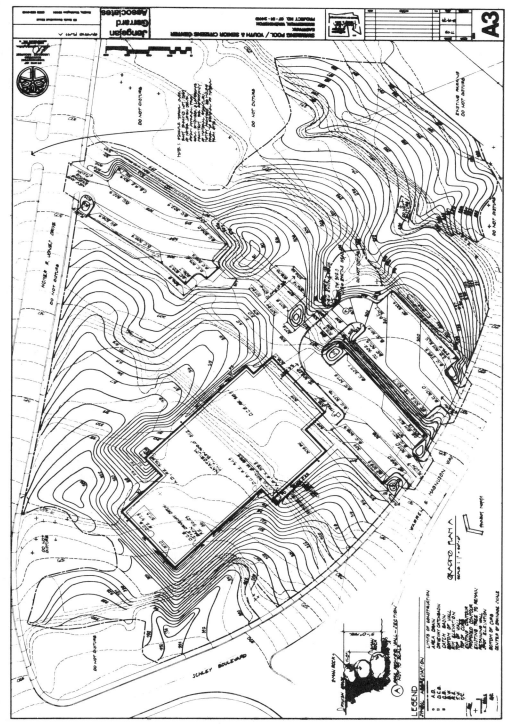

Figure 4-4(c)

ELEVATIONS

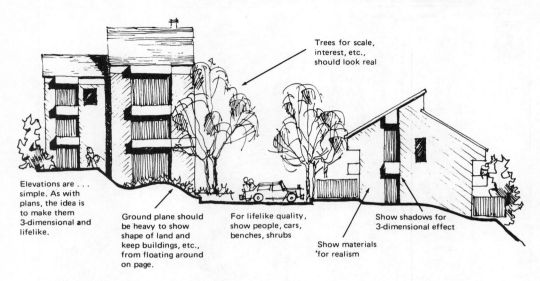

Trees for scale, interest, etc., should look real

Elevations are . . . simple. As with plans, the idea is to make them 3-dimensional and lifelike.

Ground plane should be heavy to show shape of land and keep buildings, etc., from floating around on page.

For lifelike quality, show people, cars, benches, shrubs

Show shadows for 3-dimensional effect

Show materials 'for realism

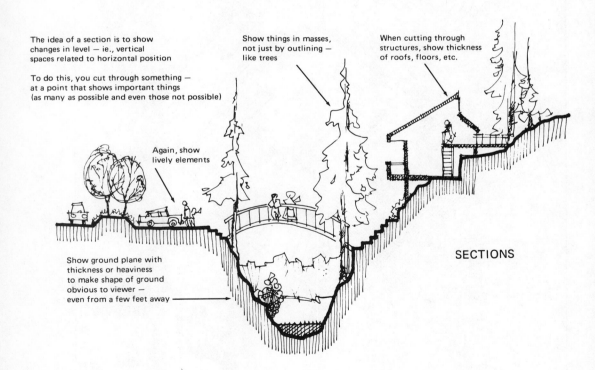

The idea of a section is to show changes in level — ie., vertical spaces related to horizontal position

To do this, you cut through something — at a point that shows important things (as many as possible and even those not possible)

Show things in masses, not just by outlining — like trees

When cutting through structures, show thickness of roofs, floors, etc.

Again, show lively elements

Show ground plane with thickness or heaviness to make shape of ground obvious to viewer — even from a few feet away

SECTIONS

Figure 4–5

lines of sight, views, usefulness of buffers, relationships between buildings, etc. They can function as a tool to check design assumptions. Spot elevations should be shown for important levels and proposed landscape elements, and scaling devices (people, cars, etc.) should also be shown. Darker lines are used to indicate those elements cut by the section, with background features drawn lighter (Fig. 4–5).

2. *Construction sections* convey technical information about materials and relationships in the third dimension to persons concerned with *actual site construction*. Their principal purpose is to show changes in level, which are depicted by spot elevations, and light horizontal lines spaced at each contour level. Spot elevations might be shown at H.P./L.P., T.S./B.S., T.W./B.W., T.C./B.C., I.E./R.E., and F.El., finish grades elevation, subgrades and existing grades, and at intersections of constructed elements. Generally, proposed planting, background features, and scaling devices are left out to assure clarity of the construction aspects.

Profiles are cut through the linear length of a road and show the relationship between existing and proposed topography (Fig. 4–6). By varying the drafting symbols, it is possible to superimpose the center elevation, curb and drainage ditch elevations, and utility lines. (See Fig. 4–7.) Volumes of cut and fill can be calculated by shading each and measuring the square measure in scale, which can then be multiplied by the width for volume.

Vertical exaggeration is sometimes used to emphasize the elevation; be sure to note any exaggerations on the drawings (e.g., 1 in. horizontal = 2 in. vertical). Exaggerations should be minimal, varying from one half to two times the horizontal scale.

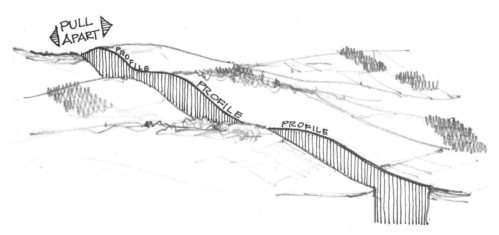

Figure 4-6

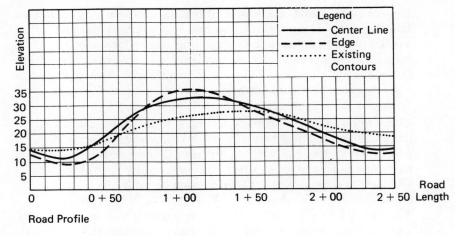

Road Profile

Figure 4-7

GRADING GRAPHICS

There are several graphic techniques that will improve the speed and accuracy of your work:

- Work on flimsy tracing paper over a print of the site plan with contours until you have it fairly well solved. Working on the print protects the original and allows you to press hard or cover some areas with graphite, magic markers, etc.
- If a grading plan is going to be an original drawing, draw the existing contours on the back of the drawing and the proposed contours on the front. This allows you to erase the proposed contours if they are drawn incorrectly without erasing the existing contours. It is important to place a clean flimsy between the rough tracing to avoid shadows on the back of the drawing.
- Where possible, draw existing contours on a site plan and have a sepia made for the grading plan. The sepia allows you to erase and correct without causing problems or damage to the original.

HINTS ON UNDERSTANDING GRADING PLANS

Some of the following is repetitious, but a review might be helpful.

1. Traditionally, *dashed* lines represent *existing* contours, while *solid* lines indicate *proposed* contours. (Existing contours are sometimes drawn as continuous lines where no proposed contours are shown, and it saves drafting time.)

2. Existing contours are usually drawn *freehand,* sometimes on the back of the sheet, and are often the lightest lines on the drawing.

3. Determine the *contour interval* (sometimes called the vertical interval), that is, the vertical distance between each contour line. This should be listed in the legend and could be 1 ft, 2 ft, 5 ft, etc. Once established, it should be maintained on the entire drawings.

4. Contours are labeled by placing the number on the *high* side of the contour (existing contours may be labeled in the middle of a contour line). Usually, only every fifth contour is labeled, with those between left unlabeled unless it becomes confusing.

5. Every *fifth* contour is drawn slightly darker and wider to aid readability and understanding.

6. A *closed* contour indicates a *peak* or a *depression.* Usually, a spot elevation is added to distinguish which it is.

7. *Spot elevations* are used to indicate critical points that can not be understood by reading the contours.

8. *Gradient* (or slope) is the fall or rise of land per horizontal unit. It is usually expressed as a *ratio* between the horizontal length and vertical rise (or fall), for example, 1:3 (1 ft vertical to 3 ft horizontal), or as a *percent gradient,* for example, $33\frac{1}{3}$ percent gradient.

9. Closely spaced contours indicate steep slopes; contours spaced farther apart indicate a gentle slope.

10. Contours spaced equally indicate a uniform slope.

11. Perpendicular to the contours is always the steepest slope and indicates direction of drainage. Called *fall line.*

12. Contours cross streams at one and only one place. In crossing a stream, the contours run up the valley on one side, turn at the stream, and run back on the other side. Since the contours are always at right angles to the lines of steepest slope, they cross the stream at right angles to its course.

THE GRADING PROCESS

Actual grading operations will be carried out during the total construction time period using different equipment. However, your grading plan will show *only* final finished grades. It is assumed that the grading contractor will figure to accommodate for subgrades, or can be directed by a note on the drawing or in the specs.

SUBGRADE — Most finished grades require the placement of some material such as bricks, concrete, loam, asphalt paving, etc., as a finish surface. These materials will be placed to conform to *your proposed grades.* However, during grading operations, it is necessary to grade out enough space to accommodate these materials. This operation is called grading to subgrade, that is, the removal of excess material to accommodate the finish landscape surface. Subgrade will vary from 4 to 12 in. depending on the amount of new material to be placed; for instance, a concrete patio may require 4 in. of space to subgrade, whereas a road surface may require 10 in. for gravel, backfill, and final asphalt surface (Fig. 4–8).

Figure 4-8
Grading to subgrade. Although the grading plan showed *final* grades, the contractor has removed sufficient material to allow placement of gravel, asphalt, topsoil, and concrete in this road project.

Two subgrading operations may concern you in the preparation of a grading plan. The first deals with stipulating the amount of soil to be removed during subgrade operation. This is often handled by a note on the grading plans indicating that 6 in. of soil is to be removed for subgrade operation, or 4 in., or whatever. The second operation is balancing cut and fill. A large subgrade operation could throw cut out of balance with fill, necessitating either removal of dirt from the site or restudying the grading and proposing another solution.

BALANCING CUT AND FILL — Grading operation has two divisions:

1. Pushing, moving, and placing soil within the site.
2. Importing or exporting additional soil to satisfy a cut or fill need.

It is generally considered good practice to avoid having to export or import large amounts of soil. To avoid excesses, it is necessary several times during design grading to do a cut and fill estimate to calculate the proposed volume of cut and fill to assure that there is a reasonable balance; if the balance is unfavorable, restudy the area and devise a grading plan that produces a balanced cut and fill.

There are several methods of calculating cut and fill, each a variation of the mathematical formula for finding volume. This will be described later.

GRADING GROUND RULES

1. Ground adjacent to all buildings should slope *away* from the structure. Where a building is located close to a steep bank, grade away from the building for 2 ft, then grade back up (Figs. 4-9 and 4-10).

2. Avoid flat grades that won't drain properly (see minimum standards of city and county or other agencies where the work is located). Rule of thumb: for pavement, *minimum* = 0.5 percent; for soil, *minimum* = 1 percent.

3. Grading must *not* extend beyond the project property line.

4. Avoid inadequate storm sewers and too few inlets (with time and experience this will become second nature). The exact number varies with the scale and scope of each project. Maintain an inquisitive attitude until you have mastered it.

5. Graded slopes and banks should not exceed natural angle of repose of soil type, or severe erosion or slippage problems may occur.

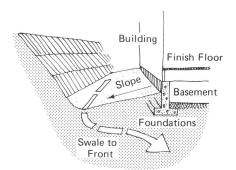

Figure 4-9

Figure 4-10
Even though the land slopes away from the building, the reverse slope drains considerable water to the low point, which is wet most of the year. However, the ducks enjoy the warm water.

6. When grading slopes, start manipulating contours at the bottom of a *cut* situation and at the top in a *fill* situation.

7. Where the land is quite flat, use intermediate contours (0.25- or 0.50-ft contours) and/or an adequate number of spot elevations (generally, areas where intermediate contours are used are marked off to indicate the new contour interval).

8. Show elevations for top and bottom of steps and walk. (Fig. 4–11.)

9. Use symbols recorded in a legend to simplify the drawing. (Fig. 4–12.)

10. Use spot elevations for clarity. (Fig. 4–13.)

11. Devise graphic methods to show retaining walls, building foundations, and curbs. (Fig. 4–14a.)

12. Strip and save all topsoil prior to grading for reuse after grading. (Fig. 4–14b.)

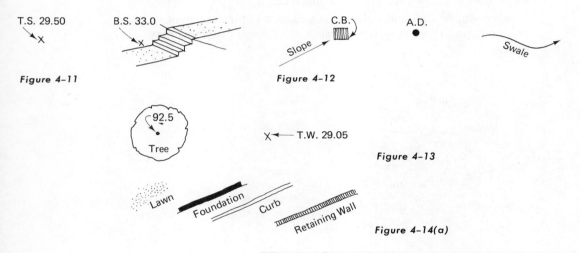

Figure 4–11

Figure 4–12

Figure 4–13

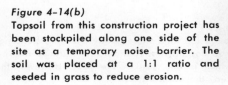

Figure 4–14(a)

Figure 4–14(b)
Topsoil from this construction project has been stockpiled along one side of the site as a temporary noise barrier. The soil was placed at a 1:1 ratio and seeded in grass to reduce erosion.

GRADING PROBLEMS TO AVOID

Destruction of existing valuable vegetation.
Extreme unbalance of cut or fill.
Drainage pockets on flat surfaces, along buildings.
Erosion due to steep grades.
Grading solutions requiring expensive landscape features, such as
walls, steps, etc.

PREPARING THE BASE MAP

An engineered survey is the starting point for developing the grading plan. Surveys usually show the legal description of the land, based on horizontal measurement from known markers or known points of reference. Surveys record both horizontal and vertical dimensions, and locate topography, structures, trees, outcrops, alignments, etc., within the property. (See Fig. 4–15.)

Figure 4-15
A large outcropping adds considerable
expense to the grading operation if it
has to be moved. Where possible,
change the design to avoid grading near
the rock. It may be possible to use the
rock outcrop as a focal point, such as in
this traffic island.

Legal description surveys of properties are called *cadastral surveys* and are prepared by licensed land surveyors, who are bonded by insurance companies for accuracy. Almost all the United States has been carefully measured by the U.S. Coast and Geodetic Survey and gridded into 31 principal baselines. From these baselines, the countryside is laid out in Ranges, Townships, and Sections. Each Township is 6 miles square, or 36 square miles in area, and is orientated north to south and east to west. Each corner is marked with stationary bronze plaques, which allow properties between to be easily located. However, discrepancies in boundaries are common and result from old time surveys that have since been changed or updated. Thomas Jefferson is

credited with development of the Township concept as a way to orga-
nize America's land resource. Each square mile of the Township is
called a section and numbered from 1–36 beginning in the N–W corner. Each section can be further divided into *quarter sections* and again
on down to small lots.

Each property boundary is described by a horizontal *bearing* or
angle, plus a horizontal *distance*. These continue around the property
until all the boundaries of the property have been described, and the
survey is closed. Property boundaries are usually composed of straight
lines that are measured *horizontally*. When working on a steep site, the
measured surface length will be greater than the recorded site length,
as property lines are legally measured horizontally. (Remember your
geometry; the hypotenuse of a triangle is always longer than either
other side.)

Coordinates are used to locate a point on a site and resemble
graph paper. To determine the point, coordinates are measured from
fixed perpendicular straight lines called axes of reference until they
cross. City maps use a crude set of coordinates to locate streets between alphabets and numbers. Each coordinate begins at some stated
or assumed datum (a given point) called the *origin,* and runs out and up
from it at right angles.

The vertical line (going from south to north) is called the Y
coordinate; the horizontal line (going from east to west) is called the X
coordinate. Generally, the X distance is stated first, followed by the Y
distance, which locates the point where they cross.

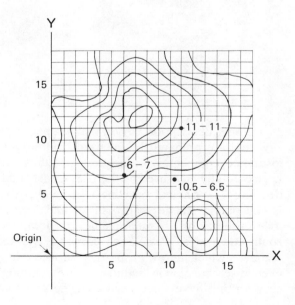

Figure 4-16

To locate a point, first establish a grid system at a convenient scale with a point of origin that can easily be located in the field. With these lines, it is easy to move along the X coordinate until you are opposite the point and record this distance. Do the same for the Y coordinate, and project the lines out or up until they meet at the prescribed point. The two distances are usually written adjacent to the point, with an arrow showing the location (Fig. 4–16).

PLANE TABLE AND HANDLEVEL

The plane table is a useful survey instrument for designers to measure and lay out simple sites. The completed survey, although not totally accurate, is fast and useful for developing base maps of small areas (1 to 2 acres). A plane table is essentially a drawing board of about 24 in.^{2} mounted on a tripod placed somewhere near the center of the area to be mapped. Rotate the sight rule around a pin in the center of the paper and sight each element, trees, buildings, steps, etc., within the survey area. At each sighting, measure the distance from plane table to element and scale the distance on the paper along the sight rule line (Fig. 4–17). By this method, each element can be set out in exact relationship. When the process is complete, the base map is almost exact enough to retrace or can be easily enlarged or reduced.

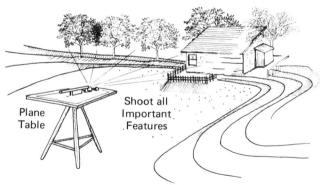

Plane
Table

Shoot all
Important
Features

Figure 4–17

HANDLEVEL

A handlevel is an invaluable field aid for determining relative elevations. The level is used like a telescope, and shows the view, a horizontal cross-hair and a level bubble. The level is moved up and down until the bubble is in the center, and the cross-hair is read against some recognizable element (stadia rod, tape measure, bump on a tree, mark on a building, etc.).

FIELD EXERCISE

Determine and memorize the height of your eye wearing normal working shoes. Aim the handlevel at a measuring stick (or stadia rod) on a wall to find out how high your eye is. When doing rough field calculations, you can use this to calculate elevations. (See Fig. 4-18.)

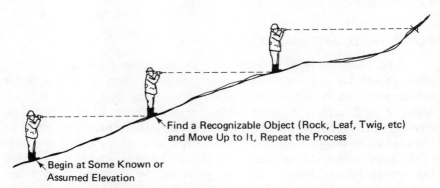

Find a Recognizable Object (Rock, Leaf, Twig, etc) and Move Up to It, Repeat the Process

Begin at Some Known or Assumed Elevation

Figure 4-18   Determining elevation using a handlevel.

EXERCISE 1

Draw Section AA three times, showing existing and proposed ground lines:

1. At the *same* horizontal and vertical scale.
2. At the *same* horizontal scale, with the vertical scale exaggerated two times.
3. At the *same* horizontal scale, with the vertical scale exaggerated three and one half times.

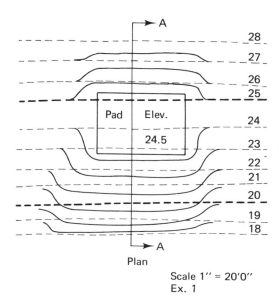

Plan

Scale 1″ = 20′0″
Ex. 1

EXERCISE 2

Prepare a Preliminary Grading Plan for Longfellow School according to the following criteria:

Maximum 1:2 cut.

Maximum 1:4 fill.

Save as many trees as possible.

Drain toward creek.

Softball and football fields: maximum 5 percent grade.

Grade track level (cross slope for drainage).

Do not extend grading beyond property line.

Finished pad elevation of four labeled buildings can vary each 2 ft.

Label all finished pad elevations.

Auditorium grade can slope up a maximum of 10 percent.

Parking: maximum 3 percent grade.

PROCEDURE — Redraw and enlarge the plan on clearprint 1000H. Determine approximate level areas. Block grade using 5-ft contours. Fill in the remainder of the contours, adjusting to satisfy your most creative grading design notions.

Enlarge this plan four times.

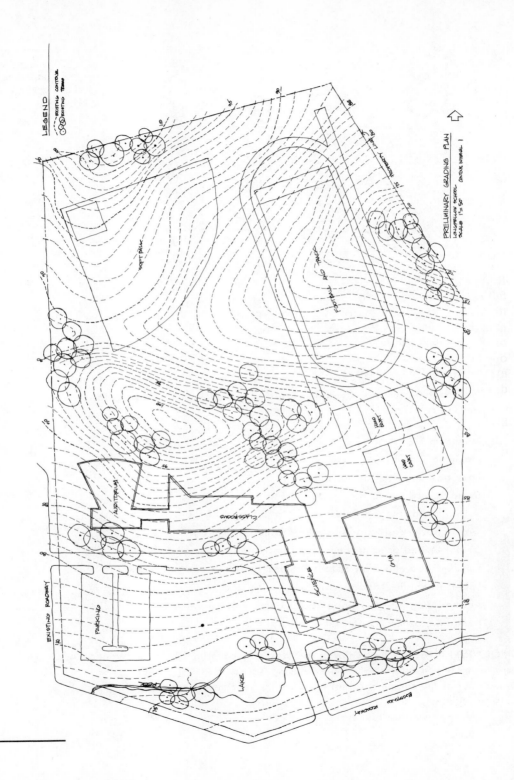

LEGEND

EXISTING CONTOUR
EXISTING TREES

SOFT PARK

FOOTBALL AND TRACK

HAND COURT

HAND COURT

AUDITORIUM

CLASSROOMS

SCIENCE

GYM

EXISTING ROADWAY

PARKING

LAKE

EXISTING ROADWAY

PRELIMINARY GRADING PLAN
LONGFELLOW SCHOOL
SCALE 1" = 50'   CONTOUR INTERVAL 1

5

DRAINAGE

Running water is the most important cause of erosion. Water from rain-fall causes erosion, which probably does more to alter the surface features of the land than all the other agents combined. The average annual rainfall in many cities is approximately 35 in. of water. Of this, 20 to 30 percent becomes runoff water flowing from the land. In developed areas this is as high as 90 to 95 percent, making much drainage more difficult. People prefer relatively dry use areas and so we must drain them. (See Fig. 5–1.)

Drainage is a symbiotic adjunct to the grading process. Every grading plan must consider and solve the drainage problem specific to it.

There are four methods by which rainfall is *removed* from where it falls:

- *By surface runoff* overland and downhill until, eventually, in many areas it reaches the ocean.

Figure 5–1
One moderate rainstorm caused this amount of erosion in a newly graded but yet unplanted bank.

• By *underground subsurface drainage* water infiltrates and moves through most soils both horizontally and vertically under the influence of gravity, although at a much slower rate than surface runoff.

• By *evaporation* from the leaves of plants, standing water, and from many different surfaces.

• By *transpiration* from trees and plants following photosynthesis.

These four methods of removing rainfall combine and become part of the *hydrologic cycle*. The cycle is complete when sufficient water evaporates, returns to the air, is transported and dispersed over land, rises with topography and wind currents, cools, and returns to the earth as fresh rainfall. (See Fig. 5-2a & b.)

Surface runoff is the primary method to remove storm water. Water is usually carried away in some sort of storm drainage system. A storm drainage system *collects, conducts,* and *disposes* of excess surface

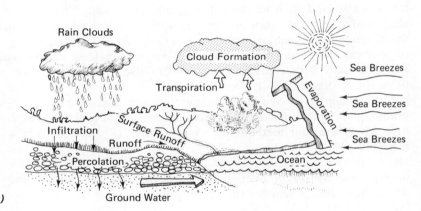

Figure 5-2(a)

Figure 5-2(b)
Corrugated metal culverts are placed under driveways where they intercept the normal drainage channel.

water caused by rainfall. Additionally, a storm drainage system can accomplish the following:

Safeguard against erosion by reducing the rate of flow and volume of water.

Reduce flooding damage to property and increase usability through elimination of unwanted water.

Eliminate unnecessary standing water that may lead to pollution and breeding of insects.

Provide better growing conditions for trees and plants by reducing soil saturation.

Improve load-bearing capacity of soils, thereby increasing the buildability of a site.

LAYOUT AND DESIGN OF DRAINAGE SYSTEM — Runoff occurs during and for a short time following the rains. Water should be collected and conducted away from use areas in a variety of natural drainage patterns, man-made open trenches, and closed pipe — called a storm drainage system.

A typical storm drainage system might begin in someone's backyard with water from the roof collected in a gutter and conveyed through the downspout to the patio. From here it may flow across the patio via gravity (the patio has a slight tilt to assure proper drainage) and onto the lawn. It would then travel across the lawn, alongside the house in a wide, gently sloping grass ditch called *a swale* to the front yard, across this lawn, and over the sidewalk (perhaps illegally) to the street. Some of the water would be lost through subsurface percolation during this process. From the street the water would flow in the gutter downhill for some distance until it reached a catch basin (Fig. 5–3.).

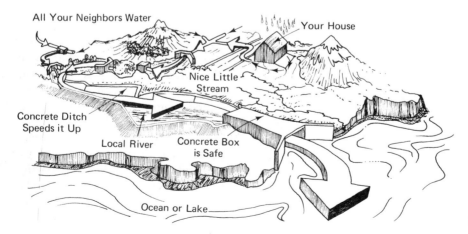

Figure 5–3

Once collected in the catch basin, the water would travel in a storm drain line (pipe) until it crosses a small natural stream, where the storm drain line would daylight (surface) and the water would spill into the stream. The water would flow through culverts (large pipes) where roadways crossed the stream, and eventually portions of the stream may have been riprapped (lined) with large rocks to prevent erosion. As more and more storm drains feed into the stream, it may be lined with concrete to speed the flow of water, and may eventually be covered for safety and other engineering reasons. Eventually, this water will discharge into a larger river, a lake, or the ocean.

Obviously, there are other ways it could have been conducted from the house, including straight away in a storm drain to the lake or river or into the sanitary sewer line (combined with household sewerage), where it would be treated prior to disposal into the bay, river, or ocean. (This practice is disappearing as it causes overflow pollution during storms and owing to the expense of treating storm water.)

DRAINAGE PROCEDURES

It should be obvious that drainage is simply a matter of *collecting, transporting,* and *disposing* of water. In preparing a drainage plan, you must determine where all the runoff will be coming from, where you will eventually put it, and how to get it there. In addition, you must determine which areas you want to keep dry. All flat use areas should be properly drained so that they are usable; this includes paved surfaces, playfields, building entrances, parking, and roads. Additionally, all sloping areas should be designed *not* to dump runoff on adjoining flat use areas. A small swale between the slope and the flat area can carry runoff away.

Runoff can originate on your site or from adjoining property at a higher elevation. Your first task is to analyze the topography, including off-site adjoining lands, to determine the overall large-scale drainage pattern. What existing patterns of runoff affect the site? Where are the high points, ridges, valleys, streams, swales, etc.? This shows where water will be coming from, what quantities you must deal with, and how it will affect your site planning. For large projects, you may want to prepare an off-site drainage pattern plan to guide you. Remember, water always travels perpendicular to the contour and faster as contours are spaced closer (Fig. 5-4).

Check in greater detail all on-site conditions to determine exact surface runoff pattern. Include high points, low points, ridges, valleys, streams, swales, points of concentration, etc. Note soil types, particularly gravelly or sandy soil, which percolate well, and clay or silt soils, which percolate very slowly. Generalized soil maps are available for most areas from the U.S. Soil Conservation Service. For specific sites, it may be necessary to dig several holes to sample the soil.

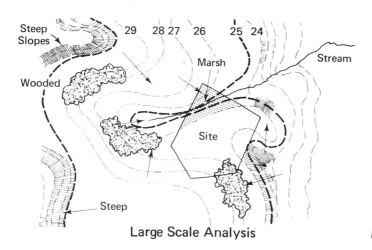

Large Scale Analysis   *Figure 5-4*

These analysis steps are too easily overlooked or considered trivial and time consuming and ignored. However, exactly the opposite is true; it is not unusual for solutions to drainage problems to be discovered during this process. You must take the time and conscientiously locate all the factors mentioned. With practice, you will develop the skill to do it quickly.

Overlay the proposed development on a summary analysis sheet. Note again where water is coming from (the highest points) and where it is going (the lowest point), and don't go against the pattern. Outline all areas that you want to keep dry, and determine fixed elevations, such as existing buildings, trees, roads, etc., that must not be changed and property lines that must not be graded or drained areas. This information is the primary data necessary to *collect* runoff; the next step will be to determine where we can *dispose* of it.

Your task will be to devise drainage systems for removing excess rainwater using these and other techniques. Depending on the size and scope of the project, you will usually be designing that portion *up to* the public right-of-way and connecting to an existing public drainage system. However, you may eventually be called upon to develop a storm drainage system for a neighborhood or a larger portion of the public community. *Remember, a storm drainage system is designed to collect, transport, and dispose.*

As usual, economy is the rule, and you will design the system producing the best results for the lowest cost. Generally, surface drainage across sloping paved and planted areas is cheaper than installing catch basins and underground drain pipes.

GOOD DRAINAGE PRACTICES

1. Gravity is the primary power for carrying away runoff. There

must, therefore, be a continuous minimum slope in the ground level to assure drainage.

2. Water flows perpendicular to the contours *always!*

3. It is ecologically better to slow down runoff water and let it be absorbed by the soil than to remove all of it through surface runoff. Duplicate natural runoff principles where possible (see hydrologic cycle).

4. Runoff water must never be purposefully directed from one property onto a lower neighboring property. It is acceptable for water that has flowed naturally from your property to the neighbors to continue, but you must never increase this flow artificially through grading.

5. Erosion is the biggest problem in drainage; slopes must be carefully calculated to ensure continuous flow, yet not so steep to erode. Plant all slopes immediately following grading.

6. Slow-moving water is likely to create a bog; water moving too fast will erode and form unwanted gullies. Somewhere in between is usually right.

7. Surface drainage is generally preferred to using underground pipes, as this eliminates the danger of pipes clogging, is less expensive, and allows more runoff to percolate into the ground (Fig. 5–5).

8. Paved areas look better when graded almost level; avoid wildly sloping paved areas.

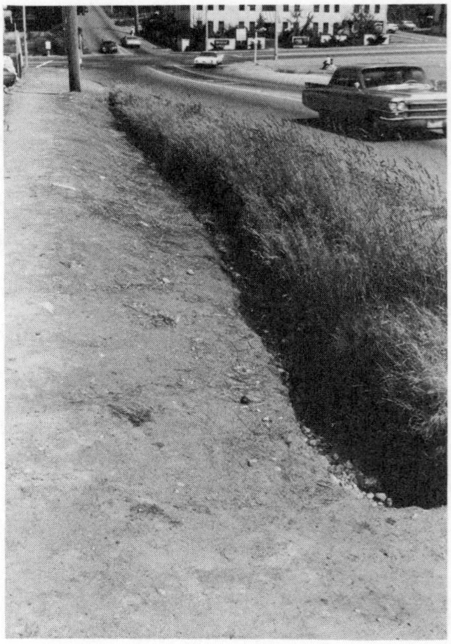

Figure 5–5
Suburban roads are usually drained via surface flow in a ditch. Vegetation improves the looks of a ditch and reduces sedimentation, and is important, but it can't grow around large parking lots.

9. Large amounts of water (such as from a parking lot) should not cross a sidewalk to reach the street drain. Install a catch basin or trench drain before crossing the sidewalk.

10. Always design a secondary drainage route to handle runoff should the primary system become clogged or constricted (Fig. 5–6).

Figure 5–6
Avoid directing water toward buildings, as the catch basin (above shadow) may become clogged and the building flooded. In this case, catch basins were installed 50 ft apart at considerable expense.

Runoff is disposed of either on or off site. Low-density projects with large vegetated open spaces can usually accommodate their own runoff needs by directing runoff onto the naturally vegetated open spaces or into a nearby stream. This is called on-site disposal. The main design task is to avoid concentrating runoff onto one location, which may cause erosion. Instead, devise a number of locations for disposal, and use particularly those areas with established vegetation or gravelly soils.

Higher-density developments usually have a public storm drainage system located in the street. Abutting projects can tie into this system to dispose of their runoff. This is called off-site disposal. This system consists of underground pipes buried 3 to 12 ft deep, with a lateral pipe connecting to each property. On-site runoff is collected and placed in this lateral for disposal by the responsible public agency. It is normal in many high-rainfall areas to have roof and basement drains connected directly to this system. Runoff from landscape development can usually be included in this same lateral connection. Some on-site water can be directed across the sidewalk to the road gutter, but the amount must not make the walk impassable or cause ice conditions in winter.

Once you have determined *where* the water is coming from, and *where* you can dispose of it, you have to determine how you can get it there. Three ways are possible:

Open system, that is, on grade (Fig. 5–7).

Closed system, underground.

Combination of open and closed system (Fig. 5–8).

Figure 5–7
An open drainage system in a suburban area. All runoff is directed toward the ditch, which in this case is paved because of the steepness of the slope. Shallow sloped swales will not erode and need only to be planted in grass.

Figure 5–8
An elegant combination surface-sub-surface system that has been clearly expressed as a design element. Why hide it? Let drainage be a conscious part of the project.

Open systems are preferred as they are less expensive to install and maintain, but closed systems may be necessary where there is a large amount of water or where gradients are minimum. Minimum gradient means that there is not enough surface fall to allow proper drainage, which necessitates the creation of steeper slopes underground. Roof gardens, parking lots, urban courtyards, and staging areas typically require flat dry surfaces that are possible only with a closed system (Fig. 5–9).

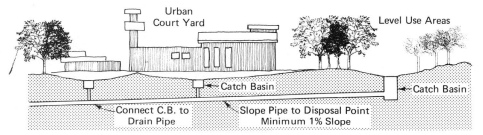

Figure 5-9   Use an underground drain line to dispose of runoff in flat areas.

Drainage systems are shown graphically with contours, spot elevations, direction of drainage arrows, and symbols designating catch basins, underground pipes, trench drains, etc. Swales are shown by pointing the contour *uphill*. The depth of the swale is indicated by *how far* uphill the contours run. Flat areas are always sloped slightly and labeled with spot elevations to indicate directions and slope of drainage. Remember, water always flows by gravity perpendicular to the contours (Fig. 5–10).

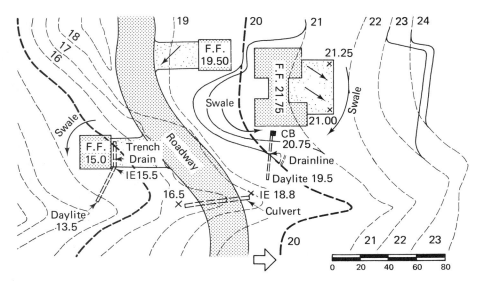

Figure 5-10

DRAWING SWALES

Swales—wide, gently sloping ditches—are probably the most frequently drawn drainage pattern. Swales are used to collect and direct runoff to a disposal area. Through careful use of swales, one can often minimize the need for expensive drainage structures. (See Fig. 5–11.)

Figure 5-11
Swale at the base of a cut bank. This swale is approximately 10 ft wide and 1 ft deep, and adequately drains an area of about ½ acre.

Swales are essentially contours drawn pointing *uphill* as a wide valley. Swale *depth* and *gradient* are the two design variables one must control.

Gradient is determined by the distance contours are spaced along the length of the swale, and should not be less than two percent to operate. To calculate the percent, divide 100 by the contour distance (assuming a one-foot contour interval); i.e., contours spaced 18 feet apart are at 5.6 percent $\left(\frac{100}{18} = 5.55\% \right)$. To find the contour distance for a given percent, divide 100 by the desired percent; i.e., for a 2.5 percent swale, divide 100 by 2.5 for 40 ft. contour spacing. (See Fig. 5–12a and b.)

Depth of the swale is measured perpendicular to the length of the swale. In the diagram, Point A is one foot deep, Point B is two feet deep. When a swale becomes deep and with steep sidewalls, it is called a ditch, and concentrates or conducts runoff. (See Fig. 5–13.)

The width, depth and slope of a swale or ditch can be calculated based on the drainage area, intensity of rain, and runoff coefficient. However, this calculation is not covered in this text. The basic principles to lay out a swale without mathematical calculations include the following:

1. The swale begins wide and shallow at the highest point, and becomes slightly deeper, steeper and wider as more runoff is added.

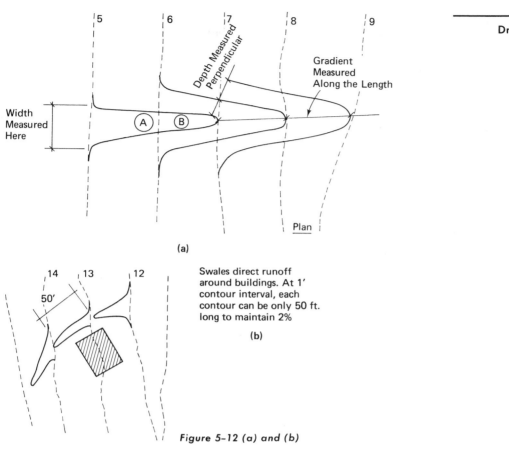

Width
Measured
Here

Depth Measured
Perpendicular

Gradient
Measured
Along the Length

Plan

(a)

Swales direct runoff
around buildings. At 1′
contour interval, each
contour can be only 50 ft.
long to maintain 2%

(b)

50′

Figure 5-12 (a) and (b)

Figure 5-13
Drainage ditch (or channel). The level
terrain necessitates a deep ditch to insure flow. Grass minimizes erosion without
noticably reducing flow.

2. Uniform or increasingly steeper gradients are preferred to gradients that start steep and then become shallow. This will prevent ponding and siltation.

3. To disperse water over the landscape, slope the swale gently and keep it wide (over 20 ft). To direct water to a catchment area, make the swale narrower, deeper and steeper.

Factors that determine drainage requirements include the following:

1. *Land use* The completeness of drainage systems varies depending on land use and density. In a built-up urban area where there is excessive runoff, water can run on the surface for only a short distance, and then must be placed in underground pipes or concrete ditches. In rural areas it is usually possible to drain active areas by letting runoff disperse over the landscape. In addition, use areas like parking lots, walks, play courts, etc., demand a dry area, whereas others, such as meadows, planting beds, forests, etc., can be used under wetter conditions (Fig. 5–14).

2. *Topography* The steeper the area, the faster it will drain. Water runs off quickly as it cannot percolate and can create a drainage problem. Drainage ditches should be provided above and below steep banks to collect runoff, and all banks must be planted immediately following grading to prevent erosion.

3. *Size of area to be drained* The area size determines the amount of water to be disposed of after a rainfall, and determines the size of underground or surface drainage structures. Size of area includes principally those areas that have been sealed from percolation, such as roads, roofs, patios, drives, etc. Typically, the larger the paved area, the larger the underground structures or surface ditches required.

4. *Type of soil* Soil type determines the rate of percolation. Percolation is movement of water through pore spaces in the soil

Figure 5-14
Almost all the rain that falls on this shopping center will be disposed of as runoff. This is contrasted with 20 percent for most areas, and demands an extensive drainage system. Typically, shopping center parking lots are sloped too steeply to assure positive drainage, and catch basins are spaced too far apart to reduce costs.

or the amount of water the soil will absorb. Fine-particle soil, such as clays and silts, does *not* percolate well; large-particle soils, such as sands and gravels, do. Therefore, if you have a sandy soil, you would expect much of the water to percolate into the soil and the runoff requirement to be minimum. One must also check the subsurface geology, for often there is a layer of clay below the sand, which limits percolation.

5. *Vegetative cover* Any thick, matty groundcover will slow the rate of runoff and reduce the need for elaborate drainage systems. Plants also deposit organic matter that absorbs and reduces runoff. If you must divert water from an area or roadway, it is best to divert it over grassed or planted areas, which will minimize the chance of erosion.

6. *Intensity and duration of rainfall* How hard it rains (intensity of rainfall) and the length of time it rains (duration of rainfall) affect the size and type of drainage system. (Rainfall data are available for most areas from the U.S. Weather Service.) Approximately one third of precipitation becomes runoff, and two thirds returns to the atmosphere by evaporation or transpiration.

GETTING ON WITH IT—Once the source of runoff and disposal methods are clearly understood, divide the total area into reasonably sized sub-drainage areas. This is a *commonsense* step involving many small decisions. Normally, the landscape design will suggest a pattern; size of area will be important, with large areas broken into several smaller units; topography may define units; use of different areas will be important. Low-lying points of concentration are obvious places for drainage structures, and all slopes should be outlined. If catch basins are to be used, a safe maximum catchment area is a 40-ft distance. Raised planters and buildings are obstacles to drainage, and may define a sub-drainage area.

Decide whether an open, closed, or combination drainage system will be best to drain each area. Quickly design a drainage system and test it; interconnect each sub-drainage area and redesign problems until the system is acceptable. Often the original concept remains valid throughout the design, but requires adjustment to work around landscape features such as trees, planters, curbs, benches, etc. Additional catch basins may be required, special swales placed in planters, or terraces introduced to increase the fall.

DRAINING FLAT AREAS

Playfields, courts, patios, roof gardens, walls, etc., require a dry, flat surface. Obviously, level areas don't drain well, so they have to be *tilted* slightly to allow water to run off. There are several traditional

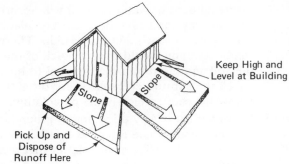

Keep High and
Level at Building

Slope

Slope

Pick Up and
Dispose of
Runoff Here

Figure 5-15(a)

drainage patterns for flat areas, including the following:

TILTED PLANE—Tilt the area in one direction, allowing the water to drain toward the low side (Fig. 5-15a). Locate building at the *high* side to prevent water from draining in. This is the simplest, easiest, and cheapest way to drain a level area, and is acceptable if the runoff can be absorbed at the low end by adjacent land. However, it creates collection problems, as runoff is distributed along the length of the low side (See Fig. 5-15b.) This leads to the second technique, which combines the tilted plane with a valley to concentrate runoff for easy collection (Fig. 5-16).

Figure 5-15(b)
A flat surface tilted toward one side can be warped to the catch basin with high points between the low catch basins.

TILTED PLANE WITH VALLEY—Tilt the plane away from buildings as above, keeping the edge along the building level. At some distance from the building, create a valley to catch the water from the tilted plane and direct it to a collection point. This usually means that the tilted plane must warp slightly to create the valley (Fig. 5-17).

Figure 5-16
Swimming pools are usually drained as four tilted planes, each sloping away from the pool coping. The coping must be kept level, and water can be collected opposite it by warping to catch basins.

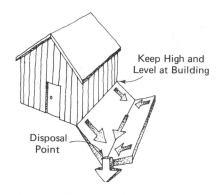

Keep High and
Level at Building

Disposal
Point

Figure 5-17

FUNNEL CATCHMENT SYSTEM — Place the drain somewhere near the center of the flat area, and slope everything toward it. It is analogous to a funnel and is used to drain many urban spaces, such as an enclosed courtyard where buildings surround the flat area. Its disadvantage is that it requires collection pipes, and if the catch basin becomes clogged, the area will flood as there is no second means for handling overflow (Figs. 5–18 through 5–20). Remember to set finish floors *higher* than the outdoor elevation, at least 6 in. (0.5 ft), and slope all areas away from the buildings (Fig. 5–21). The pavement edge along a building is usually kept level as it looks better, with drainage sloping away in another direction. Warping to form valleys to aid collection can be indicated by spot elevations, direction of drainage arrows, design sections, or notes.

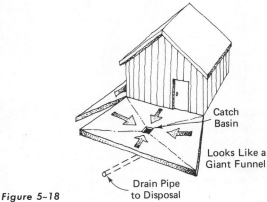

Catch
Basin

Looks Like a
Giant Funnel

Drain Pipe
to Disposal

Figure 5–18

Figure 5–19
This urban plaza is sloped toward a center catch basin. The advantage is primarily visual; the entire perimeter can be
kept level. As an aside, the slope is below minimum for bricks, and works only
because extreme care and extra cost
were employed during construction.

Figure 5–20
The sunken basketball court provides interest for the park, and space for viewers
to sit and watch. However, drainage is
subject to flooding if the catch basin becomes clogged with leaves or by children
at play. A secondary overflow is important for all use areas.

Figure 5-21
It is possible to devise special drains like this square ditch and drain toward a building; but they are easily clogged, and can overflow, causing flood damage, and they may cause someone to trip.

Drainage lines should run straight, with intersections occurring at a Y angle or catch basin so it can be cleaned out. A drainage system with the *shortest* length of pipe and fewest bends is usually best (Figs. 5–22 and 5–24). (Figure 24 a–f shows varied use of these drainage

Figure 5-22
Ditches for underground pipes are usually dug after rough grading is complete unless the pipes are to be buried very deep.

Figure 5-23
Special ditch-digging equipment can dig ditches to 3 ft deep and is useful for residential projects.

Chapter 5

Figure 5–24(a)
A trench drain can be used to center drain along narrow spaces.

Figure 5–24(b)
This center-drained play court drains to a catch basin located under the ping pong table.

Figure 5–24(c)
Amphitheaters create special drainage problems if they extend below the surrounding existing grade. Each step slopes slightly toward the center, and the runoff is removed in a catch basin.

Figure 5-24(d)
This trench drain prevents runoff from an adjacent street from entering a pedestrian area. Note however that the drain has become clogged with sediment and is ineffective.

Figure 5-24(e)
Excessive runoff should be collected *before* reaching a stairway as it will make the stairs slippery. This trench drain — using perforated, removable brick — solves the problem nicely. For narrower stairs, the landing can be warped to one side, eliminating the need for an expensive structure.

Figure 5-24(f)
Runoff can be directed toward vertical landscape elements if they are surrounded by trench drains.

Culverts should be a minimum of ten inches inside diameter to reduce clogging and allow easy cleaning. Many residential projects have used four-inch plastic culverts, but these will clog in several years, and are impossible to clean (see Fig. 5-25).

Figure 5-25
This culvert has been completely filled with silt and is no longer operative.

The closed system is useful in level areas, as you can bury drain lines progressively deeper, thereby assuring adequate fall for drainage. The pipe is laid at a uniformly sloping grade, which is determined by the designer with a profile drawn along the proposed pipe length. The pipe location is drawn as a heavy dashed line on the grading plan, with depth shown by invert elevations. An invert elevation is the elevation of the *bottom* of the pipe or the flow line leading out of the drainage structure. The elevation at the top of the drainage structure is called the rim elevation (Figs. 5-26a and b).

These five structures are intermixed as required, but used sparingly as each structure is expensive. As a general rule, 75 ft should be the maximum length of flow toward a catch basin or area drain. They are aided by curbs, gutters, swales, and sloping planes to move surface water to them. Exposed drainage structures are large and therefore become a design consideration. They are easily moved during design, and as there are numerous ways to drain any area, experiment and redesign until the drainage matches the design intent (Fig. 5-27).

Figure 5-26(a)
Institutional or public projects require large, heavy drainage structures that will be almost self-maintaining. These precast concrete catch basins have knock-out sections for inserting drain pipe and are easy to install with the aid of a back-hoe.

Figure 5-26(b)
Residential scaled projects use light-weight structures that are inexpensive to install, but require continued maintenance. This 4-in. plastic drain line can clog easily, and the clean-out does not offer enough room to work in easily.

Figure 5-27
Constructing a concrete ditch alongside a path is an old-fashioned engineering approach. It is better to direct runoff onto the lawn and carry it in a wide swale.

LOCATING DRAINAGE STRUCTURES

Locating catch basins is more art than science. Ask two designers to locate them for the same area, and invariably their plans will be different. There are, however, some conditions and common practices which can help you design the best system.

Factors which *increase* the number of catch basins:

1. High intensity of rainfall.
2. Heavy pedestrian or other use necessitating relatively dry surfaces.
3. Impermeable soils that restrict runoff percolation.
4. High percentage of paved or roofed surfaces.
5. Extensive level surfaces.
6. Cold weather conditions that may cause sheeting or standing water to ice up.

The opposite of these would allow fewer drainage structures.
Some common approaches and practices:

1. Begin by dividing the total project into smaller drainage sub-areas by *land use*. For instance, draw a freehand bubble around the parking lot, athletic field, courtyard, entrance area, etc., and then design a system to collect water using the three approaches described on page 104.

2. Differentiate between *paved* and *planted* areas by using only swales in planted areas, and a combination of swales and drainage structures for paved or roofed areas. You may eventually decide to use catch basins in planted areas, but try it first without.

3. Next, prepare a diagrammatic disposal scheme. Which areas are to be disposed directly into a public storm system, which into a retention system, which into a detention system, and which can percolate directly over the landscape? This step usually helps one understand where runoff should be directed, and the location of some structures.

4. Prepare a piping diagram, starting at the hook-up to public storm system (hopefully the lowest point) and working uphill. One hook-up should be sufficient for a small project such as apartment or office building. Draw straight lines from that point, with as few bends as possible to each drainage sub-area (as described above). Keep the pipes in roads, parking lots or open space and never go under buildings.

5. Place a clean-out catch basin wherever the pipe has to bend, and try to work it into the plan. Be flexible — move the pipe or catch basin until it makes common sense with the plan.

6. Detail design each sub-area, directing water toward the designated catchment area. Try to minimize the number of catch basins as they are expensive, but do not be too stingy. Test all circulation and use areas for positive runoff. If an area will not be heavily used, it may be acceptable to eliminate several catch basins and let the runoff drain farther as surface flow. Be sure water is positively drained *away* from the buildings.

7. Divide sub-areas into smaller areas if there are fixed elements that must be preserved (trees, buildings, benches, planters, curbs, etc.) or if the area has a complex shape or numerous vertical elements.

8. Experiment with each sub-area to determine the most efficient catch basin location. Assume that you have only one structure per area, and tilt, swale or curb the surface toward it. Evaluate the results, and add another structure if necessary. Your evaluation should examine whether the extra drainage structure costs more than the extra grading, swaling and curbing which would replace it.

GAME COURTS AND PLAY SURFACES—Such areas should appear level yet slope adequately to drain. Grading for all play facilities should be to minimum tolerances so as not to affect the game play. However, they must be sloped enough to remove standing water so that runoff does not saturate the soil. Hard courts, such as for basketball and tennis, are sloped crosswise, with one edge higher than the other. In tennis, the water runs parallel to the net toward the other side (Fig. 5–28). An alternative method is to raise the center of the court slightly and slope it to one or both ends. However, this upsets the service and play.

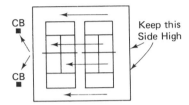

Tennis, Basketball and Volleyball

Slope across the court parallel to the net—basketball, volleyball, badminton are drained the same way.

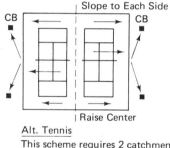

Alt. Tennis

This scheme requires 2 catchment areas.

Figure 5–28

Football, soccer, and baseball fields are normally raised in the center and pitched uniformly toward the out-of-bounds areas. A football field pitched at 2 percent would raise the field at least 2 ft in the center and perhaps slightly more. For safety, football, soccer, and baseball fields should be free of catch basins, so drainage swales have to be warped toward the catch basins, which are located out of the line of play. Approved drainage plans for common playfields and play courts are shown in Figure 5–29.

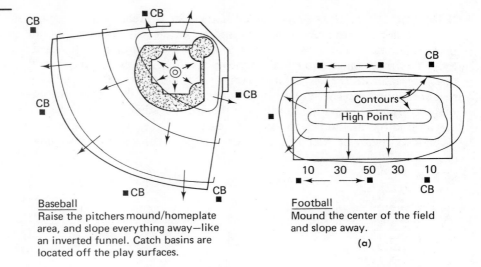

Baseball
Raise the pitchers mound/homeplate area, and slope everything away—like an inverted funnel. Catch basins are located off the play surfaces.

Football
Mound the center of the field and slope away.

(a)

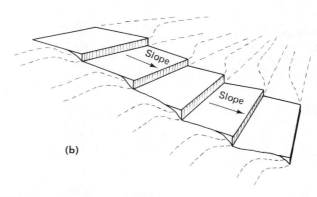

(b)

(c)

Figure 5-29(a) (b) (c)
Tennis or basketball courts can terrace down a shallow slope with each court raised above the next with a small retaining wall. The courts should cross-slope with the grade at 1-2 percent for drainage.

DRAINAGE OF STEEP SLOPES

Newly cut or filled slopes will erode and may need *interceptor ditches* or *terraces* to catch runoff. An interceptor ditch is a drainage channel located at the top of the slope to intercept water from above before it crosses the slope and causes erosion. This ditch should be sloped in one direction to carry water to a collection point for disposal or dispersal. A terrace is an intermediate level area on a long slope that collects rainwater deposited from above and prevents erosion damage below. Interceptor ditches are usually graded into each terrace. Ditches constructed in *cut* areas will usually function with a grass lining; those in *fill* areas may require a concrete, rock or asphalt lining. Filled banks are always more subject to erosion than cut banks and may require terraces every 20 ft of slope, whereas cut banks can be terraced 40 ft apart. (See Fig. 5–30.)

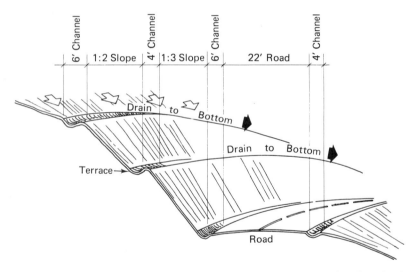

Figure 5-30 The slope and terrace dimensions of road banks can be described in a cross section.

SUBSURFACE DRAINAGE

Runoff water flows *below* the surface in the soil as well as overland. Our discussion has centered around methods to collect, transport, and distribute surface runoff, but often the problem is really below grade and these methods won't work. This section introduces subsurface drainage, and Chapter 10 will cover the details necessary to design a proper system (Fig. 5–31).

COLLECTING

Surface collection utilizes curbs, catch basins, gutters, area drains, etc.; subsurface collection utilizes gravel-filled ditches to intercept the flow and perforated drain pipe to transport it (Fig. 5-32). Water travels underground along lines of least resistance, and is attracted to gravel and then to the perforated pipe to be transported to the disposal area.

The perforated pipe is installed at the bottom of the gravel with the holes pointed down. Water fills the gravel ditch and eventually pours through the holes to be taken away (Figs. 5-33 and 5-34).

Subsurface drainage is useful for a variety of specialty problems. Basements are kept dry by installing a perforated drain line *below* the footing and backfilling with gravel. Athletic fields can be drained with

Figure 5-32
Installation of subsurface drainage laterals for a remodeled playfield.

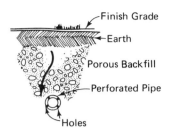

Finish Grade
Earth
Porous Backfill
Perforated Pipe
Holes

Figure 5-33

Figure 5-34
A subdrain system is like a tree; a main branch with laterals connecting to it. The larger-diameter main is intersected by laterals.

subsurface perforated drain lines to eliminate dangerous catch basins and keep the field level. Farms can be underdrained to help eliminate unwanted salt buildup. The cost for this drainage method is, however, expensive and its use is therefore limited.

TRANSPORTING

Most runoff, whether collected below grade in perforated pipes, above ground, or in structures, is transported in a closed, underground system of drain lines. This system transports water from each collection point in a tight (closed) network of pipes to a final disposal location. Pipes can be plastic (ABS, polyvinyl chloride, (PVC) etc.), Transite (a cement asbestos product), concrete, or clay, depending on code requirements and availability. Plastic is generally preferred as it is lightweight and corrosive resistant. Pipes operate under gravity flow requiring a minimum slope of 0.5 percent (one-half percent). Drain lines should be at least 6 in. in diameter for residential layouts, and larger to handle greater volumes of water or for institutional projects.

DISPOSAL

Water can be disposed of into a nearby stream, river, or public storm drainage system, or it can be distributed over the landscape or placed back into the earth through an underground drain field. An underground drain field *discharges* water by gravity through a perforated pipe laid on gravel with the holes *pointed up*. Its eventual success depends on the porosity of the soil; sandy or gravelly soil absorbs more water than clay or silt soil (see Fig. 5-35.)

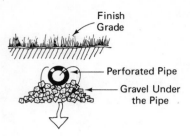

Figure 5-35

Placing water back in the soil holds promise for hydrologically balanced drainage plans, as the water table will be recharged, polluted runoff will be filtered by the soil, and the quantity of runoff will be diminished, which reduces erosion damage. The method is expensive and unlikely to be used unless a *user fee* is placed on storm water disposed through the municipal system.

FIELD EXERCISE

On a rainy day, don rain gear and umbrella and observe how well drainage of various areas really works. Discuss and answer the following questions:

1. In several parking lots, measure the horizontal distance water must travel to reach a catch basin. Measure also the thickness of the sheet of running water at 50, 75 and 100 feet. Can you walk through it without getting wet? What about in sandals?

2. Along a sidewalk, note the difference in the amounts of water on the sidewalk when it does and does not have additional runoff. Under what conditions is the walk to wet to walk on?

3. In a play court (basketball, tennis), how shallow can the gradient be and still have all the water drain from the court one hour after the storm? Is it too steep for comfortable play? (*Note:* This is a tricky question, for it is possible to construct, at very high costs, courts which are almost level but do not puddle. Any court under $1\frac{1}{2}$ percent that drains perfectly is expensive to construct.)

4. Repeat the same exercise on a drizzly day, and during an extreme cloudburst. (*Note:* Designers seldom design a drainage system large enough for the extreme condition as the benefits are seldom worth the additional costs.)

There are five basic drainage structures you must be familiar with to design a closed underground drainage system:

1. *Area drain* a drain used to collect water from a specific area and place it directly into an underground pipe. An area drain is usually located at the lowest point in the catchment area, and has a grate to catch debris and prevent clogging. It looks and is like a large version of a shower drain (Fig. 5–36).

2. *Catch basin* like an area drain, except it has a deep pit to catch sediment and prevent the pipes from clogging. It is used where there will be erosion or heavy fall-time leaf buildup as it can be cleaned out periodically. Nearby area drains or other catch basins can be connected to it (Figs. 5–37 and 5–38).

3. *Trench drain* a linear drain used to collect water along a length and place it in underground pipes. The bottom of the drain is tilted toward one end, where it is connected to the drain pipe, and the top is covered with removable grate. A clean-out pit can be added just prior to the underground pipe if necessary (Figs. 5–39a and b and 5–40.)

4. *Culvert* a pipe used to carry runoff water under driveways, roads, paths, etc. (Figs. 5–41 and 5–42).

5. *Underground pipe* pipe used to transport runoff from collection to distribution. The pipes can be either clay, concrete, plastic, or composition, and solid or perforated (Fig. 5–43).

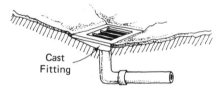

Cast Fitting

Figure 5-36

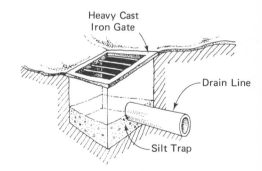

Heavy Cast Iron Gate

Drain Line

Silt Trap

Figure 5-37

Figure 5-38
This catch basin will be fitted with a cast-iron grate and set carefully to grade.

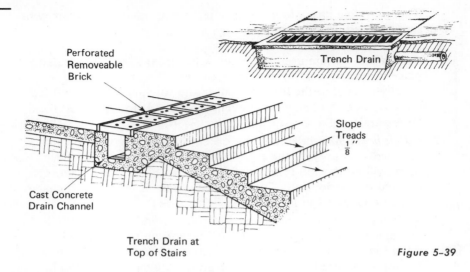

Perforated Removeable Brick

Trench Drain

Cast Concrete Drain Channel

Slope Treads $\frac{1}{8}''$

Trench Drain at Top of Stairs

Figure 5-39

Figure 5-40
Trench drains solve difficult problems, such as preventing all the uphill runoff from sheeting down this driveway.

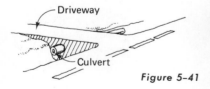

Driveway

Culvert

Figure 5-41

Figure 5-42
Culverts vary in size from 6 in. (which is hard to keep clean) to several feet. As the velocity of runoff is slowed at the culvert, siltation automatically occurs and maintenance is a continual problem.

Figure 5–43
Underground drain line is usually concrete for institutional projects; however,
clay and plastic pipe can be used. Pipe
is available in short sections and special
fittings (bends, Y's, etc.) and is fastened
together with rubber O-ring gaskets.

TERMINOLOGY

Subgrade, pad elevation, finish grade, and finish floor elevation are
interrelated but often confused terms. While it is important to understand them, it is even more important to understand that there is flexibility in adjusting them, and often a 0.5-ft shift in one elevation will
free up an entire plan. Let's start at the bottom with *subgrade* and
work up.

Site development requires removing material below the final grade
to make room for concrete, topsoil, asphalt, etc. *Subgrade* describes
the total depth of excavation necessary to add construction materials.
Pad elevation refers to the subgrade under a building, and should be
low enough to accommodate gravel, foundation, slab, etc. Subgrade and
pad elevations are usually not shown with contours, but are designated
by a note stating, "Subgrade shall be 0.25 ft [or whatever] below finish
grade."

Finish grade is the final grade when all site development is complete, that is, the final grade of the lawn, patio, drive, etc., and is designated with contours and spot elevations (Fig. 5–44).

Finish floor elevation refers to the finish first floor of a building or
to another designated floor, including the basement. Finish floor elevation should be a minimum of 7 in. above finish grade to protect wood
from coming into contact with soil and rotting. It can be more depending on the type of construction; concrete slab floors can be as close as

Figure 5–44
This worker is setting finish grade for a
walkway by leveling from offset grade
stakes. The stakes are set several feet
away from the actual work so they will
not be lost during construction.

7 in., whereas standard frame construction requires 18 in. for access under the floor (Fig. 5–45).

Setting finish floor elevations is usually a trial and error process balancing design requirements against grading problems and potentials. Keep the house close to the ground to maximize indoor–outdoor relationships and minimize earth work. Be flexible and test all alternatives. Remember to record the grades of all existing stationary objects, like trees, buildings, stairs, and retaining walls, and use them as given elevations during design (Fig. 5–46).

Figure 5-45
Form work for a slab foundation. The grade at the top of the form will be the finished floor elevation. The grade inside the forms is the subgrade of the finished floor. You will note that crushed gravel has been placed to ensure a firm footing for the concrete. The grade outside the form has been subgraded, and finish grades will probably be 6 to 8 in. below the finish floor elevation.

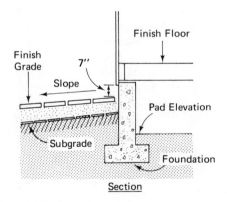

Figure 5-46

CHECKLIST FOR A SIMPLE DRAINAGE SYSTEM

1. Analyze topography:
   a. Check off-site drainage patterns. What existing patterns of runoff affect the site? What is the characteristic of the "watershed"? What extent is runoff coming onto the site?

b. Check on-site surface and subsurface conditions:
    (1) Determine the runoff pattern. Where are high and low points, ridges, valleys, streams, and swales? Where is the water collecting? Where is it going? Note areas to be drained in acres and square feet for scale reference.
    (2) Locate areas of sandy–gravelly soils that will percolate well to minimize the need for surface drainage; locate clay–silt soils that will require additional drainage. Outline matty vegetation that might absorb runoff

c. Check means of disposal. Once you've collected the water, what are you going to do with it?
    (1) On-site disposal by overland dispersal into an existing stream or via subsurface drainage.
    (2) Off-site disposal, usually into an existing public storm-water system (see also pertinent local codes).

2. Analyze use-areas for probable location of drainage structures.
    a. Points of runoff concentration are obvious places for catch basins or area drains.
    b. Flat use-areas may require drainage structures.
    c. Items that interfere with flow of water such as buildings, trees, etc., need special consideration (Fig. 5–47).
    d. Long "channels" need occasional catch basins (Fig. 5–48).

3. How close should catch basins be?
    a. Check code requirements if they apply.

Figure 5-47 Special sitting areas and planters create additional drainage problems as water must work its way around the objects. Check the plan with extreme care before construction for adequate slope and collection points.

Figure 5–48
Runoff should not flow into buildings or basements. Install a catch basin or trench drain to collect it, and warp the slopes to it.

   b.   Check drainage patterns to avoid heavy concentrations.
   c.   Check sheeting of water; avoid excessive concentrations on walkways and use areas. Typically, catch basins should not be farther apart than 150 ft.
4. Determine the best pattern of underground drain lines, and keep in mind the following points:
   a.   Start first with the highest structure and work toward the low point or disposal area. Next, reverse the procedure and locate the most reasonable point or points of disposal and work up. Several different drain lines may be necessary.
   b.   Underground drain lines should connect as *straight lines,* with change of direction occurring at a catch basin.
   c.   Avoid locating pipes under foundation walls of buildings, retaining walls, etc.
   d.   Try to follow the natural slope of the site. Avoid running contrary to the slope since this will result in deep trenches and more structures.
   e.   Unless the project is relatively uncomplicated, do not expect to connect all structures with one line. Most systems take on the appearance of a tree (multistemmed in some cases) or a series of trees
   f.   The size of underground pipe is not critical at this time and will be discussed in Chapter 10.
   g.   *Less is more.* Storm drainage can be overdone and is *expensive.*

EXERCISE
DRAINAGE

This should be an easy exercise. Basically, you will redo the second grading project (the small apartment complex), but this time include an adequate drainage system. This will allow you to reconsider your earlier study and correct any errors.

There are some considerations and clarifications:

You may change the pad elevations for any building rather than use retaining walls. Make sure to record it on the drawing. (Remember, it is easiest to set the pad elevation 0.5 ft above the contour you choose.)

Assume that there is a connection to the public storm-drainage system in the street at each parking lot entrance.

Set finish floor elevations 9 in. above the pad elevation and record it on the drawing.

Enlarge this drawing three times. Draw contours on back of original.

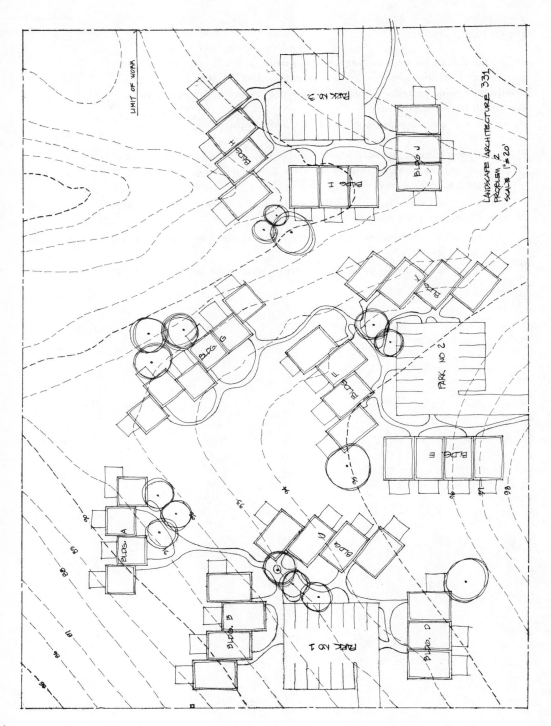

LANDSCAPE ARCHITECTURE 331
PROBLEM 2
SCALE 1" = 20'

LIMIT OF WORK

PARK NO. 3

BLDG. H

BLDG. I

BLDG. J

BLDG. C

PARK NO 2

BLDG. G

BLDG. F

BLDG. E

BLDG. A

BLDG. B

BLDG. G

BLDG. D

PARK NO 1

ROAD ALIGNMENT AND LAYOUT

That transportation is best which transports least.
Thoreau

Roads are the primary means for circulation and become the backbone of our communities. In addition to providing a flexible movement system, they perform a number of communal functions, including the following:

- Space for human activity: buying, selling, playing, working, socializing, etc. (Fig. 6–1).
- Location for our utilities: sanitary sewers, gas, electricity, water, telephone, storm drainage, etc.
- Systems of safety services, such as fire and police alarms, hydrants, street lighting, etc.
- A neighborhood setting creating a basic community image, neighborhood identity, and character.
- Routes for pedestrian, bicycle, equestrian, and other nonmotorized movement.
- Visual orientation, location, and direction.

Most existing roads do *not* serve all these purposes in a manner responsive to total community needs. Many roads are, in fact, becoming a menace to quiet, comfortable living (Fig. 6–2). In this chapter we will begin to talk about a bias designers should enunciate: the auto, although important to our life style, has intruded selfishly into many areas where it has no real purpose. Our role must be to provide for the pedestrian and other nonauto users (including the auto driver when out of the car, walking, or trying to enjoy peace and quiet at home) and for residents who live alongside the road.

This chapter will extend our skill in grading circulation routes to cover road alignment and layout.

Figure 6-1

Figure 6-2
Pave the world! Careless extension of the road across the planter, sidewalk, and into the parking lot encourages fast and careless driving and diminishes the pedestrian environment.

STREETS AND ROADS

Streets are thoroughfares in a town or city with curb, gutters, planting strips, and sidewalks; *roads* are less developed ways, usually in the country. For safety and efficiency, roads are aligned along the flattest possible routes, which minimizes grade change. Aligning roads on flat areas is relatively easy, and necessitates balancing *cost* of construction against the value of existing natural and man-made objects that might be destroyed. Roads aligned over hilly areas are a design challenge, that is, to provide a suitable road width and grade without excessive disturbance to the landscape. You will remember from Chapter 3 that there are two primary methods to move over a hill:

1. Straight up and over traveling *perpendicular* to the contours. This method minimizes grading, as the road can be aligned directly onto the land, but may create a steep route (Fig. 6–3).

2. Via a shallow gradient almost *parallel* to the contours. This method requires cut and/or fill to create a level roadbed, which may erode or slip but is convenient for most vehicles and pedestrians (Fig. 6–4).

Figure 6–3

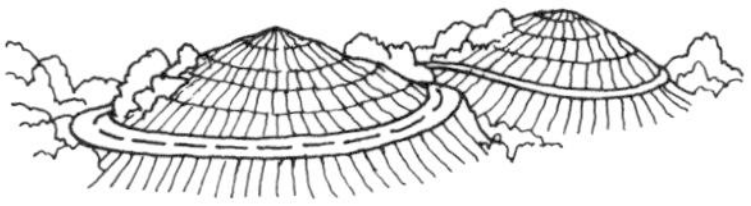

Figure 6–4

SOME GUIDING PRINCIPLES FOR DESIGNING A NEW ROAD

Safety, cost, efficiency, and amenity are used to judge the success of a particular roadway design. I would probably reverse the order somewhat, starting with *amenity,* and try to first determine the appropriate quality and character of the street. Should it be urban, rural, pedestrian, fast moving, tree lined, a shared pedestrian–auto space, etc.? (Figs. 6–5 through 6–8.) Once you understand the character you can

Figure 6–5
Rural roads can be narrow and informal, and should blend into the surrounding landscape. No curbs are necessary as runoff can be absorbed into the surrounding vegetation, and paving can be to a minimal standard.

Figure 6–6
Rural alleys and access roads that carry little traffic can be surfaced with gravel and need not be curbed. Order and organization are achieved through fences or other private-property developments.

Figure 6-7 With a little planting and maintenance, narrow alleys can be an attractive road.

Figure 6-8(a)
City residential streets can be as narrow as 25 ft to reduce the speed of travel. Parking should be allowed on both sides, with a planted planter and sidewalks on either side.

Figure 6-8(b)
Pedestrian streets should have no curbs, increased visual scale, and perhaps a randomness to diminish the linearity of the spaces.

begin to diagram origin and destinations, and analyze possible routes for development opportunities and constraints. These might include the following:

Avoid areas steeper than 10 percent.

Avoid soils subject to slippage.

Save important trees and relate road to them.

Relate road to important views.

Keep back from streams, rivers, or marshes.

Follow topography to reduce costs and improve traffic flow.

Safety can then be considered, with the principal problem being intersections, traffic generators (schools, shopping, etc.), and pedestrian conflict areas. Finally, cost can be checked and adjustments made to meet the budget. Between the 1950s and 1970s, roads were designed with the lowest possible cost as the governing rule. Straight-line connections and short-term benefits were more important than long-term costs. This is beginning to change with greater consideration being given to the quality of the finished project; but the following considerations are still important:

1. Topography and physical features. What's in the way?
2. Directness, or shortest distance between destinations. A straight line is the shortest distance, but don't be afraid to bend it to avoid valued landscape or cultural elements.
3. Maximum efficiency of construction costs. Avoid difficult terrain and unusual sites that require special treatment.
4. Available land. Parks have been considered *cheap land* in the past, and we will live to regret it. New roads should not be subsidized by park users or any other group of residents.
5. Number of users and frequency of use. This affects size and alignment, with demand theoretically increasing the width and smoothing out the alignment.
6. Running speed. Faster traffic requires a high degree of roadway refinement—larger curves, shallower grades, longer sight lines.
7. Safety:
   a. Most accidents occur at intersections
   b. Accidents increase with traffic volume, up to a point where congestion sets in.
   c. Accidents decrease with higher cross-section standards (wider lanes, structures, shoulders, better paving design, etc.).
   d. Accidents decrease with increased sight distance.
   e. Design inconsistencies are conducive to accidents.
   f. Control of access onto a road is a significant safety feature.
   g. Accidents increase with frequency of roadside attractions (service stations, signs, etc.).

RIGHT-OF-WAY

Roads are either publicly or privately owned; that is, they belong to a town, county, or state (public), or to an individual or company (private). Public roads are constructed in a right-of-way, a dedicated strip of land owned by the public and varying in width depending upon the type of roadway. Forty to one hundred feet wide is usual, with wider widths necessary for high-speed or high-volume roads. The street, curb and gutter, planting strip, sidewalk, and land necessary for construction grading must be placed in the right-of-way (Fig. 6–9). Private drives usually do not have a designated right-of-way and simply occur somewhere on a piece of land that is owned by an individual or company. One exception is a private road serving and owned by several homes. For legal purposes, this type of road will be constructed within a legally defined parcel of land.

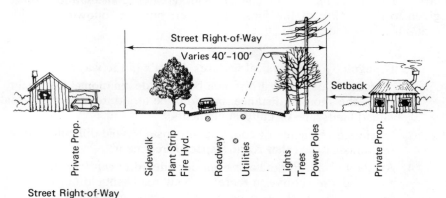

Street Right-of-Way

Figure 6–9   Street right-of-way.

Rights-of-way are usually laid out in a straight and uniform width, as narrow as possible, to "save public expense." One can easily question this cost-saving premise. For instance, a road right-of-way determined by physiographic constraints, such as including a steep ravine or stand of trees, or broadening where difficult topography occurs, or providing a buffer or sylvan pedestrian walk, may in the long run be a wise public investment (Fig. 6–10). Arterial widening programs are good examples; an insufficient right-of-way width was designated 20 or 30 years ago, and now extensive retaining walls are necessary and no room is left for street trees and the design variation that creates a quality neighborhood.

SIDEWALKS—Pedestrians require safe, continuous, pleasant places to walk, which are relatively free from automobile conflicts and noise, yet active enough to sustain interest and assure personal safety. Streets are

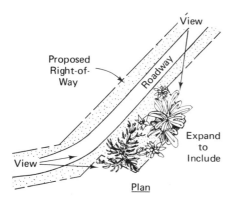

Figure 6-10
Expand right-of-way to include any important view or ecological area.

usually the most continuous, interesting, and active route; therefore, sidewalks are located parallel to the roadway. However, this produces only a fair pedestrian environment, with safety, peace and quiet, and continuity compromised by the car. Sidewalks can be located and designed to be more advantageous for the pedestrian by

Being separated from the roadway by a planted strip of land 4 to 20 ft wide (Figs. 6-11 and 6-12).

Figure 6-11   Entries to parking lots should be narrowed and organized at one place and the curb and planter reconstructed.

Figure 6-12

Allocating a wider pedestrian section and designing a sidewalk that meanders in a free-form path (Fig. 6-13).
Bending a sidewalk into any adjoining public lands such as parks and playgrounds, instead of simply following alongside the road (Fig. 6-14).

Park

Figure 6-13

Plan

Figure 6-14

Using an asymmetric road section with a wide pedestrian area on one side and a narrow one on the other (Fig. 6–15).

Developing a pedestrian walkway system *separate* from the road. This may create safety and security problems as patrolling is difficult, unless there is sufficient use to be self-policing. Costs are higher, as two sets of lights, land, drainage, etc., must be provided.

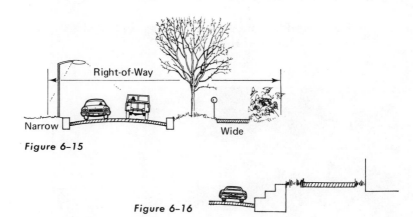

Right-of-Way

Narrow

Wide

Figure 6-15

Figure 6-16

Raising the walk, thereby creating an area superior to the auto to assure pedestrian safety. Many Southern European streets are raised 18 in. above the street, creating a marvelous platform for pedestrian activity. Access from parked cars and street crossings is more difficult, especially for handicapped people (Fig. 6–16).

Parking along the walk, which affords an additional auto barrier and measure of safety (Fig. 6–17).

Installing safe-crosses — expanded sidewalks at the intersections to make street crossing easier. As cars must slow to enter the block, a special community image is created and safe play is possible (Fig. 6–18).

Figure 6-17   Parked Car

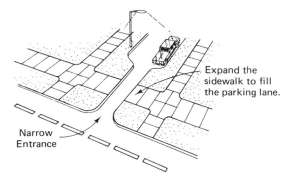

Expand the
sidewalk to fill
the parking lane.

Narrow
Entrance

Figure 6-18
Pedestrian safe cross.

Traffic in towns points out that "... the freedom with which a person can walk about and look around is a very useful guide to the civilized quality of our urban area. Judged against this standard many of our towns now seem to leave a great deal to be desired ...."

DRAINAGE OF STREETS

Roads are constructed with a somewhat level surface to move cars on, which is pitched in some direction to drain and catch runoff. The road can be drained by one of the four following ways:

1. Grading the road level across the width, but sloped over the length. This causes water to sheet down the length, where it must eventually be caught and moved elsewhere. This type of road is satisfactory for many private roads and some public roads in areas with little rainfall, as sheeting water is uncomfortable for pedestrians crossing the street (Fig. 6-19).
2. Forming a crown in the center of the road pitches water toward both sides. This is the method used on most streets as collecting water is fairly easy, and the crown separates two-way traffic.

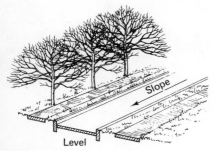

Figure 6-19

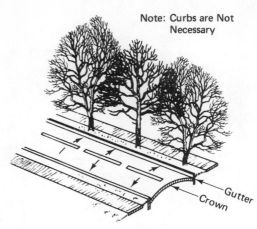

Figure 6-20
Crowning the road

A 6-in. crown is adequate for most streets up to 40 ft wide, with a shallower crown on streets to be plowed for snow removal. Water can be directed over the landscape on either side, or curbs and gutters installed to direct runoff to catch basins (Fig. 6-20).

3. Sloping the road toward one side allows water to be dispersed over the landscape or collected in gutters along that side. This drainage method is useful when the road parallels the contours, as you can take up some grade by sloping the road *with* the contours. The road is slightly more difficult to drive on, as the uphill traffic has a tendency to "slip" toward the lower lane (Fig. 6-21).

Figure 6-21

4. Depressing the road in the center allows water to collect in the middle and run via gravity to some catchment area. This system minimizes drainage structures, but the street is difficult to clean and somewhat unsure to drive on. For cleaning, a curb and gutter alongside the planter strip is still the easiest for power cleaners to sweep or wash (Fig. 6–22).

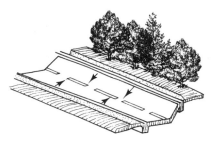

Figure 6–22(a)
Depressing the center.

Figure 6–22(b)
Narrow streets are ideally suited for center drainage, particularly if *no* curbs are used.

DRAWING CONTOURS TO INDICATE STREET DRAINAGE

We will start with the simplest situation—depressing the center of the road—because it is easy to understand, even though it is not typically used. This pattern forces runoff toward the center of the road where it travels downhill to a catchment area. (See Fig. 6–23.) The roadway must never be perfectly level, but should slope slightly in one

Figure 6–23
Unless roads are sloped adequately, water will stand in puddles for long periods. Asphalt roads should have at least a 2 percent slope.

direction to ensure adequate drainage. Contours are shown as you would show a stream or valley, with the contours pointing *up the road*. Drawing contours in a V form indicates a V-shaped depression; rounding them slightly indicates a soft, curving depression (Fig. 6–24).

A crowned road is the most typical method of street construction. The high crown in the center forces runoff toward each side, where it is collected along a curb or ditch or allowed to disperse over the landscape. The contours are shown exactly *opposite* to the center-depressed road, that is, pointed going *downhill* as a ridge would be shown. A rounded contour is typical, with drainage following routes perpendicular to the contours (Fig. 6–25).

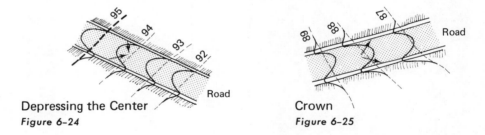

Depressing the Center
Figure 6–24

Crown
Figure 6–25

The flat cross section or roads sloped slightly to one side are easy to draw. Flat roads have the contours cutting directly across and *perpendicular* to the road. When the road slopes slightly to drain toward one edge, the contour crosses at a slight angle (remember, water always travels perpendicular to the contours) (Fig. 6–26).

Curbs are indicated by a break in the contour line, which begins again *downhill*. The contour line is actually traveling *level* along the face of the curb until it reaches the top of curb, where it becomes visible on the plan. Gutters usually follow the slope of the road and receive no special indication. However, if you want a deep gutter, or one formed as a ditch, the contour would move uphill to meet the curb or be shaped like a stream (Figs. 6–27 and 6–28).

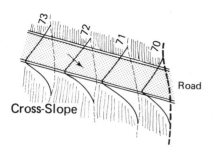

Cross-Slope

Road

Figure 6-26

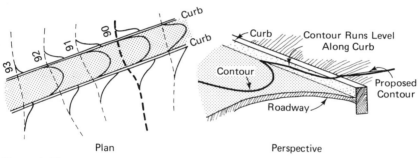

Figure 6-27 Curb inlet under construction. Water is collected in this drain by flowing through the slots or directly into the large opening in the curb. The inlet should be on a fairly flat area so that water does not rush by.

Curb

Curb

Curb

Contour Runs Level Along Curb

Contour

Proposed Contour

Roadway

Plan

Perspective

Figure 6-28

The drainages of urban and rural roads are designed from an opposite conceptual basis. An urban street is the functional catchment area for all surrounding drainage. It is at the *lowest* place in an area, with all runoff directed to it. On the other hand, rural roads are constructed *higher* than the abutting landscape, and all runoff is directed away from the road. (See Fig. 6–29.)

Rural Road Drainage

Urban Road Drainage

Figure 6-29

Rural roads are usually raised slightly above the landscape so run-off can drain away. This dam often changes to the natural drainage pattern and can cause problems to vegetation. Swales and culverts are necessary to insure a reasonably similar post-construction drainage pattern. (See Fig. 6–30.)

To help understand how contours look, draw full-sized contours with chalk on different streets or parking areas. Don't worry about precision; just approximate the contour by eyeballing a level line. Curbs and retaining walls are easily visualized this way. (See Fig. 6–31.)

Figure 6–30
Rural road raised on fill above the surrounding landscape. The road has blocked natural drainage, and has created a boggy area to the right.

Figure 6–31
Sidewalks should have a cross slope of 2 percent (¼ in. per foot) draining *toward* the street. Slope parking lots *away* from the sidewalk. The area under the bench is small, and should slope toward the walk.

ROAD INTERSECTIONS

Street intersections are best when fairly flat to allow the intersecting roads to meet on a common plane. This is illustrated in many hilly neighborhoods with streets running parallel and perpendicular to

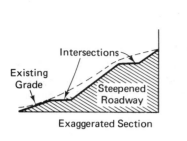
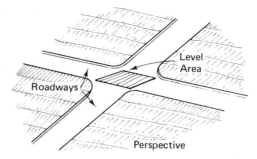

Figure 6-32

the contours. To accommodate a flat intersection, the steep street becomes steeper either before, after, or entirely between intersections.
The other street (running almost level) must warp up slightly to meet
the intersection area. Public streets generally maintain a uniform gradient between intersections, and do not vary abruptly to meet a different
grade (Fig. 6–32).

Intersections on gently sloping roads (maximum of 5 percent) can
usually slope at the same gradient if the cross streets are carefully laid
out. The cross street must have a sloping cross section or warp to one
at the intersection. The sloping cross section may be an advantage as it
minimizes grading. It is desirable to carry a flat section 50 ft on each
side of the intersection with a maximum grade of 5 percent (Fig. 6–33).

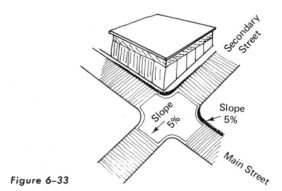

Figure 6-33

INTERSECTION ALIGNMENT

Intersections are the most dangerous part of any road system and
should be used only when necessary and made as simple as possible.
Basically, the fewer potential auto conflicts the better; therefore a T intersection (three-way) is better than a four-way (cross), which is better
than a five-way, etc. A four-way intersection has 12 more accident possibilities than a T intersection.

Ninety-degree right angle intersections are always preferred, as they slow down turning traffic, and assure equal visibility (Fig. 6–34).

Acute-angle intersections should be avoided. Drivers tend to slip through the intersection without looking and often at high speeds, thereby increasing the chance of an accident. Realign the acute angle to a 90° intersection, and use the leftover space as a small park (Fig. 6–35).

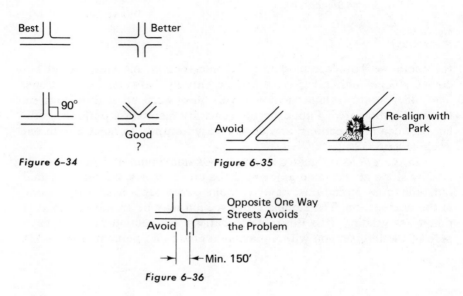

Figure 6-34

Figure 6-35

Figure 6-36

Cross intersections with a slight offset should be avoided. The double through turn decreases visibility, sets up many accident possibilities, and does not allow room between for left turn stacking (Fig. 6–36).

Intersections must not be placed so close together as to cause interruption of traffic flow. Local road intersections can be as close as 150 ft, arterial roads 350 to 500 ft, and freeway intersections approximately ¾ mile apart. Stacking room should be allowed for cars waiting to turn left.

Intersections should have a curb radius large enough to allow turning at the required speed. A radius larger than needed may cause increased traffic speeds, which will degrade the environment. The radius will vary from 5 ft for an urban intersection with a stop sign, to 10 ft for a typical neighborhood road, to 25 ft for a major road intersection (Fig. 6–37). These are

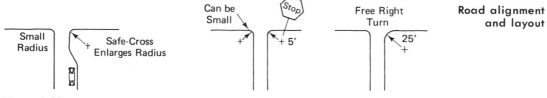

Figure 6-37

slightly below engineering standards; however, cars usually travel some distance away from the curb, thus providing a larger effective turning radius.

Large, random-shaped intersections are confusing and should be reduced to normal travel lane requirements by eliminating the excess pavement and extending sidewalks and planter space (Figs. 6–38 through 6–41).

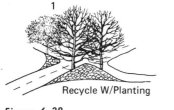

Figure 6-38

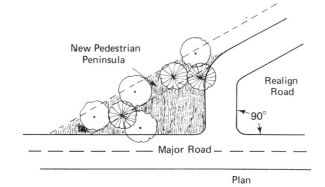

Figure 6-39

Figure 6-40
This large five-way intersection was reduced in size (and actually made more efficient) by the addition of a planted traffic circle.

Figure 6-41 Large paved areas caused by the intersection of several roads can be rechannelized by constructing *peninsulas* for planting and pedestrian use.

INTERSECTION DRAINAGE

The numerous combinations of possible intersections make categorizing drainage solutions difficult. Runoff is usually directed toward the four corners of the intersection, or toward the lowest two of a sloping intersection. Other practices include the following:

The crown of the *more important* street is carried through the intersection, with the other street warping to meet it.

Use the crown of the levelest street where a level and sloping street intersect. This will direct runoff toward the four corners.

Build up high enough in the center of the intersection to assure drainage straight away. Although contours can be used to show the general form of intersections, spot elevations may be more useful.

Street widths are determined in large part on how fast cars are expected to travel. Obviously, there is a minimum lane width necessary to accommodate the auto, probably about 9 ft. Anything wider is meant to accommodate the sway and carelessness of drivers traveling at higher speeds. Progressive cities require a minimum 10-ft travel lane, but consider 11 ft desirable. An additional 2-ft width is required when the lane is alongside the curb.

Traffic lanes are combined to make a variety of street widths for different purposes. In addition to traffic lanes, parking lanes are a minimum width of 8 ft; sidewalks and planting strip should each be 6 ft wide minimum. Combining these widths we can have roads from the smallest to the largest as follows:

One-way traffic with parking on one side. The 20-ft-wide road includes a 2-ft curb separation distance on the traffic side, a 10-ft traffic lane, and 8 ft for parking. One-way streets are usually planned in pairs, with parallel roads running in opposite directions (Fig. 6–42a).

One-way traffic with parking on both sides totals 26 ft wide, with 8-ft parking lane, two 10-ft traffic lanes, and 2 ft for curb separation. A good example is a 20-ft-wide two-way street that level, and makes it safer for pedestrians and neighbors (Fig. 6–42b).

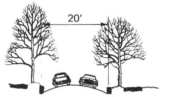

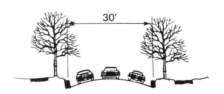

Figure 6–42

Two-way traffic with one parking lane is 30-ft wide, including one 8-ft parking lane, two 10-ft traffic lanes, and 2 ft for curb separation. A good example is a 20-ft-wide two-way street that includes an 8-ft parking lane and two 10-ft traffic lanes crowded into 20 ft. Needless to say, drivers take turns passing cars coming in the other direction. Adding 8 ft for parking on the other side totals 26 ft (two 8-ft parking lanes and one 10-ft two-way driving lane). In both instances, unnecessary traffic usually avoids these narrow roads (Fig. 6–43).

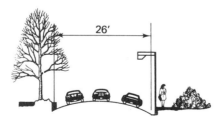

Figure 6–43

Two-way traffic with two parking lanes. This 36-ft-wide street has two 8-ft parking lanes plus two 10-ft traffic lanes allowing easy movement of cars. Two 2-way traffic lanes with parking on both sides totals 56 ft wide and includes two 8-ft parking lanes and four 10-ft traffic lanes (Fig. 6–44). This road section is used in many municipalities as *arterials* with 12- or 13-ft-wide lanes to increase efficiency. Streets used for bus routes should be slightly wider to accommodate the turning radius required to move away from the curb. Twenty feet of bus maneuvering space is required to avoid crossing the center line into oncoming traffic. The 20 ft can be two 10-ft travel lanes, or an 8-ft parking lane plus 12-ft travel lane (Fig. 6–45).

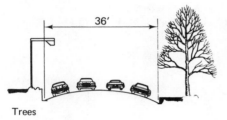

Trees

Figure 6–44

Best???

Figure 6–45

All these dimensions are minimum by engineering standards, although from an overall environmental point of view, one might consider these minimum standards appropriate.

HORIZONTAL AND VERTICAL ROAD ALIGNMENT

Roads are designed to have continuous, uniform, and free-flowing alignments that adjust in two directions—*horizontally* and *vertically*. Horizontal alignment is the to and fro direction a road assumes in the horizontal plane, and consists of combinations of straight sections (called *tangents*) and curved sections composed of an arc of a circle. (Highways use complex parabolic curves that are calculated mathematically.) These connect tangentially, that is, with the straight section at *right angles* to the radius, or the radii at 180° to each other. A horizontal curve is described by its angle of deflection, radius length, points of tangency, and sometimes length of arc (Fig. 6–46).

Vertical alignment consists of all the ups and downs necessary for a road to work. Generally, these grades will be uniform for a distance and will change gradually.

Rural roads usually have a shoulder on at least one side of the road. The shoulder also acts as a breakdown lane, and protects the

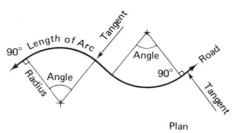

Plan

Figure 6-46   Horizontal curve alignment.

edge of the road from settlement. (See Fig. 6-47.) The junction between two gradients is a *vertical curve* and is normally calculated mathematically. We will not discuss this calculation here, but instead assume that by careful contour spacing we can approximate it. Vertical curves are soft in shape to eliminate a harsh transition between two gradients. In hilly terrain, the preferred road alignment is to have high and low points of a vertical curve coincide with the midpoint of a horizontal curve (Fig. 6-48). Generally, two sharp curves (short radius) are not connected to one another, but rather joined with a tangent (straight section) approximately 150 ft long. Larger curves (long radius) can be joined together but must always meet tangentially. Reverse curve radii join 180° apart. Sharp curves at the end of a long straight stretch or at the bottom or top of a hill should be avoided.

For convenience, the *circumference* of a circle, rather than a freehand curve, is used to describe horizontal alignments. Circumferences can be plotted and constructed easily, and cars travel safer and smoother along a uniform predictable curve. The size of the curve (radius) is determined by the speed of travel and the available space. Large radii allow higher speeds, whereas a small radius slows speeds. The formula for the circumference of a circle is $2\pi r$ ($\pi = 3.14$).

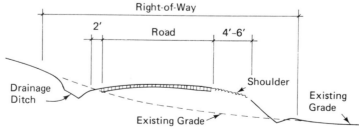

Figure 6-47

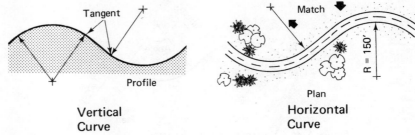

Figure 6-48

DESIGN SPEED

Speed of travel is a topic designers should become very familiar with. As speed of auto travel increases, the noise also increases. As speed of auto travel increases, compatibility with pedestrians and bicycles decreases. Cars traveling about 20 mph create excessive noise and are almost incompatible with bicycles sharing the same lane. Cars traveling above 20 mph are also dangerous to children playing near the street, and everyone knows children love to play in and around the street.

Three speed-related measures must be considered in road design—curve radius, stopping distance, and passing distance. Depending on road conditions (ice, rain, surface treatment, superelevation, etc.), the following radii and distances will serve the speed given. Interpolate for intermediate speeds and increase radius or distance for poor road conditions.

DESIGN SPEED (mph)	MINIMUM RADIUS OF HORIZONTAL CURVE (ft)
20	100
30	250
40	450
50	750
60	1100

Obviously, the exact physical site condition will be an important determinant. For instance, when planning a 25-mph design speed in an area containing fine old trees, it may be necessary to use a smaller than recommended radius and post a Reduce Speed sign.

*STOPPING DISTANCE (INDICATES MINIMUM
NECESSARY FORWARD VISIBILITY)*

Design speed (mph)	30	40	50	60	70
Min. stopping distance (ft)	300	275	350	475	600

PASSING SIGHT DISTANCE

Design speed (mph)	30	40	50	60	70
Min. passing sight (2 lanes)	800	1300	1700	2000	2300
Min. passing sight (3 lanes)			1200	1400	1600

SUPERELEVATION — High-speed roads are often banked slightly on horizontal curves to overcome centrifugal force. This allows cars to travel through the curve at higher speeds (or to satisfy a specific design with a smaller radius). The degree of superelevation is usually determined by highway engineers after considering the design speed, the horizontal curve radius, and the chance of cars sliding downhill in icy weather. The minimum superelevation height is usually twice the crown height; maximum is a 4 to 6 percent cross slope. Since superelevation increases auto speed, it should *not* be used on residential or institutional roads or for pedestrian walks.

PROCEDURE TO LAY OUT A ROADWAY

Prepare first the various analysis diagrams necessary to fully understand the lay of the land. This may include slope, drainage, existing vegetation, geology rock outcropping, and subsurface features. Combine these data with an understanding of the purpose of the road (scenic route, distribution, short access road, arterial, etc.) to determine the desired travel speed. This is a commonsense judgment weighing many factors; for instance, a scenic road, short access road, or roadway through a unique landscape should be at 20 mph, whereas a distribution road requires 25 mph and an arterial 30 mph.

Next combine the roadway speed with physiographic site conditions. Draw to scale several concentric circles on a piece of tracing paper for use as a template. The concentric circles should begin with the minimum radius for your selected design speed, and increase in units of about 5 percent. Begin freehand on flimsy tracing paper and sketch possible alignments. Use the template to help locate the curves. This is the trial and error phase of design, which includes *avoiding* desirable existing conditions (trees, streams, marshes, steep grades), aligning it over the shortest distance yet creating a character that will be remembered (varying width, twisting the route, opening views, etc.). When one solution seems superior, place your pencil on the road and slowly traverse the alignment, trying to imagine you are a passenger in the car. Look left and right, and test until you are satisfied.

VARY THE WIDTH — Most roads have been designed with a continuous width regardless of terrain, topography, existing natural conditions, need, cost, etc. There is a growing awareness that the road width should vary according to existing situations and realistic needs. The road should be narrowed to save a stand of trees or a unique rock outcropping by eliminating the parking lane, or the road can be narrower on steep terrain to reduce the amount of cut and fill.

At this point, the task is primarily of connecting tangents (straight portions of road) with curve (circumferences of circles) or in some cases curves with curves. *Block grade* the alignment to determine grading feasibility. How much excess cut or fill? How many trees must be removed? And so on. Continue developing freehand alternative solutions until you have the one that works best. Refine and put it to scale freehand, then construct the road mechanically using compass and straightedge. Grade it again, and redesign as required until it looks right.

Most streets should have a 15-ft clearance for tall trucks. This height restriction makes pedestrian bridges unattractive as users must walk up at least 36 steps and then back down, unless the topography happens to be higher on one or both sides (Fig. 6–49).

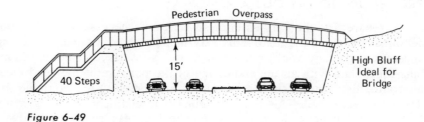

Figure 6-49

There are several helpful shortcuts to laying out horizontal curves, which stem from the need for curves to be tangential (meet at right angles) with the straight sections. When finished with your freehand design of the road alignment, convert the freehand drawing to straight lines. Draw only the center line, and don't try to connect the straight sections with curves.

To connect curves to tangents, use the template (described above) and move it over the drawing until the circumference just touches both straight sections at a point of tangency. Using your compass, punch a hole through the center of the circle, piercing also the base map below. This point becomes the center point for constructing the curve (Fig. 6–50). Tangents can move away from this curve at any point and will

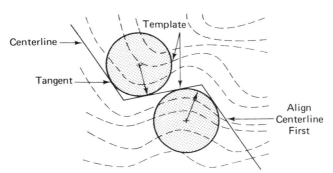

Figure 6-50   **Locating tangents**

automatically be at right angles to the radius touching that point. Be flexible, and try several radii before selecting the final one. Add an intermediate radius if necessary.

To construct a reverse curve, extend the radius as a straight line across the roadway with the required opposite radius measured along this line. Use any size of radius for the next curve, only make sure its center is aligned along the projected radius (Fig. 6–51).

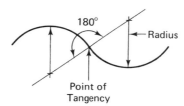

Figure 6-51

To increase the size of curve, simply move away from the road along the radius the desired distance to locate the new center point. The two curves will automatically be tangential, although at a different point of tangency (Fig. 6–52).

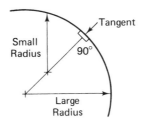

Figure 6-52

After the center line curves and tangents are laid out, edge of pavement, sidewalks, curbs, center planters, etc., can be added as parallel lines.

EXERCISE
GRADING A ROAD

On the expanded base for the roadway used in the exercise on page 141 realign the roadway according to the alignment and drainage principles discussed. In particular, provide the following

A 20-ft-wide road capable of 20-mph movement.

A 5-ft-wide walk on one side of the road.

A 5-ft-wide shoulder on the other side.

A 4-ft-wide drainage ditch where banks exceed 3 ft (drain toward the lowest point).

Culverts where necessary.

Crown the road at 6 in.

Save all possible trees.

Provide a parking lot for 10 cars within the areas shown to service a county park.

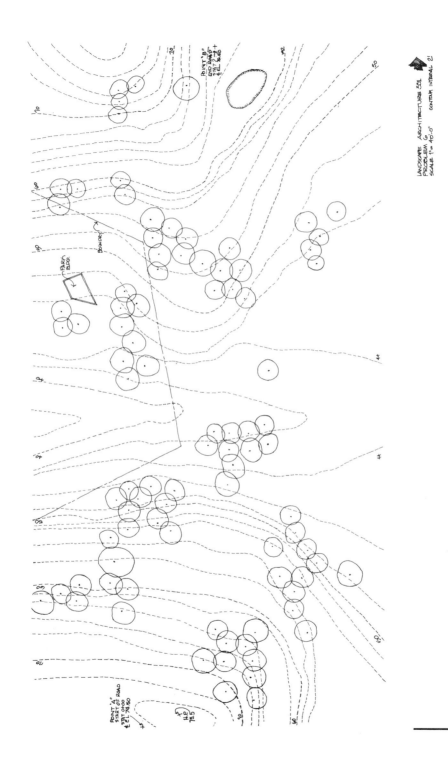

LANDSCAPE ARCHITECTURE 501
PROBLEM 6
SCALE 1"=40'-0"   CONTOUR INTERVAL 2'

PARK BLDG.

POINT "B"
END ROAD
STA 7 + 2
+ EL 86.00

BOUNDARY

POINT "A"
START OF ROAD
STA 0+00
+ EL 74.50

H.P.
76.5

GRADIENTS, CUTS, AND FILLS

The term gradient means the fall or rise of land per horizontal unit and is usually expressed in percentage. A synonym for gradient is slope. Gradients can also be expressed as a ratio, for instance, 1:3 with 3 being the horizontal distance and 1 the vertical distance. The 1:3 indicates that there is a 3-ft horizontal space for every 1-ft vertical rise. It is customary to state first the vertical distance and then the horizontal distance, that is, 1:3 in this example. (See Fig. 7–1.)

Percentages can be conveniently used to express slopes up to 1:1, with the percentage shown indicating the vertical rise per 100-ft horizontal distance. A 10 percent slope has 10 ft of rise per 100 ft of horizontal distance and could be expressed as a ratio of 1:10. Likewise, a 20 percent slope has 20 ft of vertical rise per 100 ft of horizontal distance and could be expressed as a 1:5 slope. This is carried on until you achieve a 100 percent slope, where 100 ft of horizontal distance is required for 100 ft of vertical change in elevation, or a 1:1 slope. Percentages are most useful in describing shallow slopes, as a 2 percent patio, a 5 percent bike trail, a 7 percent road. For slopes steeper than 1:1, it is customary to use ratios rather than percentage. (See Fig. 7.2.)

Figure 7–1
Grades and gradients have always been crucial in drainage, and more recently in providing barrier-free access for handicapped.

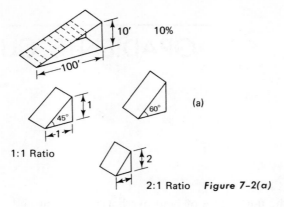

1:1 Ratio

2:1 Ratio   *Figure 7-2(a)*

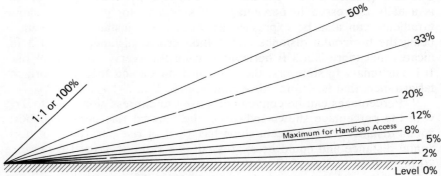

Figure 7-2(b)   Comparison of slope percentage.

DETERMINING GRADIENTS MATHEMATICALLY

The one essential mathematical formula for most grading problems is used to compute gradients. The formula will allow you to compute the following:

- The percent of slope between two known points.
- The horizontal distance between points when the gradient and vertical elevation are known.
- The vertical elevation between points when the gradient and distance are known.

As in other simple algebraic equations, when two points are known, the third can be found by multiplication:

$$\text{Gradient} = \frac{\text{rise}}{\text{run}} \quad \text{or Run} = \frac{\text{rise}}{\text{gradient}} \quad \text{or Rise} = \frac{\text{gradient}}{\text{run}}$$

Where gradient = gradient in percent
   rise = the difference in elevation between two points
   run = the horizontal length between two points

Example

Given: A length of road with point A elevation = 93.2 and point B
   elevation = 96.7.
   The distance between points A and B = 50 ft (Fig. 7–3).

Find: 1. The gradient in percent.
   2. The distance from point A to contours 94, 95, and 96.

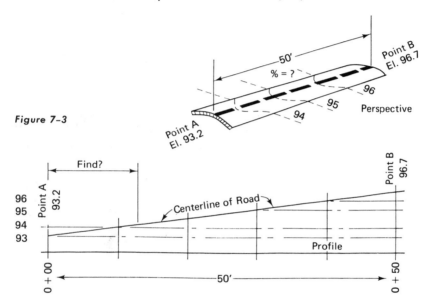

Figure 7–3

SOLUTION

$$G = \frac{\text{rise}}{\text{run}} \quad (\text{gradient} = \frac{\text{difference in elevation}}{\text{horizontal length}})$$

1. The difference in elevation between points A and B equals 3.5 ft
   (96.7 − 93.2

$$G = \frac{3.5}{50} = 0.07 \quad \text{or} \quad 7\% \text{ gradient}$$

2. To find the horizontal distance from point A to contour 94, first
   determine the elevation difference between contour 94 and point A:

$$94 = 93.2 = 0.8$$

Then

$$\text{run} = \frac{\text{rise}}{G} = \frac{0.8}{0.7} = 11.4 \text{ ft from point A to contour 94}$$

Contours 95 and 96 can be located the same way. All figures are expressed in decimals.

This calculation has been carried out for years on the slide rule using the C and D scales. However, the minicalculator has all but replaced the slide rule; it has greater accuracy and is much easier to read.

RECOMMENDED GRADING STANDARDS AND CRITICAL GRADES
(Primarily for Northern USA)

TYPE OF AREAS	IDEAL (First-class work, institutional, public)		ALLOWABLE (Utilitarian or residential work)	
	MAXIMUM	MINIMUM	MAXIMUM	MINIMUM
Streets and Drives				
Concrete (crowned section with curbs or concrete gutter)	5%	1%	11%	0.5%
Bituminous crowned section with concrete gutter	5%	1%	11%	0.5% 0.25%[a]
Bituminous crowned section with bituminous gutter	5%	1%	11%	1%
Concrete Walks				
Approaches, platforms, etc.	5%	0.5%[b]	8%	0.5%[b]
Service areas	8%	0.5%[b]	10%	0.5%[b]
Terrace and Sitting Areas				
Concrete	2%	0.5%	3%	0.5%
Flagstone, slate, brick	2%	1%	3%	1%
Lawn Areas				
Recreational, games, etc.	3%	2%	5%	1%
Mowed banks with grass	1:3	—	1:3	—
Unmowed banks with cover of vines, meadow, etc.	1:2[c]	—	1:2[c]	—

[a] If approved by local Department of Streets can use 0.25% (1/4%).
[b] Flat if cross pitch is provided for; cross pitch of 1/4 in. per ft (2%) is customary.
[c] Varies with type of soil.

RECOMMENDED HIGHWAY GRADIENTS

Although some streets in San Francisco are as steep as 33 percent, they are uncomfortable, unsafe for most drivers, and restrict flow of normal travel. When roads are designed to accommodate higher volumes of traffic at high speeds, the gradient must become very shallow. Highways are the most restrictive roads and to function properly require almost level gradients.

3%   The gradient at which slope becomes obvious (less than 3 percent normally tends to appear level); maximum gradient for Pennsylvania Turnpike, New Jersey Turnpike, etc.; gradient at which heavy trucks slow down.

5%   Practically every car can go up without changing gears, down without using brakes; desirable maximum for high-class work in city conditions.

7%   Maximum grade recommended by American Association of State Highway Officials for class D (lowest type) public road.

10% Acceptable if justified by topography. Steeper grades are sometimes used but are too steep.

A table of grading and decimal equivalents is given on page 148.

CHANGE IN GRADE

The table on pp. 149 lists the change in grade required for uniform slopes over a specific distance. The top line is percent of slope (0.5 = 0.5%, 0.75 = .75%, etc.); the left vertical line is distance in feet. To use the chart, select your percent of slope and follow down the line to the required distance, which will show the necessary change in grade. For an unlisted distance such as 66 ft, add the 6-ft figure to the 60-ft figure.

CALCULATING VOLUME OF CUT AND FILL

All grading plans reach a point where it is necessary to prepare a cost estimate and determine project feasibility by verifying balance between cut and fill. Both operations require calculating the volume of cut and the volume of fill. There are two ways to calculate volume of cut and fill; one is used when you are grading a flat area, and the other when you are grading a circulation route. Both utilize the standard formula for determining volume: *width times length times height.*

To calculate volumes of cut and fill for a flat area, measure the horizontal surface of each proposed cut and fill (width times length) and multiply by the contour interval (height) (Fig. 7–4).

To calculate volume of cut and fill for a circulation route, measure the vertical surface (cross section) of each cut and fill (width times height) and multiply that by the distance between cross sections (length) (Fig. 7–5). This oversimplification can be clarified by the following example:

GRADING AND DECIMAL EQUIVALENTS

On grading plans spot elevations are calculated and shown in feet and decimals rather than inches. This chart lists gradients (from 0.5% to 3%) and shows a change in elevation at various distances from 1 foot to 100 feet in both inches and decimal equivalents.

1″ in 16′			1″ in 8′			1″ in 5′-4″		
0.5% Grade ¹/₁₆″ fall in 1′0″			1% Grade ¹/₈″ fall in 1′0″			1½% Grade ³/₁₆″ fall in 1¹		
Absolute minimum. Can use only with the smoothest of pavings such as smooth concrete, terrazzo or marble.			*Normal minimum for pavings such as smooth and exposed aggregate concrete, brick, tile, slate and wood block. Suitable for asphalt only if water is already flowing and installation is exact.*			*Normal minimum for asphalt, redrock, flagstone, earth, and very rough exposed aggregate concrete.*		
¹/₁₆″	.0052	1′	¹/₈″	.0104	1′	³/₁₆″	.0156	1′
¹/₈″	.0104	2′	¹/₄″	.0208	2′	³/₈″	.0313	2′
¹/₄″	.0208	4′	¹/₂″	.0417	4′	³/₄″	.0625	4′
¹/₂″	.0417	8′	1″	.0833	8′	1½″	.1250	8′
1″	.0833	16′	2″	.1667	16′	3″	.0522	16′
1⁹/₁₆″	.1302	25′	3¹/₈″	.2604	25′	4¹¹/₁₆″	.3907	25′
2¹/₁₆″	.1719	33⅓′	4³/₁₆″	.3490	33⅓′	6¹/₄″	.5208	33⅓′
3¹/₈″	.2604	50′	6¹/₄″	.5208	50′	9³/₈″	.7813	50′
4¹/₈″	.3438	66⅔′	8³/₈″	.6980	66⅔′	1′-½″	1.0417	66⅔′
4¹¹/₁₆″	.3907	75′	9³/₈″	.7813	75′	1′-2¹/₁₆″	1.1719	75′
6¹/₄″	.5208	100′	1′-½″	1.0417	100′	1′-6³/₄″	1.5625	100′

1″ in 4′			1″ in 3′-2½″			1″ in 2′-8½″		
2% Grade ¹/₄″ fall in 1′0″			2.5% Grade ⁵/₁₆″ fall in 1′0″			3% Grade ³/₈″ fall in 1′		
Desirable minimum for grass, tanbark and planting areas. Maximum grade for terrace paving. Slightly *noticeable grade when related to level construction.*			*Desirable not to go above this on parking areas if you want them to appear level. Looks generally level though it is* quite *a noticeable slope.*			*Very noticeable in relation to level construction.*		
¹/₄″	.0208	1′	⁵/₁₆″	.0260	1′	³/₈″	.0313	1′
¹/₂″	.0417	2′	⁵/₈″	.0521	2′	³/₄″	.0625	2′
1″	.0833	4′	1¹/₄″	.1041	4′	1½″	.1250	4′
2″	.1667	8′	2½″	.2084	8′	3″	.2500	8′
4″	.3335	16′	5″	.4167	16′	6″	.5000	16′
6¹/₄″	.5208	25′	7⁵/₈″	.6345	25′	9³/₁₆″	.7656	25′
8³/₁₆″	.6824	33⅓′	10⁷/₁₆″	.8697	33⅓′	1′-¹/₂″	1.0417	33⅓′
1′-½″	1.0417	50′	1′-3⁵/₈″	1.3021	50′	1′-6³/₄″	1.5625	50′
1′-4³/₈″	1.3542	66⅔′	1′-8⁷/₈″	1.7396	66⅔′	2′-1″	2.0833	66⅔′
1′-6³/₄″	1.5625	75′	1′-11⁵/₈″	1.9688	75′	2′-3¹⁵/₁₆″	2.3281	75′
2′-1″	2.0833	100′	2′-7¹/₄″	2.6041	100′	3′-1¹/₂″	3.1250	100′

DECIMAL EQUIVALENTS – inches to feet

1″ = .083′	5″ = .416′	9″ = .75′
2″ = .166′	6″ = .5′	10″ = .833′
3″ = .250′	7″ = .583′	11″ = .916′
4″ = .333′	8″ = .667′	12″ = 1.0′

CHANGE IN GRADE

%	.5	.75	1.0	1.25	1.5	1.75	2.0	2.5	3.0	3.5	4.0	4.5	5.0	6.0	7.0	8.0	9.0
1'	.005	.08	.01	.013	.015	.018	.02	.025	.03	.035	.04	.045	.05	.06	.07	.08	.09
2'	.01	.015	.02	.025	.03	.035	.04	.05	.06	.07	.08	.09	.10	.12	.14	.16	.18
3'	.015	.023	.03	.38	.045	.05	.06	.075	.09	.105	.12	.135	.15	.18	.21	.24	.27
4'	.02	.03	.04	.05	.06	.07	.08	.10	.12	.14	.16	.18	.20	.24	.28	.32	.36
5'	.025	.04	.05	.063	.075	.09	.10	.125	.15	.175	.20	.225	.25	.30	.35	.40	.45
6'	.03	.05	.06	.075	.09	.105	.12	.15	.18	.21	.24	.27	.30	.36	.42	.48	.54
7'	.035	.05	.07	.088	.10	.123	.14	.175	.21	.245	.28	.329	.35	.42	.49	.56	.63
8'	.04	.06	.08	.10	.12	.14	.16	.20	.24	.28	.32	.36	.40	.48	.56	.64	.72
9'	.045	.064	.09	.113	.14	.158	.18	.225	.27	.315	.36	.405	.45	.54	.63	.72	.81
10'	.05	.75	.10	.125	.15	.175	.20	.25	.30	.35	.40	.45	.50	.60	.70	.80	.90
15'	.075	.11	.15	.188	.23	.265	.30	.375	.45	.53	.60	.655	.75	.90	1.05	1.2	1.35
20'	.10	.15	.20	.25	.30	.35	.40	.50	.60	.70	.80	.90	1.0	1.2	1.40	1.6	1.8
25'	.125	.19	.25	.31	.38	.44	.50	.63	.75	.88	1.0	1.12	1.25	1.5	1.75	2.0	2.25
30'	.150	.23	.30	.376	.45	.53	.60	.75	.90	1.05	1.2	1.35	1.50	1.8	2.1	2.4	2.7
35'	.175	.26	.35	.409	.53	.62	.70	.88	1.05	1.24	1.4	1.58	1.75	2.1	2.45	2.8	3.15
40'	.20	.30	.40	.50	.60	.70	.80	1.0	1.2	1.4	1.6	1.71	2.0	2.4	2.8	3.2	3.6
45'	.225	.34	.45	.56	.68	.79	.90	1.13	1.35	1.58	1.8	2.03	2.25	2.7	3.15	3.6	4.05
50'	.250	.38	.50	.62	.75	.88	1.0	1.25	1.5	1.76	2.0	2.24	2.50	3.0	3.50	4.0	4.5
55'	.275	.41	.55	.68	.83	.97	1.1	1.38	1.65	1.94	2.2	2.47	2.75	3.3	3.85	4.4	4.95
60'	.30	.45	.60	.75	.90	1.06	1.2	1.5	1.8	2.12	2.4	2.7	3.0	3.6	4.2	4.8	5.4
65'	.325	.48	.65	.81	.98	1.15	1.3	1.63	1.95	2.30	2.6	2.93	3.25	3.9	4.55	5.2	5.85
70'	.350	.53	.70	.82	1.0	1.24	1.4	1.76	2.10	2.48	2.8	3.16	3.50	4.2	4.9	5.6	6.3
75'	.357	.57	.75	.94	1.1	1.33	1.5	1.89	2.25	2.66	3.0	3.39	3.75	4.5	5.25	6.0	6.75
80'	.40	.60	.80	1.0	1.2	1.4	1.6	2.0	2.4	2.8	3.2	3.6	4.0	4.8	5.6	6.4	7.2
85'	.425	.64	.85	1.06	1.3	1.49	1.7	2.13	2.55	2.98	3.4	3.83	4.25	5.1	5.95	6.8	7.65
90'	.45	.676	.90	1.12	1.35	1.58	1.8	2.26	2.7	3.16	3.6	4.06	4.5	5.4	6.3	7.2	8.1
100'	.50	.175	1.0	1.25	1.50	1.75	2.0	2.5	3.0	3.5	4.0	4.5	5.0	6.0	7.0	8.0	9.0

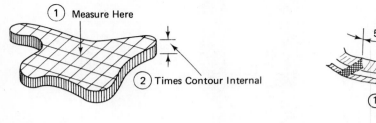

Figure 7-4

Figure 7-5

When a grading scheme is complete enough to test, place a piece of thin tracing paper over it and color all the areas of *cut* lightly in blue, and all the areas of *fill* in red. There will be a no cut–no fill line between. Next outline each proposed contour within the cut area with a *different* color pencil. To do this, start where the proposed contour leaves the existing contour, trace the proposed contour, and reconnect along the existing contour. Do the same in the fill area; that is, outline each proposed contour in a different color. The different colors help distinguish the size of each area during measurement. Number each contour area consecutively, that is, C-1, C-2, C-3 for cuts and F-1, F-2, F-3 for fills (Fig. 7–6).

Now measure separately the area of each outlined contour. Start with the C-1 (cut contour), measure and record the area, do C-2, C-3, etc., the same way, and then complete all the fill areas (Fig. 7–7).

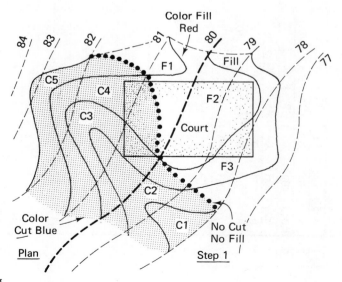

Figure 7-6

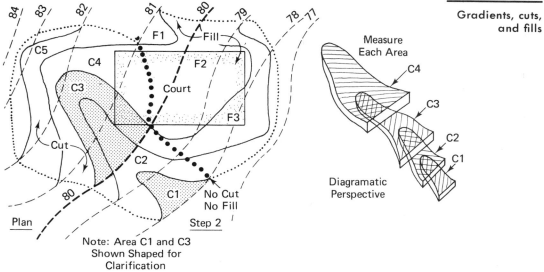

Diagramatic
Perspective

Plan

Step 2

No Cut
No Fill

Note: Area C1 and C3
Shown Shaped for
Clarification

Figure 7–7

To measure the area, use either a planimeter or overlay the area with
a fine transparent graph paper and count the squares. Do this for each
contour, noting the area of each in *square inches*. Finally, it will be
necessary to convert these square-inch measurements to square feet using the
drawing scale. This involves multiplying the square-inch planimeter reading
or graph paper count by the plan scale *squared*. For instance, if you have a
measurement or planimeter reading of 2.6 square inches, and the drawing
scale is 20 (1 in. = 20 ft), you will find the square foot measure by
multiplying 20 × 20 × 2.6 or 1040 square *feet*. This answer can then be
multiplied by the contour interval to determine the volume in cubic feet.

In practice, cut and fill calculations are totaled separately so that they
can be compared for balance. To determine the total amount of earth to be
moved, simply add the two totals. To determine the excess of cut or fill,
subtract one from the other. Cubic-foot measure can be converted to cubic
yards by dividing by 27.

STEP 1

CUT		FILL	
C-1	_____ sq. in.	F-1	_____ sq. in.
C-2	_____ sq. in.	F-2	_____ sq. in.
C-3	_____ sq. in.	F-3	_____ sq. in.
C-4	_____ sq. in.	F-4	_____ sq. in.
TOTAL CUT	_____ sq. in.	TOTAL FILL	_____ sq. in.

STEP 2

Total cut in sq. in. _____ times scale squared equals _____ sq. ft.

Total fill in sq. in. _____ times scale squared equals _____ sq. ft.

Area of cut in sq. ft _____ times contour interval equals _____ cu. ft of cut.

Area of fill in sq. ft _____ times contour interval equals _____ cu. ft of

Cut _____ plus fill _____ equals total grading.

The method just described produces a rough calculation of proposed cut and fill. You can see in the section that the shaded area of contour 2, if projected *up,* would *include* an amount *not* actually graded and *not include* an amount that *will* be graded. (Fig. 7–8). The calculation can be refined by averaging the two adjacent contours, and dividing the sum by 2. This produces an accurate average area, which can then be multiplied by the contour interval. Areas C-1 and C-2 would be added together and divided by 2, then areas C-2 and C-3, etc., and the same procedure used for fill areas.

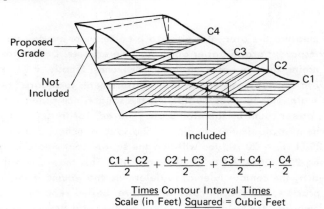

$$\frac{C1 + C2}{2} + \frac{C2 + C3}{2} + \frac{C3 + C4}{2} + \frac{C4}{2}$$

Times Contour Interval Times
Scale (in Feet) Squared = Cubic Feet

Average End Calculation

Figure 7–8 Average end calculation.

CUT AND FILL GRADING EXERCISES

1. What is the volume in cubic yards of the hill shown in Figure 7–9?
   Given: Scale of drawing is 1 in. = 20 ft.

   Contour interval is 5 ft.

   $A_2 = 0.9$ sq. in.

   $A_3 = 2.3$ sq. in.

   The answer is 4100 cu. ft or 151.85 cu. yd. This would normally be rounded up to 152 cu. yd.

2. Determine how many cubic yards of excess earth are left over from the project shown in Figure 7–10.

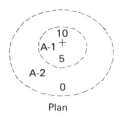

Plan

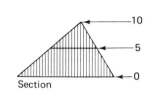

Section

Figure 7-9

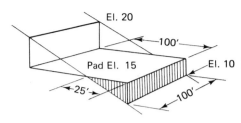

Figure 7-10

The answer is 694 cu. yd of cut and 231 cu. yd of fill, for a total of 925 cu. yd moved, including 463 cu. yd excess earth.

To calculate volumes of cut and fill for circulation routes, draw accurate cross sections at equal distances (say, 50 ft) showing existing and proposed ground lines. Areas of cut should be colored blue and areas of fill red. Next measure the areas of cut and fill separately in square inches for each cross section. This can be done with either a planimeter or by counting the squares of transparent graph paper laid over the cross section. Average two adjacent cross-sectional measurements (add both measurements and divide by 2), and convert that figure from square inches to square feet by multiplying by the proper scale squared (inches times the drawing scale squared). To complete the calculation, multiply this cross-sectional area by the interval between sections (the length) (Fig. 7–11).

Cut and fill volumes of roads can also be calculated as though they were a flat graded area. To do this, color the cut areas on the plan blue and fill areas red, outline and label each cut and fill, and measure them separately. Average adjacent contours, multiply by the contour interval and the drawing scale squared as in the above example. To keep contours in order, draw a cross section, and make sure you have

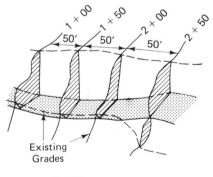

Sketch

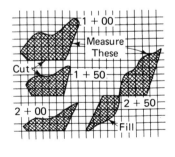

Profiles

Figure 7-11

a tabulation for each contour. Once cut and fill volume has been determined, cost factors can be applied. Designers usually apply a unit cost per cubic yard; contractors usually gauge their costs by estimating the time it will take specific pieces of equipment to do the job. For instance, a 3-yard loader can move 50 yd (for example) per hour, a dump truck can carry 7 yd, etc. The time required for each piece of equipment can be totaled and multiplied by the operating cost per hour for an accurate cost estimate.

The volume of cut and fill described will be in *cubic feet,* which can be converted to cubic yards by dividing by 27. Most cut and fill figures are given in cubic yards.

AVERAGE END GRADING EXERCISE

Determine how many cubic yards of cut is required to grade the road shown in Figure 7–12.

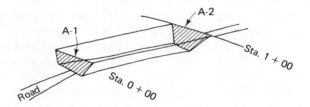

Figure 7–12

Given: Area 1 = 5 sq. in.
Area 2 = 3 sq. in.
Horizontal scale: 1 in. = 10 ft.
Vertical scale: 1 in. = 10 ft.

$$\text{Volume} = \frac{A_1 + A_2}{2} \times L$$

The answer is 1482 cu. yd.

SPECIAL GRADING CALCULATIONS

TOPSOIL STRIPPING AND REPLACEMENT — can affect your calculations on large projects. To calculate the volume to be stripped or replaced, measure the area with the planimeter, convert this square-inch measurement to square feet by multiplying by the plan scale squared, and multiply that figure times the depth of soil to be stripped or replaced. This cubic-foot volume can be converted to cubic yards by dividing by 27.

SUBGRADING — Subgrading can often throw off a balance or cost estimate. Subgrading is removing soil, which will later be replaced with gravel, topsoil, asphalt, etc. The method to calculate this volume is exactly the same as calculating for stripping topsoil; simply outline the areas of subgrade, measure, convert to the proper scale, and multiply times the depth of subgrade.

IMPORTING OR EXPORTING SOIL — To determine, subtract total cut from fill (for import figure) or total fill from cut (for export figure).

SHRINKAGE OF SOILS — It is generally known that a cubic yard of cut will not completely fill a cubic yard void when placed as fill and will shrink further over time. This loss is caused during moving, shipment, etc., and can amount to 3 to 5 percent. Therefore, when calculating for cut–fill balance, a cut figure exceeding fill requirements by approximately 4 percent will produce a *balanced result*. The exact amount of shrinkage varies with soil type, with sandy soils being most stable and organic soils and clays least stable. Most soils will shrink after placement up to about 3 percent, which can cause settlement and present some construction problems. Additionally, some clays expand when moistened, which can heave light buildings and many landscape elements.

COMPACTION OF SUBGRADE — For most flatwork (patios, driveways, playcourts, etc.) preparation of the subgrade is structurally the most critical step. If the subgrade is weak, when the pavement is loaded the surface is likely to fail and crack. No compaction is needed when the material is stable and naturally well compacted. However, the subgrade should be cleared of large stones or vegetation, which could weaken or cause the finished surface to be uneven. For less stable areas, graded, granular sand, gravel, or crushed stone should be added as base material and compacted with hand vibrators or rollers until uniformly level. The base should extend beyond the paving edge to prevent rain from washing out the material and weakening the pavement edge. Try to avoid mechanical compaction near trees as the weight can damage their roots. To be absolutely safe, include a "limit of compaction" line on the grading plan, and keep back of the drip line of trees. Any planting area that is mechanically compacted should be broken up later to make certain that topsoil and subsoil will mix to permit passage of air and water. (See Fig. 7–13.)

COMPACTION OF FILL — To ensure foundation stability, architects have traditionally located foundations on existing soils, and have avoided building on filled ground. This made good sense, as many fills consist of construction wastes dumped without compaction or concern

Figure 7–13
Compaction. This frost-free substance is being spread in 10-inch lifts and will be compacted to eliminate future settlement. Frost-free fill is made up of selected gravel and sand material which drains well, thereby eliminating winter freeze/ thaw which can damage the road. Normally, it is installed to just below the frost line.

for the quality of subbase or fill. Any building constructed on such a fill will usually settle unevenly, causing cracking and sloping floors. If buildings were constructed on fill, piles or deep footings were extended through the fill to solid earth below, often at great costs.

However, with today's efficient construction equipment and methods, it is possible to place bearing-quality fill in layers over the site by compacting it with special rollers. The finished fill is likely to be as strong as natural earth for buildings, but compaction does cause plant-root development problems. Compaction tends to reduce infiltration and increase surface runoff.

The first step in placing compacted fill is to determine the quality of the existing soil on which the fill is to be placed. If it is weak or compressible (as are many organic and clay soils), they should be removed before placing and compacting fill. Most inorganic soils are acceptable for compacted fill, with well-graded sands and gravels being the best material. Clay, silt, and fine sand are difficult to compact and should not be used. Soil is placed in layers 6 to 12 in. thick and compacted with rollers. Rubber-tired rollers are used for sand and gravel fills; a sheeps-foot roller works best on other soils. A sheeps-foot roller is a large weighted drum with short feet attached to it. Both rollers require six to eight passes over each layer of fill for proper compaction.

Controlling compaction requires supervision and inspection for quality of fill, methods of placement, moisture content, and rolling procedures. Several compaction standards can be used, with the most common being 95 percent of the standard Proctor density. Engineering experience usually dictates compaction practices, with a description of whatever existing soil is to be removed, the quality of fill, placement, and rolling procedures and testing being described in the grading specifications. The grading plan should show the limits of compaction, with care taken to avoid existing trees or future planting beds (Fig. 7–14).

Figure 7-14
Make sure to separate out roots, vegetative matter, broken concrete, and rubble from all grading projects. This material is difficult to dispose of, but can be used under planted berms as a base course provided it is covered by sufficient topsoil.

Fill should never be compacted by flooding it with water. Low moisture content is essential for compaction and flooding vastly increases the moisture content. Additionally, flooding weakens the cohesiveness of soils, and may collapse the sidewalls of trenches.

SURCHARGE—Sometimes there is too much compressible soil to remove practically before placing fill. Three choices are available: (1) build elsewhere; (2) use pile foundations; or (3) surcharge the site to compress the material. To surcharge a site, temporary fill material is piled to a calculated height, and allowed to remain for a prescribed length of time. The extra weight compresses the soil beneath until it is stable and can support the new construction. As the settlement occurs during and shortly after filling, this time period is not too long. The surcharge is removed when the compression is equal to that which would be normally caused by the weight of proposed construction. Since the surcharge will be removed, it need not be compacted during installation (Fig. 7-15).

Figure 7-15
This elevated walk was constructed on piles after surcharging, and still the earth settled and pulled away from the structure.

Surcharging is expensive, time consuming, and less than predictable. It is, however, a standard engineering practice, and many highways and buildings have been constructed on surcharged material. A soils or foundation engineer is needed to perform the calculations, supervise placement, and test settlement. The limits of surcharge are shown on the grading plan, with care taken to avoid existing trees or areas to be planted.

COST ESTIMATING

Project construction costs are estimated by applying known unit costs from previous projects to measured quantities from your present project. The procedure is in concept simple, yet requires experience to combine the proper costs per measured unit to each project. All quantities are determined by one of the following units of measure:

Square measure (square yard, foot, meter).
Linear measure (linear foot, yard, meter, etc.).
Cubic measure (cubic yard, foot, meter).
At each count (no unit of measure, just individual items).

The procedure requires recording on a cost estimate form each operation from project start to finish. For instance, grading might include a cost for layout and staking, clearing, tree removal, tree relocation, pregrading stabilization, topsoil stripping, earth to be moved (cut plus fill), earth to be exported, fill to be placed, compaction requirements, finish grading, drainage structures, culverts, topsoil placement, erosion control, etc. Once the list is complete, the units of measure can be determined. (See page 159.)

The quantity takeoff begins next. This is a laborious process of carefully measuring each operation and recording it on the cost estimate form. Make sure to cross off each item on the plan so that you don't forget anything or count it twice. The degree of accuracy depends on the state of planning, with early estimates allowing perhaps 20 percent error; a final estimate would hope for only a 5 percent error.

After the takeoff has been completed, a unit price for each operation is assigned. This is the guessing part of the operation, but can be aided by the following:

- Keeping accurate records of all unit costs of previous projects.
- Using cost-estimating handbooks, which list unit prices for many tasks and are published yearly.

SAMPLE COST ESTIMATE SHEET used for tabulating costs for a particular project. Note this sheet includes a list for both labor and materials.

Job: _____
Status: _____
Date: _____ By: _____

DESCRIPTION	QUANTITIES	UNIT PRICE LABOR	TOTAL ESTIMATED LABOR COST	UNIT PRICE MTL.	TOTAL ESTIMATED MATERIAL COST	UNIT PRICE	SUB-BIDS		

• Meeting with a contractor to review your takeoff quantities and have him suggest unit prices.
• Simulating the task by breaking it into smaller, more easily understood jobs, and determine those costs.

Costs from previous projects will probably have to be adjusted because of different site conditions. For instance, cost for disposal of soil may be adjusted because the disposal site is twice as far away or labor costs may have risen, or construction details may be tricky and time consuming, access may be restricted, etc. Allowances should be made for the contractor's overhead and profit (usually 15 percent), for contingencies (10 to 15 percent for omissions, errors, etc.), and for miscellaneous operating costs (6 percent for permits, insurance, sani-cans, etc.).

This type of cost estimate has long-term limitations as it measures only immediate out-of-pocket expenses. It does not measure *benefits,* or costs that *other people* may have to bear, or maintenance costs that may be *deferred,* or other methods of accomplishing the desired goal. It is a measure of short-term costs, which is all right up to a point; however, most environmental and ecological considerations require a broader, long-term perspective. Designers should find ways to include long-range factors in short-term cost estimates. Ecological long-term benefits associated with site development may include the following:

• Erosion control may minimize need for future replanting.
• Sedimentation reduction through proper grading may preserve a biologically productive stream or marsh.
• More expensive drainage techniques that store and reduce the rate of runoff while balancing the water table should be measured against short-term savings.
• Replanting or preserving vegetation can ameliorate many environmental pollutants with value beyond mere esthetics.
• A reduction in grading or a balanced cut–fill development reduces energy demand and may preserve an important ecological disposal site.

CONVERTING TO METRIC

The metric measuring system has worldwide usage, and Americans should be familiar with it. The basic linear measure is the *centimeter* which is about ⅜ inch long. One hundred centimeters equals a meter which is approximately 3 feet, 3 in. long. One hundred meters equals a kilometer, which is approximately 0.6 of a mile. An important square measure is the hectare, which is equivalent to 100 meters square. A hectare is approximately 2.5 times as large as an acre. (See Fig. 7–16.)

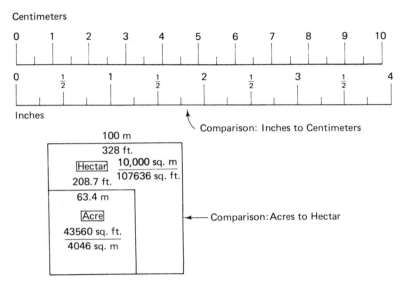

Comparison: Inches to Centimeters

Comparison: Acres to Hectar

Figure 7-16

A meter is just slightly longer than 1 yd or about 3 ft, 3 in. To convert feet to meters, multiply the feet (in decimals, *not* inches) by 0.3048. To find the number of feet in so many meters, simply divide the meters by 0.3048.

METRIC CONVERSIONS TABLE

TO CONVERT	INTO	MULTIPLY BY
inches	centimeters	2.54
inches	meters	0.0254
centimeters	inches	0.3937
feet	centimeters	30.48
feet	meters	0.3048
meters	feet	3.28083
kilometers	miles	0.6214
miles	kilometers	1.609
kilometers	feet	3280.83
acres	hectares	0.404685
hectares	acres	2.471
square inches	square centimeters	6.452
square feet	square meters	0.0929
square yards	square meters	0.836
cubic feet	cubic meters	0.0283
cubic meters	cubic feet	0.03532
cubic meters	cubic yards	1.308
cubic yards	cubic meters	0.765

COST REDUCTIONS — Moving earth is actually relatively inexpensive; we have the technology and heavy equipment to move mountains at little actual cost. However, there are factors that influence costs and can drive them up.

1. A balanced cut and fill design solution will always result in lower grading costs than an unbalanced one.
2. Removing soil from the site and disposing of it elsewhere is usually very expensive. Anything you can do (create earth mounds and the like) to avoid this will reduce the cost.
3. Importing soil is generally not as expensive as exporting it, but is enough of a problem to cause concern.
4. Stockpiling good backfill material and topsoil for reuse will save cost.
5. A grading operation that removes and places soil in one motion is the most economical procedure. If it has to be unloaded and reloaded later, additional costs will be incurred (Fig. 7–17).
6. Time of year affects costs. Winter work will be difficult; muddy, wet, sloppy conditions slow down equipment and thereby increase costs. Erosion and potential for slippage are additional cost-increasing factors.
7. Inexpensive grading requires considerable room for large equipment to operate; therefore, small urban projects will be more expensive to grade than large rural projects.
8. Rock outcrops or any mechanical constraints can increase grading cost considerably and should be avoided.
9. "High-technology dilemma." The size of modern grading equipment makes it cheaper to blast ahead, removing everything from the site. This short-term cost should be compared with the

Figure 7–17
Moving earth twice adds to the cost of grading. Design a plan that allows earth to be cut and filled in one operation. The machine is a Bobcat, which is narrow enough to be useful in tight quarters.

Cost Estimate

Sample Cost Estimate Sheet
See Also Page

Job:_____

Status:_____

Date_____ By_____

Item and Description	Quantity	Unit	Unit Cost	Item Total	Sub Total

Figure 7-18 Sample cost estimate sheet.

installation and maintenance costs of rebuilding the landscape following grading.

a. The cost of rebuilding the landscape should always be included — erosion control, replacing topsoil, trees, shrubs, groundcover, and maintenance.

b. It is usually cheaper to remove trees than to save them; the designer must list each tree that is to be saved. Don't save trees that are horticulturally or esthetically in poor condition.

c. Topsoil is easily mixed with the subsoil, and *not* stripping it may save several dollars; however, replacing it will always cost more.

THE PLANIMETER

A planimeter is an instrument used for measuring irregular areas; it is used in all grading and cost-estimating operations. If areas are geometrical in shape, it is easier to calculate the areas mathematically by measuring and multiplying width times length.

A polar planimeter is most commonly used for earthwork calculations. It is anchored to the drawing by a weighted needlepoint (called *pole weight*) about which the instrument revolves. At the outer end of the tracer arm is a *tracer point,* which is drawn around the area to be measured, following the boundary as accurately as possible. The area is calculated automatically by the revolving *measuring wheel,* which is attached to the tracer arm (Fig. 7-19).

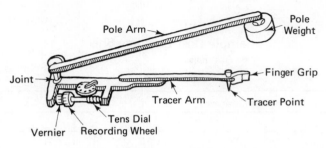

Polar Planimeter

Figure 7-19

As the tracer point is drawn around the area, the measuring wheel moves back and forth with a combination of revolving and slipping movements. The amount it has actually revolved will be a measure of the total area when the tracer point has been brought back to the starting point. Two readings are normally taken, the first in the A position and another from the B position (see Fig. 7-20), without changing the location of the pole. The average of the two will give the true area, as any instrument error will be plus in one direction and minus in the other. Two readings also allow a check, for if the two are not reasonably similar, another reading should be taken.

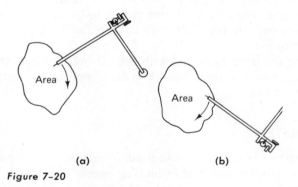

(a)   (b)

Figure 7-20

CARE OF THE PLANIMETER

The measuring wheel and bearings are very delicate, so the instrument must be handled with the care given to a fine old watch. The bearings should be kept clean and free moving and should be occasionally touched with the smallest possible quantity of fine watch oil.

It is essential that the rim of the wheel remain absolutely clean and smooth. It must not be rusty, greasy, or nicked by being bumped against drafting instruments or straightedges. The joint between the pole and tracer arms must also be accurate and kept clean.

OPERATION OF THE PLANIMETER

The surface of the drawing to be measured must be clean, even, and free from grease or the measuring wheel will give an incorrect reading. It will also give an inaccurate reading if run off and on the edge of the drawing. If the sheet is so small that this is bound to happen, readings may be taken through a large sheet of tracing paper placed over the original drawing. The table should be nearly level or the instrument may roll off or move slightly while the dial is being read, creating errors.

When ready to measure, the instrument is placed on the drawing with the pole located so that the tracer point can reach all parts of the outline. The pole should ordinarily be *outside* of the area. Choose a starting point that can be easily identified as the stopping point, since it is important that the tracer return exactly to the point from which it started. On all good instruments, there is a spring mounting pin to prick a hole in the paper marking the start. The outline should be traced in a *clockwise* direction so that the reading will be positive. The difference between the starting and finishing readings will be the measure of the area. Set the instrument at zero to start so that there is no possibility of error. The second reading can be taken without resetting to zero, and should be approximately twice the first. Some machines are reset by pressing a button, which makes resetting very convenient.

READING THE PLANIMETER

Planimeters in this country are calibrated to read in *square inches*. Newer planimeters have digital readout scales that can be read directly; older machines have four dials that must be read. If the instrument is in proper adjustment, one space on the horizontal disk will equal 10 sq. in. (10.00); one numbered division on the recording wheel will represent 1 sq. in. (01.00); and one small division, $\frac{1}{10}$ sq. in. (00.10). One division of the vernier will then represent $\frac{1}{100}$ sq. in. (00.01). The four figures are always entered in the record to eliminate possible errors in the placing of the decimal point, even though the first three may be zeros (Fig. 7–21).

Four measurements are taken for each reading; one from the horizontal disk, two from the large vertical wheel, and one from the small vertical wheel. A four-place tally sheet will help to clarify readings until you develop proficiency. In the example:

1. Read first from the horizontal disk and place the number in the ten's column. For this example, the number is 0. The number

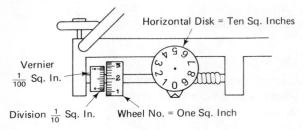

Horizontal Disk = Ten Sq. Inches

Vernier $\frac{1}{100}$ Sq. In.

Division $\frac{1}{10}$ Sq. In.   Wheel No. = One Sq. Inch

Figure 7–21

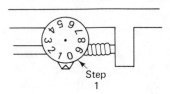

Step 1

Figure 7–22

must be *past* the pointer for all readings, a confusing point, which can be verified by looking at the next reading (Fig. 7–22).

2. Read next from the large vertical wheel, choosing the whole number that is past the center vernier on the smaller disk. In this example the number is 1 (Fig. 7–23).

3. Read next on the large, vertical wheel the largest division past the center vernier on the small disk; in this case the division represents 8.

4. The last reading is tricky and is read on the small stationary wheel. The one division that perfectly lines up with a line on the larger wheel is the reading; in this case the number is 6. This reading may be clearer if you use a magnifying glass (Fig. 7–24).

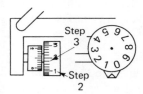

Step 3

Step 2

Figure 7–23

Step 4

Figure 7–24

PLANIMETER CONSTANT — Most planimeters have a slight built-in error or planimeter constant, which must be compensated for at the end of all your calculations. This error is corrected by multiplying the total measured area by the planimeter constant. The constant is usually marked on the instrument at the factory, or can be calculated by measuring a known area and comparing the answer. There is usually a circular testing measure supplied with the planimeter so that the test can be quickly made. It is easier to use a planimeter constant than to attempt to adjust the planimeter to read directly in inches.

For example, suppose that the testing measure used is a 3-in.-radius circle. The planimeter is run around the circle and measurements compared. The actual area of such a circle is 28.27 sq. in. Suppose that the instrument gave a reading of 27.64. Dividing the correct area by the measured area, we find the constant:

$$\frac{28.27}{27.64} = 1.02, \text{ planimeter constant}$$

and all readings taken from the drawing will be converted to exact square inches by multiplying the readings by the constant. The constant correction need be applied only once to the total sum of the readings.

CAUTION — Planimeters are very delicate instruments and any damage, even when not apparent to the naked eye, will result in a loss of accuracy. Hence, observe the following precautions:

- Treat the axle of the measuring roller with the utmost care, protecting it against jar and pressure. If the bearing points of the measuring roller are damaged, the instrument will not be accurate.
- The measuring roller should never be turned by hand when resting on a working surface. Lift the instrument to turn it. The measuring roller is made of hardened steel. To avoid rust, which may affect accuracy, don't touch it with your fingers.

USE OF PLANIMETER IN CUT-FILL CALCULATIONS

1. Outline the total area of cut and total area of fill.
2. Outline and label each contour of cut and fill with a different color.
3. Measure each outlined contour with the planimeter and record separately in square inches.
4. Total all the areas of cut and all the areas of fill on separate lists.
5. Apply the correction factor (planimeter constant) to each amount.
6. Multiply the corrected total measurement by the drawing scale squared.
7. Multiply these amounts by the contour interval to convert to cubic feet.
8. Divide by 27 to determine cubic yards.

QUESTIONS

1. A sanitary sewer is designed primarily to carry
   (a) storm runoff.
   (b) domestic wastes.
   (c) none of the above.

2. The angle of repose is the
   (a) slope a pile of dirt will assume with retention.
   (b) slope a pile of dirt will assume without retention.
   (c) slope a pile of dirt will assume when wet.
   (d) slope a pile of dirt will assume when frozen.

3. A 5 percent slope is equivalent to
   (a) a 5:1 slope.
   (b) a 1:10 slope.
   (c) a 1:20 slope.
   (d) none of the above.

4. A 1:10 slope is the same as a
   (a) 5 percent slope.
   (b) 10 percent slope.
   (c) 20 percent slope.

5. A stair with a tread–riser relationship of 6:12 is steeper than a stair with one of 5:15.
   (a) true   (b) false

6. Manholes, man-sized circular pits, are used to enter the lines or to look down their length.
   (a) true   (b) false

7. Septic tanks and their drain fields work well when
   (a) soil is impervious and water table is high.
   (b) soil is impervious and water table is low.
   (c) soil is pervious and water table is high.
   (d) all of the above.
   (e) none of the above.

8. The main advantage of a flat area created by cutting into the bank is that the ground will be stable.
   (a) true   (b) false

9. In grading, handling runoff _____ is the most reliable method.
   (a) on the surface of the ground.
   (b) under the surface of the ground.

10. A catch basin is designed to catch
    (a) fur-bearing mammals.
    (b) sediment and/or debris.

11. Which of the following soils have poor load-bearing qualities when wet?
    (a) sandy loam
    (b) clay
    (c) gravelly loam

12. Drainage is a symbiotic adjunct to the grading process.
    (a) true   (b) false

13. Runoff is likely to be highest from a
    (a)   pasture.
    (b)   forest.
    (c)   suburban area.

14. With respect to newly cut or filled slopes, one primary rule is to
    (a)   prevent water from running over the slope.
    (b)   direct runoff onto the slope.
    (c)   make the slope too steep so that vegetation won't grow.
    (d)   none of the above.

15. A trench drain is
    (a)   a square drain.
    (b)   a long linear drain.
    (c)   a pit filled with gravel.

16. A culvert is a
    (a)   trench in which utilities are laid.
    (b)   pipe used to carry runoff water under driveways, sidewalks, etc.

17. An area drain is
    (a)   the same thing as a catch basin.
    (b)   used to collect underground water adjacent to foundation
          footings.
    (c)   used to collect water from a specific area and place it into
          underground pipes.

18. The finish flow elevation shown on a plan usually refers to
    (a)   finished elevation of the basement.
    (b)   finished elevation of the first floor.
    (c)   pad elevation.

19. It is probably less expensive in the long run to place all drainage
    underground rather than handle it on the surface.
    (a)   true   (b)   false

20. Slopes of less than 4 percent seem flat.
    (a)   true   (b)   false

21. The slope of a mowed lawn must be kept under (choose the best
    answer)
    (a)   25 percent.
    (b)   45 percent.
    (c)   60 percent.

22. Lawn areas of less than 1 percent
    (a)   will drain adequately.
    (b)   may not drain adequately.

23. Storm drainage systems (underground) are necessary when
    (a)   development is dense.
    (b)   excess runoff occurs after almost every rain.

(c) surface water runoff will inconvenience adjacent land users.

(d) all of the above.

(e) none of the above.

24. Transpiration is a part of the hydrological (water) cycle.

(a) true (b) false

25. The most important cause of erosion is

(a) wind.

(b) running water.

26. Water flows

(a) perpendicular to contours.

(b) diagonal to contours.

(c) parallel to contours.

(d) none of the above.

27. An open drainage system is one that

(a) is underground.

(b) is easy to inspect.

(c) is sloped sufficiently to prevent sediment accumulation.

(d) all of the above.

(e) none of the above.

28. Most underground drain lines require a minimum slope of above 1 percent or $\frac{1}{8}$ in. per foot.

(a) true (b) false

29. If you were asked to grade a slope at 20 percent and the contour interval of the map you were using was 2 ft, how far apart should you draw the contour lines for the slope?

(a) 5 ft

(b) 10 ft

(c) 15 ft

(d) 20 ft

(e) none of the above

30. If you were asked to lay out a trail at 10 percent on a map whose contour interval was 5 ft, how much distance on the plan should you allow between contours before the trail could cross the next higher or lower contour line?

(a) 25 ft

(b) 50 ft

(c) 75 ft

(d) 100 ft

(e) none of the above

WHEN NOT TO GRADE

We have been discussing mechanical methods used to manipulate ground form to create flat use areas. We talked tangentially about possible environmental problems associated with creating large, flat use areas. This section will help make these problems clear, and point out substitute grading methods to accommodate human needs without causing unnecessary problems. The environmental problems include the following potentials:

Interruption of drainage patterns.

Loss and mixing of topsoil through erosion.

Loss of vegetation.

Natural disasters.

Loss of unique habitats.

Esthetic degradation.

Interruption of natural drainage patterns can concentrate runoff elsewhere. This new concentrated runoff pattern, if not carefully planned, can cause erosion, downstream sedimentation, flooding, visual degradation, and possible loss of a natural stream. Approximately 30 percent of our rainfall is removed by runoff in natural conditions, whereas development speeds runoff and increases it up to 90 percent. This increased speed and excess runoff changes a stream's dynamic balance.

Lawns actually shed most of the water that falls on them, as the soil has been compacted by mowing and use and dense roots prevent infiltration. Forest soils store as much as 50 times more soil moisture than urban lands.

Loss of topsoil is more important than normally realized, particularly where topsoil is in short supply. We owe our existence to

COMPARISON OF URBAN AND FORESTED RUNOFF

	FORESTS (in.)	50% IMPERVIOUS (in.)	100% IMPERVIOUS (in.)
Precipitation	40	40	40
Interception	5	3	2
Overland flow	(0)	(18)	(36)
Soil moisture storage	(6)	(3)	(2)
Evapotranspiration	15	12	2
Runoff	20	25	36

( ) Indicates temporary storage

plants—trees, shrubs, and groundcovers—as producers of energy, food, and pure air. All plants require water and nutrients to grow, and these are most efficiently obtained from topsoil. Elimination of precious topsoil hampers plant life, which eventually affects us. Topsoil is manufactured naturally by weathering and decomposition of parent and organic material over a long period of time. Approximately 1000 years is necessary to build 1 in. of topsoil. *All* grading operations disturb topsoil, leaving some eroded, some mixed with subsoils, and some lost. Our design decisions and care determine how much we lose; it *is* possible to minimize the loss (Fig. 8–1).

Figure 8–1

Loss of vegetation has both long- and short-term effects. We are absolutely dependent on plants for our own survival. It has been estimated that approximately 75 mature trees are necessary to replenish the oxygen used by every urban dweller. Plants are climate moderators, causing beneficial changes in air temperatures, surface radiation, rainfall, etc. Plants help control erosion by reducing the rate of water flow and binding the soil in its root system.

To date we have been generally unconcerned about the actual value of plants. What is the replacement value of a 40-year-old elm or fir? The question is impossible to answer. However, we may say that the cost is whatever additional expense is required to *not* remove it. If it is necessary to replant following grading operations, this cost must also be figured in. The time is near when we will be able to accurately express the value of each urban plant, and that will help designers argue for plant preservation.

Natural disasters such as slides, slippage, floods and earthquakes, can be compounded by excessive or careless grading. Slide- and flood-prone areas can usually be detected in advance and should be avoided. The cost of repairing a slide is usually in excess of the value of the built facility and is often borne by the public. Determining slide hazard requires understanding the characteristics of local soils and their geological structure. This information, combined with topographic conditions, determines which areas are likely to slip:

1. Steep banks are most likely to slip and fine soils (clays, silts) on steep banks slip easiest. As the soil becomes water soaked, it gains weight until eventually gravity pulls it away. Sandy soils will stand at a steeper slope without slippage as they drain better. If you avoid steep areas, the chance of slippage is decreased.

2. The layering of soils, particularly in glaciated areas, can cause slippage if friction between soil types is increased by heavy loading or lubricated by increased water. A slip occurs when the shear stress between layers exceeds the shear strength.

3. Any weight increase or retained water increases the chance for slippage on steep banks. Deep pile foundations diminish the danger but usually at great expense.

4. Many layered soil profiles include impermeable clay layers beneath gravel or sandy layers. The sand–gravel drains well until it hits the impermeable layer, where it moves laterally and lubricates the clay layer. If the clay layer is inclined, the soils above may eventually slip away (Fig. 8–2).

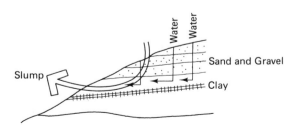

Figure 8-2

5. Earthquakes are altogether a different problem. There *are* known and suspected problem areas. Your best bet is to pay particular attention to the known problem areas, to heed any warnings, and consult an expert if you must work in the area.

6. Many natural disasters are triggered by work done on property hundreds of yards apart. For instance, removal of the toe of a bank for construction of a swimming pool may cause a house above to slip. This relates to the familiar rule, "Everything is connected to everything else." Connections are often difficult to perceive except by hindsight.

Unique landscapes and sensitive habitats should be avoided at all costs. These include land that is very steep, marshes, bogs, or rock outcroppings where the soil is obviously a problem that will require expensive grading techniques. Land rich in wildlife or other biotic life should be conserved for its own value.

VISUAL DEGRADATION—Modern site plans are designed to accommodate the automobile and to serve utilitarian purposes—delivery, parking, industrial processes, etc.—with forms and sizes not particularly satisfying to the pedestrian or easily integrated into subtle landscapes. Grading often removes all existing site qualities, and unless extensive landscape development is carried out, the places will be uncomfortable for most "people requirements" (Fig. 8–3).

Figure 8–3
This four-wheel vehicle is small, turns on a dime, and doesn't tear up the landscape. It is perfect for small projects in tight or sensitive areas.

GRADING DESIGN METHODS

There are many solutions to substitute for mechanical grading when one of the preceding problems arises:

REDUCE THE AREA TO BE GRADED — Accept the challenge and admit that there is *no proper* way to accommodate the development program. Try to strike a compromise; for instance, the building can be built, but access and auto parking should be kept back a certain distance. There are many cottages constructed carefully on difficult sites with only a narrow foot path leading to them. Another way to reduce grading is to reduce the amount of land covered by buildings. We live, work, and learn in a one-story world. By simply adding another story, the required flat land area is reduced by half. Roof gardens and parking under buildings reduces grading, although, at an increased cost (Figs. 8–4 and 8–5).

Figure 8–4
Terrace up a steep slope until it is almost vertical.

Figure 8–5
Eliminate the car from steep sites to minimize grading. A funicular railroad provides easy (though expensive) access on steep slopes while minimizing the environmental impact.

BREAK THE LARGE, FLAT USE AREA INTO SEVERAL SMALLER ONES — Most suburban projects have traditionally been built on one large level area to reduce grading cost. However, special site conditions may necessitate splitting or terracing the project and placing various portions of the building on different levels (Fig. 8-6). On very large and very small projects this may not add much cost and may produce interesting side effects. This technique allows most existing site features, such as trees, rock outcroppings, and streams, to be saved, which should enhance the site plan (Fig. 8-7).

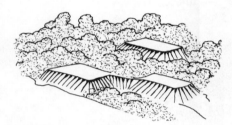

Figure 8-6 Stepping separate flat areas down the slope reduces grading and minimizes retaining walls.

Figure 8-7

CHANGE BUILDING ORIENTATIONS AND SITE CONFIGURATIONS TO RUN PERPENDICULAR OR PARALLEL TO THE CONTOURS — whichever way minimizes the impact of grading. A building parallel to the contour may require considerable cross-grading to permit access and drainage; one running perpendicular to the contours can adjust to grade and therefore require very little grading (Fig. 8-8).

CONCENTRATE THE DEVELOPMENT — assume that the grading will do maximum damage to a minimum amount of space, leaving the balance of land in natural condition. This is contrary to the typical suburban concept of minimal damage to the entire area. By concentrating the development, buildings may be entered at different levels to reduce the need for expensive elevators (Fig. 8-9).

REGROUP SMALL LAND PARCELS — One large parcel may overcome difficult development problems. Unfortunately, most land has been subdivided into ownership parcels by surveying techniques rather than by

(a)

(b)

Figure 8-8 (a) Perpendicular to contours. (b) Parallel to contours.

ecological parameters. This left many parcels too small to handle the
kind of environmental problems found in the 1970s. Additionally, most
property owners expect to use their land regardless of the environ-

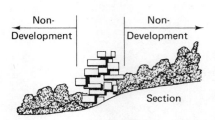

Figure 8-9 Concentrate development.

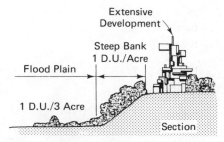

Figure 8-10 Transfer development rights.

mental consequences of development. Incentive zoning can offer bonus privileges to owners who join together to create a large enough land area to solve some long-term problems. What happens to the marsh owner who feels he has a right to develop, but clearly should not, while the land on a nearby plateau offers few environmental problems to defer development? Is there a way to combine these two areas (and whatever is between) to share in the profit of a development plan that preserves the marsh and builds on the plateau? (Figs. 8–10 and 8–11.)

COST ACCOUNTING — Any site evaluation should include both long- and short-term costs. Add the costs for maintenance to initial construction costs for each alternative solution. Test a variety of solutions from no grade to extensive grade. Test honestly; add costs to replace landscape elements removed, and add costs borne by other parties (the local municipality) and in the chain of ecological events for large projects. Cost accounting is a form of impact evaluation and is a valuable tool for assisting designers in implementing the proper approach. Many states have reasonably strong laws requiring impact statements

Figure 8-11
Parking is located on one side of this creek, with access to the houses over this foot bridge. This solution minimized grading impact on the stream, and provided a very quiet living situation.

for work that may cause environmental problems. However, cost accounting will require development of more sophisticated site analysis techniques.

HOW TO PREVENT EROSION
DURING CONSTRUCTION

The greatest chance for erosion occurs during and immediately following construction, when existing vegetation is removed, steep banks are created, drainage patterns are concentrated, and soil is exposed. Secretary of Agriculture Freeman reported in 1967 that "Farmlands converted to suburban uses can increase soil erosion from 50 to 2300 tons per square mile per year." Once soil is exposed, rain or wind can easily loosen soil particles and transport them as suspended particles. However, a carefully planned grading document can reduce erosion by avoiding grading on sensitive sites during the rainy season, minimizing the removal of vegetation, saving topsoil, replanting immediately, and developing temporary diversion channels and sediment traps to slow runoff and trap sediment.

Erosion is a process of detachment and transportation of soil particles. Rainfall detaches the soil particles, and runoff carries them down the slope. The soil particles are deposited as water slows down and spreads out. Five principles are involved in controlling erosion:

- Using land with soils suited for the development.
- Leaving soil bare for the shortest possible time.
- Reducing the velocity and controlling the flow of runoff.
- Detaining runoff on the site to trap sediment.
- Releasing runoff slowly to downstream areas.

These steps are carried out *mechanically* and *vegetatively*. Mechanical measures used to reshape the land should be held to a minimum to make the site suitable for its intended use without increasing runoff. New slopes should be less than their natural angle of repose, and stumps, other decayable material, and loose soil should not be used for fill.

A preventative *pregrading* operation should be carried out on large projects to reduce the damage from erosion, runoff, and sedimentation. This early grading is normally carried out 3 to 6 months before rough grading, and includes moving small amounts of soil to create dams and channels to collect eroded topsoil when the actual site grading takes place. Pregrading equipment should be small in size, and the work carefully located to minimize impact. Small rubber-tired equipment and handwork with seeding immediately following is best. Bales of straw are often used to slow runoff and trap sediment. They should be placed across drainage swales perpendicular to the line of runoff and fastened with long wooden stakes. Runoff filters through the bales, and sediment is trapped behind. Sediment should be removed periodically.

It is advisable to consider what the likely effect of the worst possible rain on a 1-year cycle would be to adjoining properties.

Silt traps should be located where changes in the rate of flow from fast to slow occur, as silt will be deposited there.

Fill banks are more subject to erosion than cut banks as the soil is loosely compacted. However, fill banks are easier to plant and usually revegetate quicker. Terrace across long slopes to break the flow of runoff. Each terrace should be just wide enough for a drainage ditch to carry runoff. Construct diversions of channels and ridges to intercept and divert runoff on long shallow slopes. It may be necessary on steep banks with highly erodable soils to pack broken rocks over the entire bank. This method works, although it is expensive, difficult to plant, and looks bad for many years.

All graded areas should be planted immediately following disturbance. Planting can be accomplished by hydro-seeding—a special grass seed, fertilizer, and binder blown mechanically over the graded area. It can also be hand or mechanically planted and should be tailored to special site conditions. Grass is used most for erosion control as it is low in cost, easy to maintain, and lasts a long time.

Spreading topsoil on steep slopes is futile as it will only wash away. Experience has shown that effective plant cover can be established on subsoil provided adequate fertilizer is applied. Erosion control nets (burlap or jute) can be used in steep areas. Maintenance will be necessary in almost all cases—to water, repair eroded areas, channel water properly, and replace any plants that die.

Fall and winter grading should be avoided on steep or sensitive sites as plant roots do not have sufficient time to take hold. The best time to grade is in early spring, as the rains are subsiding and planting will be sufficiently mature to reduce erosion the following winter. Spring and fall are the best seeding time for erosion control grasses. If you must seed at another time, use a quick germinating annual grass first, followed by reseeding with perennial grasses.

Mulch can be used to protect new slopes during plant growth time. Mulch is an organic or inorganic surface cover that holds soil in place and allows vegetation to root. Mulch reduces the speed of runoff, allowing more water to infiltrate the soil, which helps establish plants. It also reduces the loss of soil moisture through evaporation. Almost any local material such as leaf litter, tobacco stems, corn stalks, sawdust, or excelsior can be used. Grain straw is cheaper than hay, and all can be applied at the rate of $1\frac{1}{2}$ to 2 tons per acre.

Erosion-control netting may be required on steep slopes. This heavy jute or plastic net is available in several sizes, from 2 in. for

Figure 8-12
An engineering approach to erosion control which "works," but shows little respect for the neighborhood. Use nonplanting techniques only as a last resort.

steep slopes to 6 in. for shallow slopes. The net catches and retains eroded soils on the low side of each square, allowing plants or grass to continue to grow. Planting to reduce erosion depends more on its covering capacity to reduce raindrop impact than the soil binding effect of its root system. The more cover provided, as in forestland, the more effective the control. (See Fig. 8-12.)

Asphalt, although usually used for paving roads, can also be used to stabilize soil and promote seed germination and growth. A medium curing asphalt-spray mulch can be sprayed on a steep area after it has been seeded. During germination the asphalt holds in moisture and absorbs heat. As it dries, it cracks, allowing vegetation to grow through while still stabilizing the soil. In time the asphalt film disintegrates.

A combination straw and asphalt mulch can also be used. After the soil has been final graded, a layer of straw mulch is laid on top and a mixture of water and seeds blown over the mulch. The final step is to spray with asphalt as mentioned above. A variation on this method is to prepare the ground and then simultaneously spray asphalt seed and mulch over the soil.

OTHER NONGRADING TECHNIQUES

There are many ways to create flat use areas using variations of mechanical methods or substituting architectural and retaining elements.

INCREASE THE BANK STEEPNESS — Making an area flat creates two types of land, *the flat area* and the *steep bank* necessary to reach existing grade. The steep bank is unwanted, but is necessary to create the flat area. The flat area is what you want — a place to use and the reason for grading. There are several possible modifications to adjust the *steepness of bank:*

Tipping the flat area to run slightly uphill.
Adjusting the steepness of the bank.
Constructing retaining walls instead of earth banks.
Terracing.

Tipping the flat area to run slightly *uphill* is a common practice in grading parking lots. The auto (and many other functions) can operate on an area that is slightly tipped. By tipping the area you *reduce* the height of the bank necessary to reach existing grade. Additionally, you ensure positive drainage, reduce the amount of grading, and avoid large steep banks. On the other hand, it is possible to make the flat area too steep, which may look bad or not function properly. Anything over 8 percent should not be suggested, or should be very carefully thought out (Figs. 8–13a and b).

Figure 8–13(a) The forecourt of these garages has been tipped and each garage raised one ft to reduce the amount of grading.

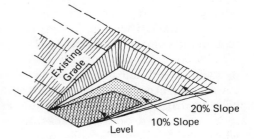

Figure 8–13(b)

Steepness of the bank necessary to reach existing grade may be adjusted depending on conditions and the amount of available land. A small urban site may need a relatively large flat area and require a very steep bank to save room, whereas a rural site may have adequate room for a long shallow bank. This depends on existing conditions; that is, trees or other features worth saving may preclude a long shallow bank, or an existing soil that does not stand steeply when graded may eliminate the steep bank (Fig. 8–14).

CONSTRUCT RETAINING WALLS — This eliminates the need for sloping banks, and thereby saves horizontal space. Retaining walls are expensive and should be used where space is premium, to solve special problems, or to create an architectural effect.

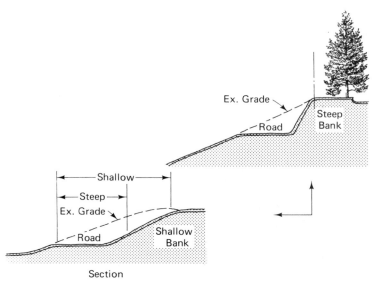

Ex. Grade

Road

Steep
Bank

Shallow

Steep

Ex. Grade

Road

Shallow
Bank

Section

Figure 8-14

Retaining walls are designed to retain an embarkment or an abrupt change in surface levels. They are an important potential solution for any grading scheme and can be constructed of rock, masonry, concrete, timber, or steel. As a general rule, they are expensive; however, cost should not keep a designer from *exploring* their possible use in a grading design.

Retaining walls will generally *not* be used on large lots or in rural areas with an adequate amount of open space to accommodate gentle banks. However, in urban areas where the amount of land is limited and there is *not* enough room for banks, retaining walls may solve the problem (Figs. 8-15 and 8-16).

A retaining wall is essentially a steep bank — very steep, in fact, *vertical*. It eliminates the 2:1, 3:1, or 4:1 bank necessary to accommodate the angle of repose of most soils. As the wall is vertical, contours running through the wall are *not* shown in plan form. The contour lines run into the wall at one end and emerge from the wall at the other end. Depending on the height of the walls, three, four, or five or more contours may run into each end and out the other. The retaining wall is usually darkened on the drawing, and spot elevations are used at top and bottom of wall and at any critical intermediate points. A retaining wall must be long enough to accommodate the bank as it returns to the original grade near the end of the wall (Fig. 8-17).

TERRACING — The bank may be adjusted by *terracing;* that is, instead of one large bank and flat area, use several flat areas and several small

Figure 8-15
Broken concrete can retain to about 8 ft if it is battered back slightly. The finish has a rough texture that is pleasing to look at, is easy for unskilled labor to install, needs minimum footings, and uses up unwanted concrete rubble.

Figure 8-16
Two short retaining walls with planting between softens the harshness of tall retaining walls and increases the apparent size of a small garden.

banks. This eliminates a large, ugly bank by dividing it into several smaller ones, which may make it easier to plant, to control erosion, and to drain. Terracing is often used in parking lots; in fact, all four examples can be seen around most new urban developments (Figs. 8–18 and 8–19).

POLE FOUNDATIONS CAN SUBSTITUTE FOR FLAT GRADED AREAS—The existing ground form continues under the pole platform with minimal disturbance to vegetation, drainage, topsoil, etc.; the trick

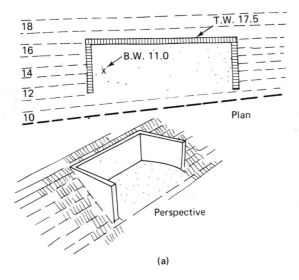

Plan

Perspective

(a)

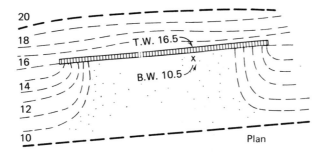

Plan

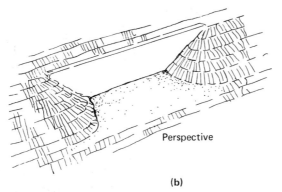

Perspective

(b)

Figure 8-17 (a) Wing walls contain the slope and are typical of daylight basements. (b) Without wing walls, the bank wraps around and joins the wall.

Figure 8-18 These apartments are terraced down the slope, which improves tenant privacy and visual appearance, as well as reducing the amount of grading.

Figure 8-19
Special care is necessary where the grade changes to avoid too steep a bank. Typically, a retaining wall extends a short distance perpendicular to the building, and then the grade feathers into a warped bank.

is to avoid the use of large equipment, which would do damage during construction. Pole holes should be hand dug, and foundations should not run across the grade forming a dam. The platform should be high enough to allow sunlight under for proper plant growth. House, garden, and parking decks are particularly well suited for pole construction on steep sites (Fig. 8–20).

Figure 8-20

Figure 8-21 The foundation of this building has been extended 8 ft to the ground and then boulders
added for landscape effect.

Buildings can terrace down the slope on poles, thereby eliminating
unsightly foundation when viewed from beneath. In certain areas, fire
from below is a problem, but this can be reduced by using fire-retard-
ant plants. The use of bridges to avoid large landfill operations is a logical extension of pole construction.

*EXTENDED BUILDING FOUNDATIONS CAN REDUCE GRAD-
ING, PARTICULARILY ON FILL SLOPES* – By this, we mean to construct the foundation and footings on the sloping grade, then build up
architecturally to the platform. This foundation system is most suited
to small structures, as large buildings tend to look awkward or out of
scale with the bank (Fig. 8–21).

There are many other methods that a talented designer can devise
to do the job properly and accommodate human needs within a frame-
work of natural processes. The number of times you will use *restrained
grading* techniques is increasing as we use up our easily developed
land and shift to the remaining difficult sites. Grading has become more
than mechanical manipulation of contours; analyze the site condition,
devise alternative development concepts, test and reanalyze, and pay
attention to problems. There are usually solutions, although sometimes
at higher costs. Where no reasonable solution exists, the project prob-

Figure 8-22
Bridges reduce the amount of grading on steep sites.

ably should not be done unless the risks are fully understood and enough funds allocated for proper maintenance and repairs (Fig. 8–22).

GRADING TO SAVE A TREE

A mature tree requires 15 to 20 years to grow, and may cost $2000 to replace. If one exists on the site, all efforts to save it should be employed, including the following:

Doing absolutely no grading under the drip line is the safest way to ensure saving the tree. Many heavy-foliaged trees shield themselves from rainfall and depend on these outer roots for water. Running grading equipment over these roots compacts the soil, and may restrict the flow of necessary water.

Never fill above or cut below the existing ground level of a tree (Fig. 8–23).

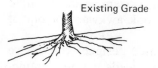

Existing Grade

Figure 8-23

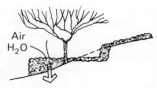

Air
H_2O

Figure 8-24

Use stacked rock walls at some distance from the tree to form wells for minor cuts and fills. Stacked rocks allow air and moisture to penetrate around the tree trunk and base and require no extensive foundation. This method is somewhat expensive, but should ensure saving an irreplaceable tree (Fig. 8–24).

Figure 8-25

Figure 8-26

Construct a deck around a tree, rather than cutting or filling to achieve the flat use area. Decks require minimum footings, and can be adjusted as needed around the trees (Figs. 8–25 through 8–28).

Figure 8-27 The road has been constructed too close to tree, and it will probably die in a few years.

Figure 8-28 Don't be afraid to move a large tree. This 10-in. caliber *cedrus deodara* was successfully moved with one piece of equipment in approximately 2 hours.

In difficult conditions, survey the situation closely with the help of a horticulturalist to determine special conditions that may allow grading beyond reasonable expectations. Check also on the health of the tree to be sure the tree is worth saving.

Adjust the design to save the tree; new roads can be raised, lowered, jogged, or split to accommodate a tree.

See if the tree is worth moving, and if there is a place to move it. With modern tree-moving equipment, it is possible to move most trees easily.

If all else fails, demand as much root space as possible, grade around it, and hope. The addition of evapotranspiration retardant sprays and installation of deep watering pipes may help.

PSYCHOLOGICAL EFFECTS OF GRADING

There are certain landforms and visual arrangements that affect people in specific ways and that should be used when appropriate. Two opposite design approaches to grading can be generally stated thus:

Architectural—parallel and perpendicular, with all lines, shapes and forms crisply defined and molded to convey a message of man's handiwork and separation from nature. (Fig. 8–29)

Natural—with size, shape, and grade carefully conceived to blend in with nature.

Using one approach rather than the other is personal and depends on design philosophies and the specifics of each project. Whichever is chosen, it is important that the architectural approach be truly archi-

Figure 8-29
Architectural landform grading.

tectural and that the natural approach be uncompromisingly natural. In general

Architectural grades will be parallel and perpendicular with slopes steep, uniform, and straight, with a sharp definition between existing grades and new use areas. Forms should be bold, with corners sharp and defined, and finish details such as planting designed to parallel, reinforce, and heighten the graded effect (Fig. 8–30).

Figure 8–30

Natural grading should create banks that approximate existing slopes. Concave and convex top and toe of banks are more pleasing than typical straight slopes. The junction between proposed and existing grades should be rounded to smooth the transition. Special small equipment and handwork will be necessary for both approaches following rough grading (Fig. 8–31).

Boring

Figure 8–31

Once the basic design philosophy or concept has been established, there are a number of other psychological factors that can be used to guide the design:

Convex or concave forms are more pleasing to the eye than straight planes (Fig. 8–32). Concave forms generally appear lighter and more elegant.

A rise in grade is dramatic and gives a feeling of expansion or vastness, but reduces circulation ease (Fig. 8–33).

Figure 8-32

Figure 8-33

Figure 8-34

Figure 8-35

The steeper the slope, the greater the spatial break between the adjacent plane (Fig. 8–34).

Valleys afford a complete visual composition. Open and rounded valley forms are expansive; steeper and angular valleys appear secluded (Fig. 8–35).

Downward or declining landforms give a sense of refuge, confinement, protection, privacy, and of being in harmony with the forces of gravity (Fig. 8–36).

Horizontal or open, flowing space provides for easy, safe movement and a free choice of direction but often results in monotony (Fig. 8–37).

Figure 8-36

Figure 8-37

Symmetrical plans indicate man's control of the landscape. Symmetric landforms require precision in detail and bold forms to succeed (Fig. 8–38).

Asymmetric ground forms depict freedom and bring man into harmony with nature (Fig. 8–39).

An axial plan becomes highly directional, orderly, and dominating, but often monotonous. It is *not* conducive to relaxation, appreciation of nature, or to freedom of choice (Fig. 8–40).

Figure 8-38
Symmetric design combined with strong
architectural land forms is an efficient
design approach for an athletic complex.

Figure 8-39

Figure 8-40

Flowing shapes and continuous forms and spaces connote a
feeling of relaxation (Fig. 8-41).

Flat sites are monotonous and usually convey a rather neutral
landscape quality (Fig. 8-42).

Figure 8-41

Figure 8-42
Flat sites can be manipulated by major
grading, planting, and constructing
buildings. Digging a lake and using the
spoils to build large earth berms is often
successful.

Paths that loop and switch back along a steep grade reduce the
apparent height and length of a climb (Fig. 8–43).

Conversely, paths or walkways that travel in a straight, unbroken
climb to the hilltop increase the apparent distance and height and
are more tiresome in ascent (Fig. 8–44).

Figure 8-43   Figure 8-44

Retaining walls create a more formal feeling than natural slopes
(Fig. 8–45).

A change in level is the classic way to introduce surprise and
variety.

A slope upward from the house is less satisfactory and will
appear cramped unless extensive concave grading is done. The
view up the hill is foreshortened, reducing apparent size of garden.
Drainage is difficult (Fig. 8–46).

A cross fall presents a great design challenge—buildings appear to
slip sideways unless they are designed to grow out of it (as a
Swiss chalet does). Land shaping can help.

Straight lines are strong, bold, and lead forward. Horizontal lines
are subtle, and exude peace and quiet, restfulness, etc. Diagonal
or zigzag lines are busy, active, dynamic, erratic, and many
directional (first this, then that way). Curved or rolling lines are
similar to horizontal lines—calm, and tranquil.

Figure 8-45

Figure 8–46
These townhouses have, a constant drainage and sedimentation battle at their
back door. Try to avoid building so close
to a steep bank.

BERMS

A berm is an earth mound or a large pile of carefully formed earth used for some special design effect. They can create privacy in a back-yard, act as a noise barrier, make level land appear steeper, or use up excess fill. Berms may be rigidly architectural or smooth-flowing natural forms. Smooth-flowing berms must be carefully formed and fine graded to blend into the surrounding landscape or they can easily look like an "elephant burial mound" and appear awkward. Architectural berms appear satisfying with straight lines, uniform slope, and crisp angular corners. Planting architectural berms is difficult, for plants usually grow large and soft enough to eliminate the bold design, whereas planting free-flowing berms is a simple matter as plants enhance the free-flowing ground form. Architectural berms are improved with sharp edges at the top and toe of the bank (Figs. 8-47a & b); naturalistic berms should be molded to flow freely, with the top and toe disappearing.

There is a tendency among designers to design "little berms," which often look contrived; design the berm large enough to *be* something. There is nothing wrong with a 4-, 5-, or 6-ft-tall berm. Berms should generally be steep, but not so steep as to erode or not support plant life. A 1:3 slope can be mowed and 1:2 is acceptable for shrubbery or groundcover. The main disadvantage of berms is they require

Figure 8–47(a)
Architectural landforms are created by spacing contours equally, with abrupt changes between horizontal and sloping surfaces, and with precise corners. (See grading plan for this earth mound.)

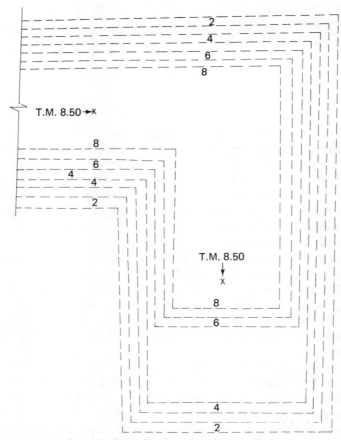

Figure 8–47(b)   Grading plan for an architectural berm.

Figure 8-48(a)
A *berm* adds topographic interest to flat
sides, and blends different uses together.

Figure 8-48(b)
Berms can screen unwanted views such as
this parking lot. If additional earth were
available, this berm should be raised 2 ft.

more horizontal space than building a fence or a retaining wall
(Figs. 8–48a and b.)

Berming around buildings provides excellent insulation against
heat loss or gain and noise. Water, drainage, and dampproofing are necessary. With proper design, it is possible to bury the north, east, and
west walls and reduce heating requirements by 40 percent.

BERMS AS NOISE BARRIERS — Effective noise barriers to protect
houses from highway noise can be graded with excess earth. The berm
must be tall, necessitating a wide base and considerable land. A precise
section through the housing and highway helps indicate how high the
berm must be, with units *below* the berm top effectively protected, and

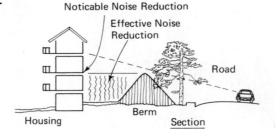

Figure 8-49

those below the sound line receiving noticable reduction in noise. (See Fig. 8-49.)

Berms shaped like a long prism are most efficient to construct, and can be at a 1:1 slope ratio if planted and maintained. However, if more room exists, the inside can be contoured and used as a park/playground. (See Fig. 8-50a and b.)

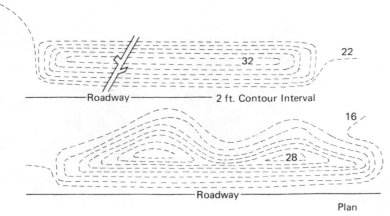

Plan   Figure 8-50(a)

Figure 8-50(b)
Planted earth berm to shield the apartments from a noisy road. Note the combination bike and sidewalk, with bikes riding on the asphalt strip traveling in the same direction as the cars.

STREET SYSTEMS

The many pervasive, undesirable effects of our street system are now known facts. Auto emission pollutes the air and often reaches concentrations that cause health hazards. Noise from engines, tires, and the streamline effect touches every metropolitan area, whether from the freeway or nearby arterials. Visual and esthetic pollution is caused by wider pavement, fewer trees, expanded parking areas, and larger signs that demand attention at high speeds (Fig. 9–1). Public roadways occupy 25 to 35 percent of our urbanized land, and seem likely to grow larger. On the other hand, roads serve our life style, afford considerable personal freedom, allow us to visit friends, travel to work, etc. The objective must be to design alignments that balance freedom of travel with a high-quality environment for abutting land owners.

Our society has many engineers advocating expansion of the road network, and does not need additional spokesman. The real need is for counterbalances—designers who are advocates for the non–auto user or the auto user when out of his car. Such designers would champion the pedestrian, bicyclist, children at play, home and apartment dwellers, etc., and would attempt to assure that autos don't intrude unnecessarily. He would probably work at two levels:

1. Arguing for proper land uses abutting each type of road; that is, a major road with heavy traffic, noise, and emissions should *not* have residential uses abutting it.
2. Designing a proper road layout to minimize undesirable environmental effects. This suggests matching road type with desired travel needs and providing wider sidewalks, higher curbs, adequate tree and shrub planting, depressing roadways, creating berms, placing signs, narrowing or reducing auto lanes, etc.

Figure 9-1
Endless asphalt and concrete; unless we are careful, the whole world will be paved.

These positions need not be wholly one sided, but instead designers should determine the *real* requirements and purposes of each road, and attempt to structure or redesign it to assure high overall environmental quality. To do this, it is essential to have insight to the standards, techniques, and methods used in the civil engineering of road systems.

Streets are organized in *hierarchical networks* with each higher level of road serving an increased volume of traffic at a faster speed and covering a longer distance. This can be compared to a tree with the decreasing size and connection of trunk, limb, branches, and twigs analogous to freeways, arterials, local, and feeder roads. Each satisfies certain collection, movement, and distribution purposes. The hierarchical approach is not a formula for rubber-stamp application, but is rather a way to conceptualize alternative solutions to each problem — and then adjust designs as required. There are five basic street patterns that guide the conceptual organization of street alignment projects:

1. *Radial* — major roads leading to the center, and the center becoming very important (Fig. 9-2).
2. *Ring* — major roads concentric to each other (Fig. 9-3).

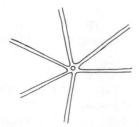

Figure 9-2   Radial pattern.

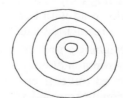

Figure 9-3   Ring pattern.

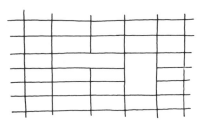

Figure 9-4 Grid pattern.

Figure 9-5 Hierachial pattern.

3. *Grid*—the most typical pattern in the United States; uniform and geometric with square, triangular, or hexagonal patterns. The grid distributes traffic uniformly over the land (Fig. 9–4).
4. *Hierarchical*—like a tree or river, with specialized roads serving a specific number and type of traffic (Fig. 9–5).
5. *Linear*—straight major roads serving adjacent developments via minor roads connecting to them (Fig. 9–6).

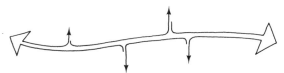

Figure 9-6 Linear pattern.

Obviously, these basic patterns can be combined, producing a *radial–ring* or *linear–grid,* for instance, or they can be repeated at small intervals as $\frac{1}{2}$-mile-radius radials. Each has unlimited expansion by simply extending the grid, radial, or linear street outward or adding another concentric ring.

These conceptual road patterns serve two important uses for the designer: first, most existing road patterns fit into one of the categories. You should be able to determine how an existing road relates to the larger system and treat it accordingly. Second, in designing a total street system, you will have several conceptual alternatives to begin with. A warning: the conceptual diagram is seldom a perfect solution and should be reworked and adjusted to conform to topography, vegetation, outcrops, land unit types, your intuition, etc.

A hierarchical system can be designed into each basic pattern by controlling access and varying the road width. The designer has two major choices:

1. *Jointed system*—most roads interconnected allowing direct and easy access to all parts of the neighborhood or community. This

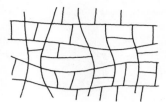

Figure 9-7   Jointed system.

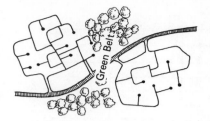

Figure 9-8   Disjointed system.

produces a uniform pattern, with uniform distribution of traffic and ultimate flexibility (Fig. 9–7).

2. *Disjointed system*— several roads form small neighborhoods, which connect to a main road to connect to other neighborhoods. Cul-de-sac and loop roads (roads to nowhere) serve this type of network and can be combined in many patterns to guarantee quiet and safety.Open space and green belts can fill the space between (Fig. 9–8).

ROADWAY CLASSIFICATION

Community roads are ideally classified into three categories, each serving a special purpose: (1) major, (2) local, and (3) feeder roads (Fig. 9–9).

Major roads provide efficient routes from point to point in the greater community. They should carry heavy traffic loads at relatively high speeds, and provide external access to individual communities. The roadway design should reflect the detached nature of this road system; it need not compromise for minor land features. Sidewalks should *not* be provided; parking should *not* be allowed; auto access from adjacent land should be limited. Planting should be bold, with enough room

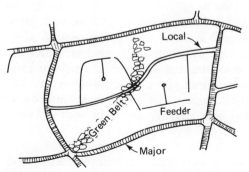

Figure 9-9   Conceptual hierarchical street layout.

allowed for structural noise barriers protecting adjacent communities. Most communities really don't have many of these streets. Our interstate highways are extremely overscaled and not at all community roads; perhaps a broad boulevard comes closest to describing it. (See Fig. 9–10.)

Figure 9–10
Carefully designed major road under construction. The center island and planter strip will soon be planted with trees and grass. Note the road is only one lane wide in each direction, with a painted bike lane. However, no parking is allowed and the road can carry a high volume of traffic.

Local roads serve as a distribution system within the community. These roads connect with major roads and act as linkages between development areas. They should serve both autos and pedestrians and have parking where it does not conflict with movement. Their configuration and alignment should follow the form of the development that they serve. Most arterial streets fall crudely into this category, although existing site conditions seldom influence arterial alignment, the pedestrian is minimally served, and they are disastrous to all unfortunate abutting residents. In the long term, arterials may be improved by slower speed limits, more public transportation, better integration of the pedestrian routes with the surrounding architecture, and various road treatments to assure a higher standard of environmental quality. It may be necessary to have additional local roads to relieve the congestion of existing arterials, without causing adverse damage to existing land uses.

Feeder roads should relate directly to the development that they serve, with their configuration determined by the adjacent development. They should become the shared domain of both pedestrian and auto users. Auto speed should be carefully controlled so that children can play safely and enjoy the outdoors in relative quiet. Most neighborhood streets could fit into this category with minor changes in configuration. The apartment parking street is another American feeder road example; the European expanded street node is a better example (Fig. 9–11).

Figure 9-11
A feeder road—narrow to reduce speed of travel, with sidewalks and landscaping for pedestrians. Note that parallel parking is organized and defined by planted islands that "capture" the no-parking area and a curb that makes the street appear narrower.

ROAD CAPACITY

Roads are "designed" to carry a predetermined number of cars. Transportation planners use surveys, charts, and trends to predict future traffic demands, which are then passed on to engineers for use in design and construction. We are generally much better at designing roads to meet a capacity than we are at determining what the capacity should be, partly because we spend more time and effort at designing them, and partly because predicting is still a guessing game.

Determining the capacity of each traffic lane is partly technological, partly luck. Traffic planners usually begin with an assumed maximum traffic lane capacity at *ideal* conditions. Capacity is expressed as vehicles per hour per lane at ideal conditions. This is calculated at an assumed speed of travel with sufficient lane width, easy grade, no interruptions, etc. From this assumed maximum capacity, deductions are made for any factor that interrupts the flow, such as steeper grades, intersections, narrower lanes, commercial areas, left turns, many trucks, etc. The maximum capacity for each lane under ideal conditions at 25 mph is 1200 vehicles per hour.

The process of determining road capacity seldom includes questions relating to the quality of the finished environment. I feel the designer's role in determining road capacity must assure a proper environmental balance after the road improvements are complete. The following are questions that you might ask to this end:

Is the projected capacity based on rush-hour peak loads or is there really a constant 8- to 10-hour per day need. If the need is just for rush hours, what happens if rush hour is extended 1 hour, or if more buses are added, or car pools developed, or anything else which reduces the number of vehicles during that time?

Where is the road going? If it is only, say, four blocks long, is it worth speeding traffic up and increasing capacity for such a short distance? Most street improvements are planned in short increments, and soon become self-serving by extending the problem a short distance and creating road-widening demand further on.

What noise and pollution problems will result from the increased capacity? Auto-generated noise is very difficult to control, and it cannot be done with street trees. Concentrations of emissions can cause health hazard to abutting residents, and runoff can pick up oil and grit that pollutes nearby streams.

Who benefits and who loses from the "improvement"? If a neighborhood is going to suffer environmental problems from a roadway benefiting nonneighborhood users, what special benefits should they receive? Landscaping? Tax reduction? High-quality design? Zoning change?

Are there other means to satisfy the demand; what about improving bus service, constructing bicycle trails, foot traffic, or sharing rides, etc.?

Should we purchase truly adequate right-of-way, buying all the houses on one side of the street to correct all the problems? If so, is it worth the cost and political headaches?

Speed of travel is a topic designers should become very familiar with. As speed of auto travel increases, the noise also increases. As speed of travel increases, compatibility with pedestrians and bicyclists decreases. Cars traveling about 20 mph create excessive noise and are almost incompatible with pedestrians and bicycles sharing the same lane. Cars traveling above 20 mph are dangerous when children are playing near the street, and everyone knows that children play most of the time in and around the street.

To increase the potential road speed, designers can consider the following:

Straighten the alignment—smooth out the curves and make it as straight as possible

Widen the roadway—the wider each lane is, the faster you can drive.

Separate traffic lanes—a barrier or planting strip, which removes the danger of oncoming traffic, allows drivers to speed up.

Use one-way streets—avoids conflict with oncoming traffic.

Limit access—the fewer distractions from driveways, businesses, etc., the faster cars can travel.

Increase speed limit — just say it is okay to travel faster.

Smooth the road surface — the smoother, the faster.

Simplify the route — eliminate confusing elements (signs, scenery, etc.).

Add signals — traffic lights assure a clear way at each intersection.

Eliminate off-street parking — reduces visual conflict as cars park and leave.

Improve street lighting — increases speed at night.

Build pedestrian overpasses — reduces conflict.

Widen the shoulder — actually a road-widening device.

Superelevate — bank curves to compensate for gravity forces.

Obviously, if one wished to slow down traffic, the opposite treatment should be employed. The point is, we must decide where cars should travel fast, and where they should travel more slowly, and design the total streetscape to best satisfy those conditions.

Several types of roads have a high potential for serving both pedestrians and autos, the so-called "roads that don't go anywhere." Developers have found the *cul-de-sac* to be the most popular street to live on. It is a safe place for children to play, quiet, and imageable. To ensure fire and police protection, public policy usually dictates that cul-de-sacs not exceed 500 ft in length. They could functionally become longer, with a maximum length of 1000 ft. One thousand feet is quite long and could occasionally be blocked by accident, utility break, falling tree, repairs, etc. Such a tie-up would not affect regular traffic, but emergency vehicles might be more severely affected.

The maximum length for higher-density clusters should not exceed 600 ft. If the cluster has over 100 units, a loop road returning to the same entry is better. Clusters over 300 units should have two entries, or at least an extra exit. These figures depend on the condition of the abutting road, and should be adjusted if the abutting road is heavily traveled.

The turnaround can be a circular drive or simpler hammerhead design requiring a backup maneuver. Some cul-de-sacs provide no turnaround space, but utilize driveways at the end of the road (Fig. 9–12).

Recommended minimum turning radii for a complete U-turn are shown in the following table:

VEHICAL	RADIUS
Compact car	15
Standard American car	19
Pickup truck	19
Delivery van	24
Forty-foot bus	43

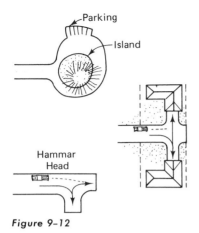

Hammar
Head

Figure 9-12

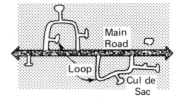

Main
Road

Loop

Cul de
Sac

Figure 9-13

Loop roads can be longer than cul-de-sacs, as they *rejoin* a larger through road. Cul-de-sacs can be attached to the loop road, providing additional quiet neighborhoods for many families (Fig. 9–13).

Grid system streets can be converted to a hierarchical system by adding traffic control structures that create a series of cul-de-sacs and loop roads. The work is accomplished by changing the form of inter-sections to divert unnecessary auto traffic and reduce the speed of all auto travel. A converted neighborhood will be quieter, safer for children to play in, and better for pedestrians and bicyclists. The traffic-control structures include the following:

Diagonal diverters at the intersection in kitty-corner fashion (Fig. 9–14). Drivers must slow down at the intersection and turn left or right. Pedestrians can walk across the diverter without confronting moving traffic. (See also Figs. 9–15–9–18.)

Figure 9-14
Diagrammatic street diverter.

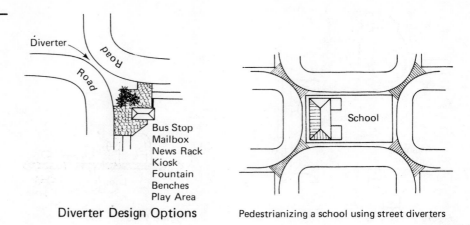

Diverter Design Options

Pedestrianizing a school using street diverters

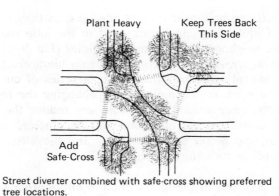

Street diverter combined with safe-cross showing preferred
tree locations.

Safe-cross and street diverters can be combined on wide
streets where parking is to remain improving pedestrian
crossing in all directions.

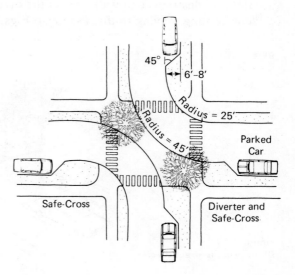

Figure 9-15   Diverter design options

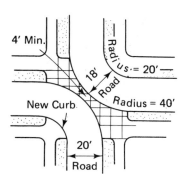

Street diverter—minimum design standards for two-way auto traffic. Compact cars can pass easily at slow speed, while large cars must negotiate it one at a time.

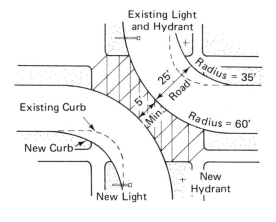

Engineering design standards for street diverters meet emergency acess requirements and will satisfy most traffic engineers.

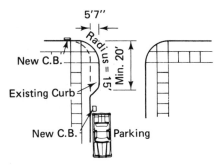

Figure 9-15 (continued).

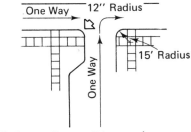

Reduce radius on all 'no turn' corners

Pedestrian safe-cross narrows the roadway at the intersection by extending the sidewalks (Fig. 9–16). This slows traffic, warns drivers of pedestrians, and reduces the crosswalk length. The safe-cross can also be used to define parking spaces by jutting out where no parking is allowed (Fig. 9–17).

Small circular traffic islands within the intersection allow continuous flow through the intersection, but at reduced speeds.

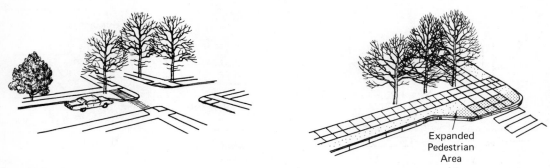

Figure 9–16

Expanded
Pedestrian
Area

Figure 9–17
Pedestrian safe-cross expands the side-walk into the parking lane at the inter-section. Parking is prohibited near the intersection, so no spaces are lost. Trees, benches, bus stops, etc., can be added to the "captured" space.

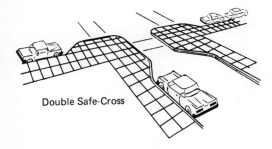

Double Safe-Cross

● Remove Pavement
● Install Curb
● Drain
● Plant

45° Angle

Curb

Varies

Min. 3'0"

5' to 7'

Mid-Block Safe-Cross

Figure 9–18   **Pedestrian safe-cross design options.**

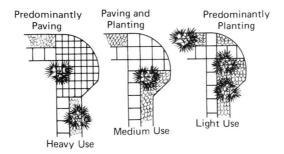

Predominantly Paving

Paving and Planting

Predominantly Planting

Heavy Use

Medium Use

Light Use

Safe-Cross Paving Patterns Tailored to Serve User Demand

The safe-cross occupies a space approximately 6 feet wide by 20 feet long, replacing a portion of a parking or traffic lane. Remodeling an existing intersection involves removing and realigning the curb, modifying drainage structures, laying new sidewalks, planting, and installing necessary street furniture.

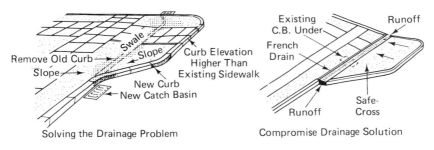

Solving the Drainage Problem

Compromise Drainage Solution

Figure 9–18 (continued).

Closing sections of a street for use as people-oriented commons. Although this provides inexpensive open space where it is needed most, it is inconvenient for abutters and may be difficult to implement (Fig. 9–19).

Creating cul-de-sacs with a hammerhead turnaround or using opposite driveways.

Devise a system of short one-way streets to slow traffic down and add land to the pedestrian domain. A one-way system requires less pavement than two-way and can increase pedestrian safety if auto speeds are held down. Intermix one- and two-way streets to confuse the "uninitiated driver" while serving those familiar with the area (Fig. 9–20).

Figure 9-19
This cross street is being closed to through traffic. The street portion has been removed, and the sidewalk will be reinstalled 6 in. above street grade with a small driveway for neighborhood access.

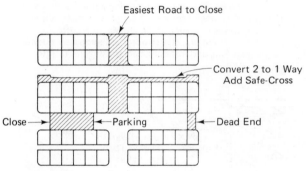

Figure 9-20 Plan showing alternative road recycling opportunities in an existing neighborhood.

Diverter projects have been successfully developed in many cities, with overwhelming support *after* they are properly installed. Many neighborhoods experience uncertainty during the planning stages; the following hints may help to persuade them:

Minimize the amount of change in each neighborhood. Do as *little* to the streets as is necessary to eliminate nonneighborhood through traffic. The principal objective of a system of diverters is to eliminate unnecessary through traffic, while allowing access for residents and guests. The traffic circle seems to serve this purpose better than all other methods, as it slows traffic without restricting the direction of travel. Diverters and one-way streets restrict movement, and often force a longer journey for neighborhood residents. A typical layout is shown in Fig. 9-21 and 9-22.

Work with the fire, garbage, and bus departments to assure that their vehicles can comfortably maneuver within the proposed system. The best way to satisfy everyone is to set up a test with small cans and have a fire engine, garbage truck, and bus move through it.

Check to see where through traffic will be diverted and verify that no unnecessary damage will be suffered by people using those streets.

Listen carefully to people in the neighborhood and respond to their requirements.

Figure 9–21
This landscaped traffic island has reduced through traffic and confusion in its residential neighborhood. However, had it been constructed as a peninsula, it would have been larger and more effective.

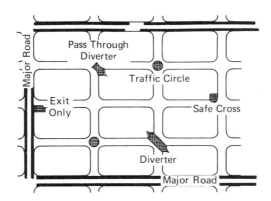

Neighborhood plan: Diverters, safe-cross, one-way streets and traffic circles can be used in combination to exclude unwanted traffic from a neighborhood.

Figure 9–22

(a)

(b)

Figure 9-23(a) Long straight roads are boring, create undefined neighborhoods and cause auto drivers to speed up. (b) To correct these problems, design bends or T intersections into the road system.

OTHER STREET LAYOUT CONSIDERATIONS

Minimize unnecessary through traffic on local streets — Designate some streets for higher volumes of through traffic, which theroetically reduces unnecessary traffic on local streets (see Fig. 9–23a and b.)

Interconnect all parts of a neighborhood — Ideally, neighbors should be able to walk or ride to a friends house without traveling out of the way or too indirectly.

Consider carefully the placement of traffic generators within the neighborhood — Schools, shopping areas, churches, offices, etc., cause congestion and require special treatment.

Vary width and design of different-purpose streets — Feeder roads should be narrower than arterials or collector roads, and perhaps landscaped differently (Fig. 9–24).

Design local streets to discourage high speeds — Curves, defined parking, narrow road section, speed bumps, signs, etc., should be used to keep traffic to 15 to 20 mph. (Many traffic engineers say 25 mph is better; I disagree for neighborhood streets.)

Devote a minimum amount of land to streets — Some urban areas have 30 percent of their land tied up in streets through inefficient planning. Use cul-de-sacs, internal private drives, narrow streets, and clever planning to reduce the length and to some degree the width of roadways.

Figure 9-24
Bend roads to open up a view. Long straight roads are boring and should bend or meet a T intersection occasionally to *enclose* the street.

Reduce the number of intersections — Intersections slow traffic and cause the greatest number of accidents.

Make sure there is sufficient room to permit easy development — Often roadways cut parcels into awkward sizes and diminish the use of valuable land.

Relate roads to topography — Follow topography to reduce costs and improve traffic flow. Valley floors, for instance, are natural locations for roadways (Fig. 9–25).

Figure 9-25   Follow the valley floor, *but* keep to one side.

STREET PAVING — Most urban and suburban regions now use bituminous (asphalt) paving installed over a gravel base. This material is satisfactory, durable, easy to install, patches easily, and is inexpensive. However, its color and texture are not too attractive (Fig. 9–26).

Figure 9-26

Gravel roads are suitable for rural and infrequently used areas and are good looking as they blend into the landscape. Gravel has a tendency to move to the side under heavy traffic and must be graded and renewed from time to time. Pea gravel and large crushed gravel are hard to walk on, which is one disadvantage.

Paving blocks (granite, brick, and heavy scored concrete) can be used on steep grades for traction and are attractive as their color, size, and pattern can be controlled. However, in many areas, materials and skilled installers are unavailable, making them expensive to construct.

All roadways should have an adequate gravel base course to protect against soil, climate, or heavy use problems. Generally, sandy or gravelly soils drain well and require limited bases; heavy or poorly drained soils should be removed and replaced with an engineered gravel fill. Roads in severe frost areas used by heavy vehicles should have a gravel base extending below the frost line to minimize heaving damage.

Curbs are utilitarian rather than decorative elements that channelize and direct the movement of cars and runoff. Curbs protect pedestrians, trees, and planter strips, direct and assist drainage, define parking, and establish a positive limit on car encroachment. Curbs should be 6 to 8 in. high; they can be taller to protect pedestrians if a stepped curb is used. They must be strong enough to resist auto tire impacts and are usually constructed of concrete or asphalt, although wood can also be used. Curb cuts and sloped ramps should be installed at all intersections for handicapped and bicycle access (Fig. 9-27.)

Many engineers tend to overuse curbs, placing them on all new roads. This adds costs, channelizes drainage, and in rural areas makes the country look like the city. Omission of curbs allows the road to blend in with the landscape, and allows runoff to disperse in small quantities over the total landscape. Installing curbs visually separates

Figure 9-27 Construction of new curbs. Note the two trees that were saved, and the handicapped ramp in the lower right corner. The asphalt paving will be installed after the curbs.

Figure 9-28 Rural road without curbs.

the street from the landscape, and directs runoff to collection points where concentrations are often too high for the landscape to absorb it (Fig. 9–28). A storm drainage system is almost always necessary when curbs are used.

BARRIER-FREE ACCESS AND CIRCULATION FOR THE HANDICAPPED

People in wheelchairs, grandparents pushing prams, bicyclists, elderly with a cane, and many other people require circulation routes that are flat to slightly sloped. Free movement for handicapped is a problem and public recognition is long overdue. Many states and local authorities recognize this shortsightedness and are beginning to require a secondary access for handicapped. Most designers plan circulation routes without regard for the handicapped, and attempt to work in some handicapped access *after* major design decisions have been made (Fig. 9–29). Ramps are tacked on in some way, or long obscure routes are proposed, creating a general feeling that handicapped are second-class citizens. A preferred method is to accept barrier-free access* from the start, and use handicapped access as a prime design concern. There are times when conditions won't work exactly as you would want, but the overall job will always be superior. It is unnecessary to give up a change in level because of the handicapped; just provide a separate route with slope, change of grade, and connections between carefully designed to assure free access to those confined to wheelchairs (Fig. 9–30).

*A continuous, unobstructed, path of travel 32-in. wide by 80-in. high and not exceeding 8 percent throughout the site and building connecting all designated accessible facilities.

Figure 9-30 An 8-ft-wide ramp allows easy passage in both directions, and will be used by many others besides the handicapped.

Figure 9-29 Ramps can be integrated into the landscape *if* they are thought about early enough.

The most critical concern in grading for the handicapped is to assure that there is a continuous route that does *not* exceed 8 percent. Eight percent is one foot rise per 12.5 feet of linear distance. There must be *no* steps or curbs that may create a barrier. Eight percent is the accepted maximum, though designers occasionally build 12 percent curb cuts when space is tight, while those confined to wheelchairs would prefer a maximum 5 percent limitation. (See Fig. 9–31 and 9–32.)

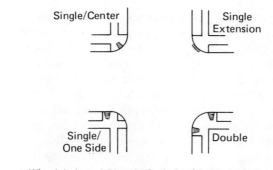

Single/Center

Single Extension

Single/ One Side

Double

Wheelchair and Bicycle Curb Cut/Ramp Locations

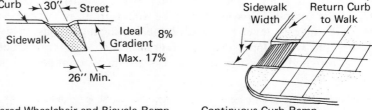

Figure 9–31(a)

Flared Wheelchair and Bicycle Ramp

Continuous Curb Ramp

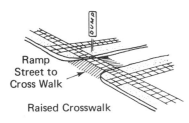

Ramp
Street to
Cross Walk

Raised Crosswalk

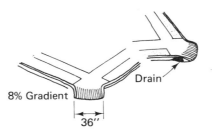

8% Gradient

Drain

36″

Extended Wheelchair Ramps   *Figure 9–31(b)*

Figure 9–31(c)   Existing curbs can be converted for access by adding an asphalt ramp out from them. However, this may interfere with auto movement and is not the preferred method.

Figure 9–31(d)   A ramp constructed at the apex of the corner radius serves circulation for both cross-street directions. The scored lines help blind people find the corner.

Figure 9–32
Ramp/stair combinations are difficult to work out because of the long length needed for the ramp. They often appear awkward as in this example, but they do provide direct and equal access for the handicapped—a feat not normally accomplished.

FIELD EXERCISE

Rent a wheelchair and spend one full day confined to it. Try to go from your home to work or school, to shop, and play. Experiment also on known gradients (5 percent, 8 percent, 12 percent) and on a long (over 100 feet) 8 percent gradient.

BARRIER-FREE ACCESS — Pedestrian overpasses can work efficiently for pedestrians if the roadway is depressed slightly, and the overpass arched. This eliminates the need for steps on the overpass, and assures easy access for handicapped. Depressing the road also creates a barrier to those who find crossing the street easier than using the overpass. In urban conditions, the road can be as steep as 11 percent, while the overpass arch should not exceed 8 percent so that the handicapped can use it. (See Figs. 9–33, 9–34 and 9–35.)

Figure 9–33
Pedestrian overpass (see grading plan). The arched form requires minimum structive at the center, which also decreases its required height. Note the smooth concave and convex ground form under the bridge.

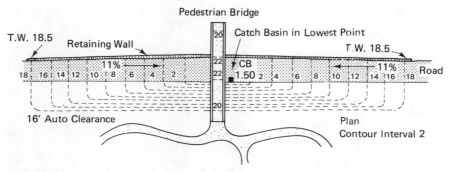

Figure 9–34

Figure 9-35 Converting for handicapped access often results in awkward routes. This path would be better if it were straight or angled slightly.

BIKEWAYS

Higher projected use of bicycles creates an entire new set of problems for traffic planners. There is much to learn, and we will only be able to introduce the problem. Basically, bikers require conditions similar to the pedestrian—minimum conflict with the car, gentle grades, quiet safe route, visual interest and beauty along the way. However, bicycles are not as maneuverable as pedestrians and travel faster, creating conflict when they share the same route. There are three basic ways to accommodate bike trails:

A separate bikeway is best. One can be located along an abandoned railroad track, a closed road, shoreline, utility easement, through different parks, etc., on a trail designed for exclusive bike use (Fig. 9–36).

In the street, but separated from cars and pedestrians. This solution is appropriate on arterials where the speed of traffic is too fast for bikers (Fig. 9–37).

Road

Separate Route

Figure 9-36

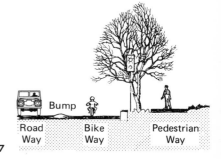

Bump

Road Way

Bike Way

Pedestrian Way

Figure 9-37

Figure 9-38

Posting a slow auto speed limit (say 15 mph) along certain streets and designating the street a bikeway. This allows bikers to travel in the road without excessive danger, and does not eliminate parking or auto traffic. Through auto traffic must be accommodated elsewhere or the route will fail (Fig. 9–38).

WHERE SHOULD IT GO? — There are several logical ways to handle a bicycle:

In places of low congestion and low bicycle demand, let the bicyclists ride either on the sidewalk or in the street, being careful to avoid both pedestrians and automobiles.

As bicycle traffic increases, convert a two-way street to one-way, and designate the captured lane as a bicycle route. Costs are minimal as no new land must be purchased, and with careful planning a one-way street system can satisfy the movement requirements of most neighborhoods (Fig. 9–39).

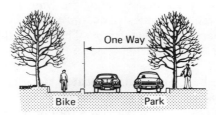

Figure 9-39

Narrow the travel lanes of existing roads, and designate the excess for bicycle use. Many streets have 12- to 14-ft-wide travel lanes, which could be reduced to 10 ft. Cars cannot travel fast in a 10-ft lane, but that is appropriate for compatibility with the bikeway. Two-way roads can even be narrowed to a point where it is impossible for two cars to pass, say 12 to 15 ft wide, forcing one car to pull into a vacant parking place to allow the other to pass. The captured space can then be used for bikes, but the bike route *must* be separated from the road or cars will use it.

The most complex question is, should there be two separate lanes, one in each direction, or one lane serving both bicycle directions. One lane serving both directions is the easiest and least expensive to construct, but a one-lane route may not be convenient in urban areas and may even present some safety hazards. As a general rule, in the United States, bicycles are ridden on the *right side* of the road in the same direction as automobile traffic. For two-way auto traffic, it is best

Figure 9–40(a)
Bicycle routes in suburban or rural areas *should* be two-way as distances are long, interruptions few, and the cost lower.

to provide a path in each direction to simplify bike access and egress and to increase the speed and pleasure of the ride. (See Fig. 9–40a.)

BIKEWAY DESIGN

WIDTH REQUIREMENTS — The absolute minimum one-direction bikeway width is 3 ft, 6 in.; the recommended minimum width is 5 ft, which allows 18-in. sway on each side, or space enough for another bike to pass carefully. The absolute minimum two-way width is double a one-way width or 7 ft; a comfortable minimum is 8 ft. If it is suspected that the route will be heavily used, or used during peak periods, additional width will be required for rider comfort. If users are to be mixed [i.e., recreation (slow traffic) with commuters (motivated riders)], additional width is required. If for any reason you can squeeze out more room, *do it,* for bicycle popularity is on the rise.

LOCATING THE BIKEWAY — The most desirable locations to the least desirable are as follows:

Next to the curb, and without any parked cars to interfere. This location affords sidewalk protection on one side, is easily accessible to bikers, allows fast riders to pass using the street, is easy and safe from both left and right turns, and places the bikeway in the pedestrian domain.

On the street side of parked cars. If parking must remain, a bikeway on the street side of cars is preferred as bikers are visible to drivers, can access the route easily, make safe turns, and pass slower bikes in the street. They must, however, be alert for car-door openings and for cars moving in and out of parking spaces.

Between parked cars and curb. Where space is plentiful and parking must stay, locate the bikeway between curb and parking. The bikeway can become part of the sidewalk, which is an advantage, and there is little auto conflict except at intersections.

A median bikeway would be two-way, with each bike traveling next to automobiles moving in its direction. Space should be generous, at least 12 ft wide, to allow landscaping and some barrier. The median bikeway should be used as an excuse to develop a distinguished boulevard with tree planting, lighting, and other amenities.

Steepness of the bicycle route is a judgmental factor. Routes on the whole should not exceed 7 percent grade. Grades less than 200 ft long can be up to 15 percent, although this is not desirable. Subtract 1 percent for each additional 100 ft of slope length; therefore, a 600-ft grade should not be over 11 percent. Grades over 1000 ft long should be kept at 5 percent or less, if at all feasible.

Moving over steep terrain can be accommodated either by a long, shallow ramp, or by a short, relatively steep ramp. Both accomplish the goal with the same expenditure of energy; however, psychologically, the short steep ramp may be preferred because many bicyclists will push their bike up a ramp in any event. (See Fig. 9–40b.)

Figure 9–40(b)
A 30-in.-wide ramp parallel to a stairway facilitates bicycle travel. Those not hardy enough to ride up it can easily push their bikes. This ramp is entirely too steep for wheelchairs, and should not be expected to serve this purpose.

The future transportation importance of bicycles is not yet recognized by most people, and it may be difficult to construct bike lanes on all new roads. As a stepback position, be sure to allocate sufficient width so that a lane can be constructed in the future *without* relocating curbs and trees. One way to do this is to offset the street within the right-of-way, leaving more room on one side of the road for the future bike lane. Try to allow 3 ft for a small planting strip, 8 ft for the bike lane, 3 ft for planting, and 6 ft for sidewalk as a minimum (20 ft total).

BIKEWAY DESIGN CRITERIA

DESIGN CONSIDERATIONS	GUIDELINES
Handlebar width	18 in.
Cycle length	5 ft, 6 in.
Pedal clearance	4 in.
Vertical clearance	7 ft minimum
Horizontal bikeway clearance minimum	$1\frac{1}{4}$ ft
Speed, recreational commuter	10 mph 15 mph
Bikeway width for two-way traffic	5 ft, 3 in. minimum, recommended 8 ft
Grade in percent	Maximum for short runs, 15% Recommended short run maximum, 10%. Recommended maximum, 5%
Radius of curves	Minimum 8 ft, 15 ft average, recommended, 20 ft
Bikeway capacity	4 ft wide = 1000 bikes per hour/one way

AUTOMOBILE PARKING

Parking the automobile is *the* major site-planning problem. Depending on conditions, 200 to 400 sq. ft per car is required for parking and maneuvering, a very large amount of land (Fig. 9–41). On the other hand, cars are becoming smaller, and energy conservation efforts may reduce the number and use of vehicles, thereby reducing the amount of required parking.

SIZE REQUIREMENTS FOR PARKING

The amount of space required for parking varies according to three factors:

Figure 9–41
The fight for extra parking often results in poor lot layout. This lot slopes too steeply, sheets run off across the sidewalk, and invade the pedestrian domain.

1. *General size of cars to be parked* — Areas designated for compact or sports cars can be smaller than lots that accommodate both large and small cars.

2. *Nature of the user* — Assigned, private parking used by the same person each day can be smaller than public parking in a shopping center or along the street, which will be used by many different people. The familiarity of assigned users plus a feeling of neighborliness reduce scratches, dents, etc., while parking or opening doors. Shopping center spaces must be larger to handle the frequency of parking and facilitate loading groceries.

3. *Size of available land* — Designers tend to increase proportions when land is plentiful and to reduce standards or design cleverly when land is scarce.

As a general rule of thumb, we suggest using a minimum parking space dimension of 8 ft wide by 18 ft long with a 20-ft backout space. These dimensions are *functional minimums;* that is, they will "work" for all sizes of modern cars, although large cars will have to park slowly to avoid accidents. Public parking spaces for shopping, office, etc., require slightly larger dimensions — 9 or 10 ft wide with 22-ft backout space.

For open lot or on-street parking, there are three general parking configurations: (1) perpendicular, (2) parallel, and (3) diagonal.

Perpendicular parking is the most efficient in terms of land utilization and traffic flow. Its layout is linear, with cross section including 18-ft stall space plus a 20-ft maneuvering aisle. It can be as long as you need with 8-, 9-, or 10-ft-wide parking bays added ad infinitum. A single loaded bay is 38 ft wide; a 56-ft width allows for double loading and more efficient land use. Traffic can flow in two directions, which eliminates the need for separate entry and exit (Figs. 9–42 and 9–43).

Figure 9–42
Landscape planters should delineate all parking lots, and can replace No Parking signs. Note the path in front of cars for easy pedestrian entry and egress.

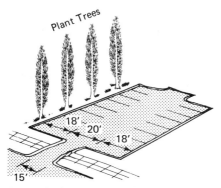

Figure 9-43   Perpendicular parking.

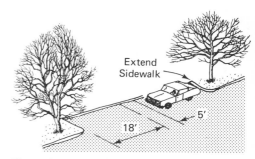

Figure 9-44   Parallel parking.

Parallel parking is useful along streets as drivers can use the street for maneuvering. Required dimensions are 18-ft stall length plus 5 ft for maneuvering by 8 ft wide. Space can be conserved by combining one 5-ft maneuvering area for two cars. Parallel parking spaces can be delineated with expanded sidewalk or planter strips marking areas that should *not* be parked in (Fig. 9–44).

Diagonal parking is useful if the site is long and narrow. Basically, the same 8- by 18-ft stall and 20-ft backout space is required, but as the arrangement is aligned on the angle, its perpendicular distance is shorter. The 45° angle is used most, and requires a 14-ft-wide backout aisle and approximately 20 ft of stall width. Diagonal parking operates only one-way, is tight for maneuvering, and has poor sight lines, which are its main disadvantages (Fig. 9–45).

Access and egress to the lot should be organized and minimized to a one-point location. The continuous rolled curb, typical of used car lots with access over the length of the lot is visually degrading and infringes on pedestrian-comfort and safety. For access and egress, a 10-ft-wide drive and apron is adequate for up to 10 cars. This does not allow cars to enter and exit at the same time, but this conflict should be infrequent and cause minimal inconvenience to the drivers. For lots for more than 10 cars, a 16-ft-wide apron provides adequate room for simultaneous entering and leaving.

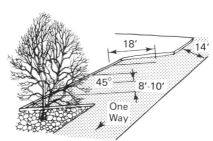

Figure 9–45
Diagonal parking.

Figure 9-46
An excellent pedestrian system with paved crosswalk, handicapped ramps, planting, etc.

Besides being planted with trees and properly screened from view, all parking lots for more than 10 cars should provide safe pedestrian access from car to destination, and vice versa. For the designer, this requires evaluation of origin–destination routes and development of a sensible pedestrian pathway. In busy parking lots, a sidewalk should be planned to lead pedestrians from their cars to the shopping area (Fig. 9–46). This consumes room, but protects the pedestrian and improves visual appearance. Trees should be planted around and through all lots, at a minimum rate of three trees per two cars.

Locate parking areas perpendicular to the final destination and install a sidewalk between two parking bays. One planted walkway will serve as a collector for up to five bays of parked cars. The walk should be a minimum of 5½ ft wide, allowing for auto overhang of 15 in. on each side. If cars back in to the parking space, the sidewalk must be wider to accommodate the larger rear overhang (Fig. 9–47).

Figure 9-47
This planter strip serves double duty, as an informal pedestrian walk and to shade and screen the cars.

Perpendicular parking along roads in apartment complexes is becoming common. For safety and amenity reasons, it is preferable to route the sidewalk *in front* of the cars, using a diagonal connector walk. The sidewalk can then serve as a bumper stop for the parked cars and collect drivers as they leave their cars. The walk width should be a minimum of 4½ ft to allow 15-in. front auto overhang.

PARKING ARRANGEMENT SUGGESTIONS

1. Tandem parking (one car behind another) reduces the amount of land required by eliminating one backout aisle. Tandem parking is useful for second car, boat, or camper storage and where daily use of the inside "trapped" vehicle is limited or can be coordinated (Fig. 9–48).
2. Parking areas can serve multiple uses as a playcourt for basketball, volleyball, and bicycle riding if care is taken during layout. Car wash and repair and laundry drying are also possible.
3. Children automatically gravitate to parking areas, which suggests play areas be located at the end of a lot with necessary precautions such as signs, bollards, speed bumps, etc. (Fig. 9–49).

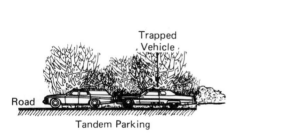

Figure 9–48

Figure 9–49

4. Avoid perpendicular parking opposite parallel parking as it is easy for the perpendicular cars to hit the parallel cars while backing out (Fig. 9–50).
5. Design special parking lots for *small cars* and locate them close to the destination as an incentive. Spaces can be 7½ ft wide by 15 ft long.

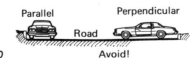

Figure 9–50

Figure 9-51
A proper parking arrangement with the
walkway in front of the cars. Note that
the cars overhang about 15 to 18 in., so
the walk must be at least $4\frac{1}{2}$ in. wide.
The berm to the left of the walkway
shields the cars visually from the park
beyond.

6. Store infrequently used recreational equipment, using tandem parking some distance from daily use areas.
7. Avoid locating perpendicular or diagonal parking on busy streets as maneuvering is dangerous.
8. Sidewalks should be located *in front* of perpendicular parked cars to ensure pedestrian safety. Children walking behind parked cars are not visible to a driver backing out (Fig. 9–51).
9. Temporary parking on weekends or at special events can often be satisfied by parking "in the road" and temporarily routing road traffic in only one direction.
10. Older parking lots can be restriped to reflect increased numbers of smaller cars. Use the extra space for landscaping or pedestrian circulation.

SCREENING PARKING LOTS

The parked auto is generally considered an undesirable visual element and efforts should be made to screen it from view. There are several design possibilities, each demanding extra room and increasing the cost of parking. However, this cost should be looked at as a requirement to more evenly distribute the actual costs for auto use (Fig. 9–52).

Tree planting between each row of cars and around the parking lot perimeter provides visual screening from above and from a distance, which is often an important consideration. Shrubs between trees block the near pedestrian view (Fig. 9–53).

Berms. Berms are earth mounds that physically and often gracefully block views. Berms are useful in suburban or rural

Figure 9-52
The view from above is now a major concern in urban areas, and it is improved only by tree planting.

2 Trees per 3 Cars

Figure 9-53

W/Planting

Parking

Figure 9-54

situations where there is adequate room to blend them back into existing topography (Fig. 9–54).

Fences and walls offer immediate, effective and inexpensive methods to screen unwanted views. They require little space and can be designed to solve difficult problems. Trees should be planted along with berms and fences to soften the overall view (Figs. 9–55 a and b).

Sinking the parking lot is an expensive but effective technique. Excavated earth can be added to the perimeter to construct a berm, which reduces the overall amount of grading and disposes of cut material (Fig. 9–56).

Grassed parking areas, paved with cobbles or bricks spaced so grass can grow between them, improve the look of empty lots. This solution cannot support continual or heavy use, but suffices for occasional parking, such as at a summer park or sports arena. Grasscrete, a waffle-like, cast concrete paver with holes for grass to grow through can be effectively used (Fig. 9–57).

231

Figure 9-55(a)
This narrow row of tall shrubs visually screens the parking lot from passing pedestrians. A row of trees would improve the landscape; however, most store owners feel the trees block views of their stores from passing automobiles.

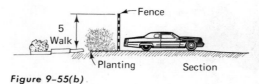

Figure 9-55(b)

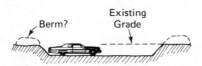

Figure 9-56   Sinking the lot.

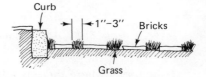

Figure 9-57

PARKING LOT DRAINAGE

Parking lots can be drained by one or a combination of the following:

By tipping the total lot and sheeting the water along the length (Fig. 9-58a).

By tilting the lot and draining the water to one side (Fig. 9-58b).

By warping the lot and collecting water in a corner (Fig. 9-58c).

By draining to the center in funnel fashion (Fig. 9-58d).

By depressing the center over the length and draining along the center line (Figs. 9-58e through 9-58g).

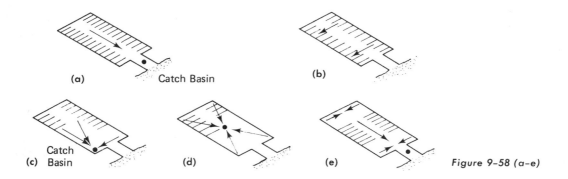

(a)   Catch Basin

(b)

(c) Catch Basin

(d)

(e)

Figure 9–58 (a–e)

Figure 9–58(f)
Draining toward the center is inexpensive as only one collection point is required. This 200- by 70-ft parking lot is drained to one catch basin, although two grates are used for the collection. Should the catch basins clog, the overflow would run across the sidewalk and be collected by the city's storm drainage system beyond. The lot is efficient by all standards except amenity. There are no trees, no planting, no pedestrian walkway, and no concern for the views into the lot at either end. Strictly a functional parking lot.

Figure 9–58(g)
All parking lots over six cars must have a catchment area to collect water before it runs across the sidewalk. Large amounts of water sheeting across the sidewalk are uncomfortable for pedestrians and may freeze in winter. This lot was warped to collect water at the corner.

Once runoff is collected, it can be transported through a storm drainage system, released over natural plantings, or percolated into the ground through drywells or drainfields. The drywell/drain field system filters out some unwanted oils, grease, and dust particles that collect on the lot. However, heavy amounts of oil will gum it up. Any runoff that is likely to lower water quality should be discharged through an oil–grit separator.

OIL-GRIT SEPARATION

Oil residues from roads and parking lots can pollute streams if discharged as part of runoff. To prevent this, an oil trap should be installed in catch basins prior to discharging runoff into the stream. Oil traps operate on the principle that oil is lighter than water and *floats,* while grit is heavier than water and *sinks.* Two types of separators are commonly used—a simple, inexpensive cover attached to the discharge pipe of catch basins, and an expensive, specially constructed tank used to treat large quantities of runoff from airports or freeways.

The inexpensive cover utilizes a long, downward pointing elbow attached to the discharge inlet. Runoff can enter the discharge pipe only from below the flow line, thus trapping the floating oil in the basin. Grit settles to the bottom, where it must be removed periodically. The elbow should extend down about 24 in. to within approximately 6 in. of catch basin bottom, allowing room for silt to settle. Water remains in the catch basin between storms, with the oil floating on top. When it rains, runoff fills the basin until it is higher than the discharge flow line, at which time water automatically flows into the discharge pipe from below.

During dry periods, the trapped water usually evaporates, and the oil settles into the silt and should be removed. If it is not, most of it will float to the top following the next rain and again be prevented from entering the discharge pipe. The system prevents most oils from entering the stream, but it is not totally effective as portions of oil are soluable and therefore discharged through the elbow. (See Fig. 9–59a and b).

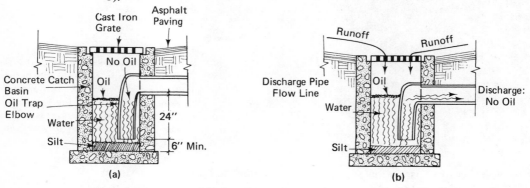

Figure 9–59(a) Section—between storms. (b) Section—during a storm.

Runoff from highways or airports is diverted through a large separator, where it passes through a series of compartments with baffles and diffusers. The diffusers slow the water, allowing heavier grit to settle out, while oil baffles trap floating oily substances before the runoff is discharged. Separators can be constructed to meet different levels of purification, quantity of water entering the system, and how long oil and grit have collected on the road. The longer the period of oil collection between rains, the more oil and grit that have to be removed. Water separated from oil should be passed over gravelly soil to further filter pollutants before it reaches natural water bodies. The process is simple, but the design is complex and the unit expensive; therefore, each unit is carefully located to handle runoff from a large area.

SPECIAL DRAINAGE AND GRADING PROBLEMS

This chapter will introduce advanced grading and drainage concepts and techniques. It is not a complete coverage of the subject, but simply an introduction, including (1) reducing the peak intensity of runoff, (2) designing natural waterways, (3) special grading-drainage problems, and (4) use of soils information in grading and drainage.

REDUCING THE PEAK INTENSITY OF RUNOFF

We have discussed the hydrologic cycle and the balance between runoff and the form of the land as it occurs in the natural system. For review, this balance slows, stores, and disperses rainwater through transpiration and evaporation from trees and vegetation, surface runoff and via streams until the water reaches a lake or ocean, and percolation into the soil with subsurface drainage; the rate of runoff is slowed by matty plants that cover most of the vegetated areas of the world. When man builds, he seals off large areas of land by paving roads and parking lots and by constructing covered areas under roofs. This diminishes the natural efficiency of the hydrologic cycle and produces large quantities of runoff that must be artificially carried off during and immediately following peak rain periods. This runoff must be diverted through underground structures and eventually dumped into the nearest creek or stream. The streambed, through erosion, sedimentation, loss of vegetation, and other processes, begins to change character and lose quality and appeal (Fig. 10–1).

Figure 10-1
This former small creek has been lost to urbanization through careless drainage practices.

Luna Leopold* lists the four major effects of urbanization on the hydrologic cycle as follows:

- Increased volume of runoff through elimination of native plant material that previously slowed down runoff. This additional volume of water cannot be absorbed by the natural stream, and may erode and cause downstream flooding.
- Increased speed of runoff, which decreases the time required for runoff to reach the stream. Vegetation removal is again the culprit, and water reaching the stream faster may exceed the stream capacity, causing erosion, sedimentation and flooding.
- Increased temperature and pollution of runoff reaching the stream. As water moves over pavement it is warmed and picks up pollution, which raises the stream temperature and upsets its ecological condition.
- Increased visual degradation of the stream caused by erosion and pollution. Vegetation may be eroded away, water colored brown by sediment, and trash swept away by runoff and lodged in the streambed.

*U.S. Geological Circular #614. "Effects of Urbanization on the Hydrological Cycle."

Figure 10–2
Large parking lots are a principal cause
of all these problems.

OTHER HYDROLOGICAL IMPACTS
CAUSED BY URBANIZATION

Increased overland flow; 100 percent paving will produce at least 90 percent runoff (Fig. 10–2).

Erodes stream banks, which increases sedimentation, turbidity, and reduces the stream channel size, which destroys gravel spawning beds (Fig. 10–3).

Reduced evapotranspiration through the destruction of vegetation.

Decreased channel size through the deposition of sediments, reducing water storage areas and leading to increased flooding.

Reduced groundwater resources through paving aquifer recharge areas and reducing infiltration. This leads to greater fluctuations in groundwater flow with more water in the winter and less in the summer.

Figure 10–3
Sedimentation is a major problem with all surface drainage systems. Culverts should be oversized, and maintained every other year.

Water pollution; fertilizers and toxic wastes from industrial and commercial land uses lower water quality.

Increased discharge velocities caused by channel straightening and riprapping.

Reduced fish populations: gravel spawning beds destroyed, streamside vegetation destroyed, temperature raised, and toxic substances added to the water.

These effects usually occur in the following chronological order:

Early: Decrease in transpiration
         Increase in surface runoff
         Increase in land erosion
         Some lowering of the water table
         Contamination of wells and streams

Middle: Accelerated land erosion
         Accelerated stream sedimentation
         Increased surface runoff
         Reduced infiltration

Late: Lowered water table
         Lowered base flow in streams
         Higher peak flow in streams
         Increased pollution of streams
         Change in channel quality

The volume of surface runoff can be increased several hundred times by paving areas that were formerly planted. A theoretical study covering 1 square mile of slightly sloping land found the dramatic increases in peak discharge shown in the following table:

DEVELOPMENT TYPE	DESCRIPTION	PEAK DISCHARGE (GAL/MIN)
Wooded	Normal forest growth	30,000
Rural	50% forest, 50% farm	50,000
Suburban	40% wooded, 40% lawn 20% roof and paving	140,000
Urban	50% lawn and garden 50% roof and paving	360,000

Besides increasing peak discharge, urban areas absorb and store 100 to 200 times *less* water in the soil than forested areas do. Paving close to existing vegetation reduces groundwater infiltration and can seriously affect that vegetation. (See Fig. 10–4.)

Figure 10-4
Grasscrete paving helps reduce urban runoff while allowing percolation. The paver—a concrete block with many holes—allows grass to grow while also withstanding foot and auto traffic.

ZERO PERCENT INCREASE IN RUNOFF

There is growing realization that most rainwater should be held where it falls until *after* the storm subsides. Traditional development practices collected all surface runoff and placed it immediately in a storm drainage system. This removed the problem from each site, but transferred it downstream, where the cumulative impact caused flooding. To minimize downstream flooding and reduce the cost of storm drainage systems, many communities are adapting a zero percent increase in runoff ordinance. The ordinance requires certain new developments to hold most rainfall on the site until after the rain subsides. Runoff can then be released slowly into nearby streams without causing flooding or degrading the natural stream.

There are two basic approaches to zero percent increase in runoff—*Permanent retention* and *Temporary detention*.

1. *Permanent retention* can be used when soil conditions are pervious and allow excess runoff to be disposed of through percolation. Such a soil would contain a high proportion of gravelly or sandy soil, over which runoff can be directed and permanently absorbed.
2. *Temporary detention* merely detains runoff on your property until the storm subsides and runoff can safely be added to the public storm sewer. This requires some sort of holding basin capable of storing excess rainwater and a mechanism to slowly release the water into the stream or drainage system. This delays discharge of surface water from developed areas and somewhat duplicates the normal rate of runoff of natural vegetated areas. By maintaining a low, continuous release into the stream, degradation is reduced.

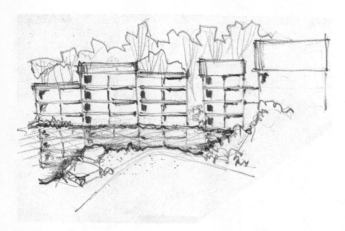

Figure 10-5
Detention ponds can be worked into existing sites as a positive feature.

Detention ponds or holding basins can be created in any natural depression, valley, or low-lying area to store stormwater during a rain (Fig. 10–5). Holding basins should be designed with a small pipe near the bottom to release water slowly during and following the rainfall. This release should be sized to duplicate the volume of runoff normally released from the area previous to development. It is also necessary to provide an emergency flow at the top for extreme rain periods (Fig. 10–6).

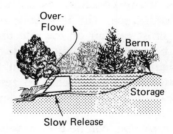

Figure 10-6   Section

This detention method assumes that heavy rainfall occurs only once every four to five days, thereby allowing release of water between rain periods so that storage from the next rain can take place. A carefully designed holding pond can serve many recreation uses during the summer. The sides must slope gently, and it should be landscaped and planted in grass; the slow release pipe must be maintained to assure against a muddy, saturated area (Fig. 10–7).

Holding basins can also be constructed on the roofs of shopping centers or industrial buildings. This requires (1) a flat roof and (2) a device to block the downspouts to raise the water level 1 or 2 in. New,

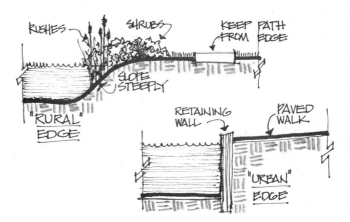

Figure 10-7
A detention pond can become the visual focus of a building if its edge is integrated into the landscape and the pond designed to fit in.

smaller downspouts should be installed to remove water at a rate duplicating the natural runoff *prior* to the building. With this system, small amounts of water would be continually removed from the roof, and when the rain ceased, the bulk of it would be released over several hours (Fig. 10–8).

It would, of course, be necessary to provide emergency downspouts at a higher level to prevent roof collapse during heavy rain. Most industrial roofs are designed to support 2 to 3 in. of water with no danger of collapse. This same system could obviously be used for all residential structures with flat roofs. It is conceivable that buildings with sloped roofs could construct underground storage tanks that would store the water during peak rain periods and disperse it slowly following rainfall (Fig. 10–9).

Shopping centers, industrial parking lots, and other large paved areas such as playfields can also be used as holding basins. Generally, shopping volume is reduced during storms, so the loss of parking

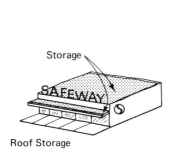

Roof Storage

Figure 10-8

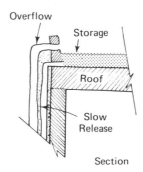

Slow Release Mechanism

Figure 10-9

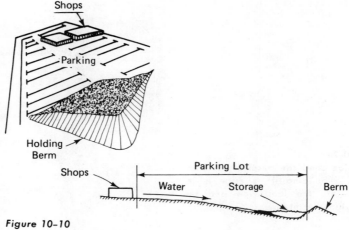

Figure 10-10

spaces presents little problem. The water should drain from the bulk of the parking lot toward one corner, where it would be contained by berms. By careful planning, the holding basins can be designed to minimize the loss of parking (Fig. 10-10).

Select a low-lying area away from the store and grade it with dams and berms to retain water. The area should have a slow release pipe to allow portions of the water to drain off continually, leaving most of the water stored until the rain ceases. It could then be released over several hours as in previous examples.

The most common method of permanent retention, after determining that the ground percolates adequately, is to construct a small drain field. The selected area is excavated to about 30 in., backfilled with 6 in. of gravel, perforated pipes laid, and backfilled with selective gravel fill to grade. Collected runoff can then be disposed of in the drain field. The drain field can be paved (as a parking lot) or planted in grass or ground cover. Never build over the drain field as water may damage the foundation. (See Figs. 10-11a and b.)

Runoff can also be directed over gravelly soil in low density developments if it is not steeper than 8 percent and presents no problems abutting properties. It is advisable to use a silt trap with either method.

Calculating the size required for percolation is a fairly complex process and can not be fully discussed here. The size depends on:

1. The permeability of the soil.
2. The size of area to be drained.
3. The intensity of rainfall (rain per period of time).
4. The duration of rainfall.

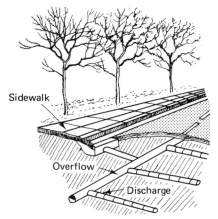

Sidewalk

Overflow

Discharge

Figure 10-11(a)   Roadbed cut away.

Figure 10-11(b)
A subsurface percolation system. Parallel
ditches are dug 15 to 20 ft apart to a
depth of 2 to 3 ft and perforated pipe is
laid in the bottom. Gravel is added and
the water directed through the system by
gravity. Note the concrete clean-out structure in the lower corner, which distributes
water into two laterals.

However, with good draining soils, the amount of land required is
not excessive, with one square foot of drain field disposing of runoff from
up to 20 square feet of parking lot. A 20-car parking lot could be percolated by a 10 × 35 foot drain field if the soils percolate well.

Two problems with detention ponds are that (1) sediment builds
up and they become filled with vegetation, and (2) unless carefully designed, they look bad. Flow problems increase and slow eutrophication
begins to develop. The sediment problem can be corrected by maintaining and dredging the pond every 4 to 5 years, but that adds to the
drainage system cost. Integrating the pond into the landscape involves
siting it so that it becomes a part of the surrounding, and then grading
it to blend in (Fig. 10-12).

The Rational Formula—Q = CIA—is used to calculate the quantity of runoff in minor drainage design and for making preliminary calculations. In the formula Q = CIA:

Q equals the quantity of runoff in cubic feet per second which can
be used to determine pipe size or retention/detention requirements. It
can be converted to gal/sec by multiplying by _____ .

C equals the coefficient of runoff and indicates the proportion of

Figure 10-12
All runoff from this hospital is diverted into its retention pond, which has been landscaped and planned as the focal point for most of the rooms.

precipitation that is runoff. Low numbers (0.1–0.3) are used for forested areas and indicate a minimum amount of runoff, while high numbers (0.7–0.95) are used for urbanized or paved surfaces, indicating that most of the precipitation is carried away as runoff.

I equals the intensity of rainfall in inches/hours and combines how hard it rains (intensity) and how long it rains (duration). This figure can be taken from weather bureau monographics or calculated, and is normally based on a storm cycle (occurrence). A short storm cycle (5–10 years) is used for residential developments while a longer one (25–50 years) is used for commercial developments.

A equals the area in acres and is measured according to whatever coefficient category the land is in (i.e., forest, paved, lawn, etc.).

These three letters —C, I, and A—are entered into the formula and produce an estimate of the quantity of runoff. The formula is accurate for areas up to several acres, so larger plots must first be subdivided.

DESIGN METHODS TO PRESERVE STREAMBEDS AND NATURAL WATERWAYS

Rapid urbanization during the past 25 years has caused wooded and grassy areas to be replaced with buildings, streets, and parking lots. Because of this, the amount of runoff from winter rains has increased dramatically. Occasionally, during years with heavy precipitation, we have witnessed disastrous flooding and extensive property damage. As flooding became more of a problem, federal and local flood-control projects began appearing throughout the country. These projects were often supervised by engineering and rural-related agencies using hydraulic and rural design practices for urban flood prevention. Engineering practices included the construction of channels, pipes, riprap, stream straightening, etc., rather than natural retention or land use control measures. Over the past 25 years, a large number of natural wooded creeks have been converted to concrete channels. Unfortunately, urbanization increased at a faster rate than channel construction, and the flood danger has not really decreased. Cities are paying a high price to control floods by losing substantial parts of their natural environment as streambeds are modified and channelized.

HYDROLOGICALLY SIGNIFICANT COMPONENTS OF A WATERSHED—The following watershed components need to be protected from development through conservation measures to retain their hydrologic functions.

ELEMENT	*VALUE*
Surface water and streams	A vital function of a stream is its ability to cleanse runoff of most pollutants. This is dependent on diverse plant and animal life and relatively constant temperature and flow.
Marshes	Accommodate floodwater and tidal surges, act to trap sediment and other suspended materials and include nutrients important to wildlife habitat.
Floodplains	Areas adjacent to streams subject to regular flooding. Delineation of boundary depends on flood frequency (a 5-year flood will inundate less land than a 100-year flood). Flooding is only a problem when buildings in the floodplain are damaged. Filling floodplains reduces their capacity to store water, causing flooding elsewhere.
Aquifer recharge area	The aquifer where it surfaces at the ground; about 25 percent of all precipitation falling on these areas infiltrates into the aquifer. Landfills, industrial uses, septic tanks, filter fields, and leaking sewer systems can pollute the aquifer and should *not* be located near the recharge area.
Poorly drained soils	Soils with a periodically high water table. Septic tanks and leaking sewers are not suitable in such areas as effluent will seep into groundwater or adjacent lands.
Erosive soils	When located on steep slopes present serious erosion hazards and must be protected during construction.
Steep slopes	Development will increase surface runoff, eroding soils normally not prone to erosion.
Woodland	Despite high evapotranspiration losses, woodland is the ideal drainage basin cover, as erosion is prevented, little sediment is lost, and infiltration is increased, augmenting year-around stream flow.

Although most flood-control projects utilize *hydraulic efficiency* as the design criteria, there are alternative waterway and streambed designs that preserve the natural environment and control flooding *when* combined with zero percent increase in runoff techniques. Over the long term, considering maintenance costs and amenity value, it is possible for designed waterways and landscaped streambeds to cost less than construction of concrete channels. Designing natural streambeds to solve flood-control problems involves the use of interdisciplinary design teams. The design process includes survey and analysis of existing conditions, developing conceptual approaches and alternative designs, cost–benefit evaluations for each design, selection of the final design, and development of implementation techniques. Long-term costs and benefits must be included, with an accurate value placed on esthetic values.

One obstacle to overcome is public agency guidelines, which foster and make easy the implementation of engineering flood-control solutions. For instance, the Corps of Engineers will fund only for construction of channel improvements and *will not* fund floodplain acquisition. Generally, long-term maintenance costs are not important in federal assistance programs as the local jurisdiction is responsible for maintenance. In addition, ownership of the creek is often by two abutting property owners, and frequently the center of a creek marks a political boundary separating two cities. This makes cooperation in flood-control planning difficult, and limits public access along private portions of the stream in built-up areas (Fig. 10–13).

There are design techniques that can accommodate increased runoff without channelizing the stream. These techniques may be useful for all or just small portions of the stream, and may be combined in different stretches to accommodate problems. In certain instances, it may even be necessary to channelize. The point is to avoid single-purpose

Figure 10–13
Bridges help preserve creeks and streams. Most stream crossings are constructed by filling the ravine, which changes and may destroy the creek. A bridge does not change the hydraulics or functional characteristics of a stream.

channelization treatment applied regardless of specific conditions. The following solutions are attainable in many neighborhoods and present realistic alternatives to channelization, while retaining wildlife habitat and providing a natural recreational resource for the neighborhood. Each solution depends on maintaining land that can be flooded to store water during and immediately following rainfall.

PRESERVING THE NATURAL FLOODPLAIN

The simplest solution is to determine the land that floods naturally (called floodplain) and restrict the amount of building on it. This area would retain its natural qualities, be economical to maintain, and is adaptable to different land configurations and sizes. Floodplains serve as open space and can be safely used for recreation, forestry, and farming. Floodplain zoning is difficult to enact in built-up areas as pressure for intensive land use works against it. In most cases, low density development can occur on the floodplain provided the owners are aware of the potential flood danger. It may even be possible to acquire critical developed land abutting streams and put it back into public ownership as open space and floodplain (Fig. 10–14).

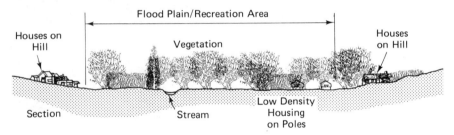

Figure 10-14

CREATING AN ARTIFICIAL FLOODPLAIN — If the natural floodplain has been limited in size by urban encroachment, it may be possible to build levees at the extreme limits of the remaining stream corridor and create an enlarged artificial floodplain (Fig. 10–15). Yearly flooding would be contained, whereas infrequent major floods may not be contained. However, it is doubtful if complete safety from major floods can be expected in urbanized areas. Reconstructing a natural environment for multiple use and visual enjoyment requires careful landscape treatment of the new berms (Fig. 10–16).

STREAMBED CLEARING AND ENLARGING — This approach tries to balance correcting hydraulic deficiencies with retaining desirable natural amenities. Certain critical areas are widened and cleared to increase

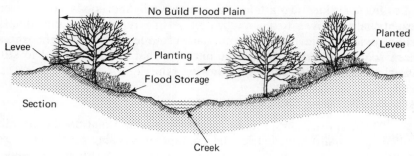

Figure 10-15

Figure 10-16
This stream running through a small housing community has been preserved with buildings constructed high enough so that the stream can overflow its banks on occasion. A walk system allows people to enjoy the stream, and its banks have been landscaped with trees that can stand occasional flooding.

the flow, while the best landscape features, which give the area natural quality, are preserved. This approach is useful where the stream is narrow or where urbanization has enroached (Fig. 10-17).

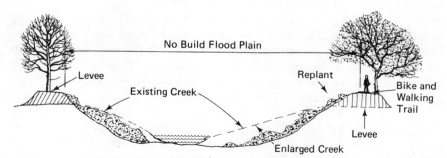

Figure 10-17 Enlarging the creek basin. Note the creek bottom was *not* lowered, as that would create a pond and eventually silt up.

CREATING A SECOND PARALLEL STREAM — This method can supplement the capacity of an existing creek without requiring any modification to the natural stream. This may be possible where the existing stream is constricted or does not operate for some physical reason. Natural rivers actually dig a second channel in braided portions of the stream, which remains dry during most of the year, but fills during serious storms. It may not be necessary to create the second channel the entire length of the stream, and it would be desirable for the second channel to be landscaped (Fig. 10-18).

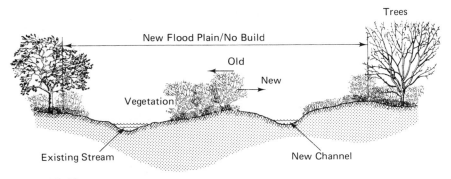

Figure 10-18

ENLARGING, MODIFYING, AND RIPRAPPING — To improve flow and reduce erosion, riprap can be installed on the outside shoreline along a bend in the stream. Typically, the inside radius and straight sections need *not* be riprapped (Figs. 10-19 and 10-20).

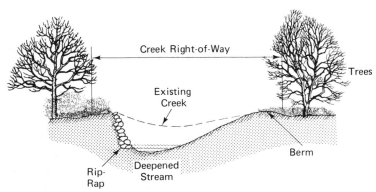

Figure 10-19

Figure 10-20
Building too close to the stream necessitated this extensive riprapping and destroyed most of the natural stream qualities.

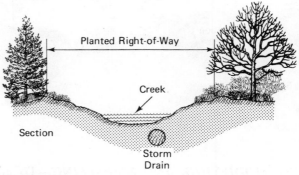

Figure 10-21

ADDING AN UNDERGROUND PIPE TO THE CREEK BED — This solution locates a large pipe somewhere within or near the stream channel to carry excess stormwater runoff. Excess water would be diverted into the pipe, with normal runoff carried by the stream (Fig. 10–21).

Stream planting should use native vegetation for easy acclimation and low maintenance. Begin with trees, and overplant to account for loss. Twiggy shrubs, vines, groundcovers, and grasses should be added.

In summary, we must find ways to handle our runoff problem, yet retain the natural amenity that streams and creeks provide. There are implementation problems; this method of landscape treatment is not practiced by most flood-control agencies. The main problem is inadequate cost accounting; these techniques may cost more to install, but long-term maintenance costs plus amenity value will increase the benefits. Designers should play a persuasive role in assuring maintenance of our natural streams.

SPECIAL DRAINAGE
AND GRADING PROBLEMS

RETAINING WALLS—We have suggested minimizing the use of re-taining walls, but they should not be taboo. On small sites, a retaining wall may solve an impossible grading problem, and if carefully designed can add three-dimensional richness. Walls create a more formal feeling than natural slopes, so use them carefully. It is sometimes possible to develop a series of low retaining walls to scale down the wall size and create the necessary flat area (Fig. 10–22).

Any concrete retaining wall more than 2 ft high should have a solid footing extending below the frost line and should be adequately reinforced. Walls over 3 ft high should be engineered by a qualified structural engineer.

Figure 10-22
Combining a low retaining wall with a small slope reduces the apparent height of the bank.

GRADING FOR RETAINING WALLS—Although a retaining wall creates a vertical slope, constructing it requires removal of earth be-hind it so that footing, formwork, and foundation drains can be in-stalled. The footing width of a typical cantilever retaining wall can be approximately 40 percent of the height. (This figure will increase if the soil is not firm, or the backfill well drained, or if there is a surcharge caused by a steep slope above.) About one third of the footing is nor-mally in front of the wall, with the other two thirds behind. Therefore, if you were constructing a 6-ft-tall wall, the footing would be approxi-mately 30 in. wide, with 10 in. in front of the wall, and 20 in. behind. In addition to the 20 in., the excavation must be large enough to allow workers to install the formwork, or about 2 ft, and the slope back prob-ably cannot exceed a 1:1 ratio. Adding all this gives a total of 9 ft of graded space beyond the face of the wall (Fig. 10–23).

Figure 10-23
View of retaining wall under construction. Note the gravel drain and waterproofing painted on the wall.

If you wish to construct this retaining wall on the property line, it will be necessary to obtain permission from the neighboring property to dig out to accommodate construction. If there is a building right on the neighbor's property line, you are safer to move the retaining wall in several feet.

All retaining walls should have drainage designed to release water trapped behind the wall. *Weepholes,* pipes 3 to 6 in. in diameter and spaced about 8 ft apart, are the easiest way to drain exterior walls. Gravel backfill is necessary to prevent silting. *Footing drains,* continuous drains behind the wall near the footing that daylights at each wall end, can also be used. All drain lines must be installed *lower* than the basement floor to assure proper drainage and must be sloped toward a collection point. Footing drains should be backfilled with clean gravel. Any nearby clay should be removed, as it is not easily drained and may shrink and swell. A fiberglass soil separator is useful to reduce the chance of soil clogging the gravel. Avoid backfilling the excavation with construction wastes, as the voids will attract water and leakage might occur. Waterproof all basements with asphaltic coatings prior to backfilling.

WATERPROOFING BASEMENTS — Surface and subsurface water must be removed from all basement areas lest it leak into the basement. Three actions are necessary: (1) slope the surface adjacent to the

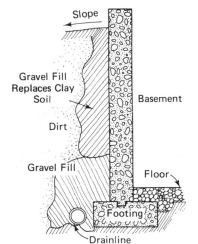

Slope

Gravel Fill
Replaces Clay
Soil

Dirt

Gravel Fill

Basement

Floor

Footing

Drainline

Figure 10-24

building away at 2 percent, (2) waterproof the exterior of the basement wall, and (3) prevent subsurface water from reaching the wall by subsurface drainage. Footing drains, perforated pipe laid in a trench *below* the footing level and backfilled with gravel, are the least expensive drainage method. The drain may also be located several feet away from the wall to intercept water (Fig. 10–24).

NO FOOTING RETAINING WALLS—*Gabion walls* can be built in many sizes and shapes to protect steep slopes or line streambanks. The plastic-coated wire baskets are filled with rocks by a backhoe with selective hand packing. Gabions do not require a footing, and are able to adjust slightly to conform to existing streambank configuration (Fig. 10–25).

Figure 10-25
Gabion retaining wall. Each gabion is approximately 3 by 4 by 12 ft long, and in this example, they are stacked two high with a slight batter to prevent tipover.

Crib retaining walls consist of small individual pieces like Lincoln logs that lock together into a series of squares, known as cribs. Each crib is filled with soil, and retention is provided by the weight of the soil binding the interlocking pieces. No foundation is necessary, and plants can be grown in the spaces between parts. Reinforced concrete is typically used for the units.

Broken concrete can also be laid up as a retaining wall to a height of about 5 ft without a footing. The wall must be constructed on firm subgrade and battered back slightly (Figs. 10–26 and 10–27).

ROOF/DRAINS AND DOWNSPOUTS

A large percentage of rainwater is collected in roof gutters and must be disposed of. There are ways to dispose of it by connecting the downspout to (1) the sanitary sewer system, (2) the storm sewer system, or (3) the garden or a drywell.

Water-quality/quantity problems may result from roof/drains that are connected directly to storm or sanitary sewers. Roof/drains can add substantial volumes of water to the sewage system, which may exceed the system's capacity during moderate to heavy storms. This can cause rainwater and untreated sewage to bypass the treatment plant and overflow into local waterways, causing localized flooding, erosion problems in streams, and reduced groundwater supply. Local streams that depend on groundwater to maintain stream flow during summer months are deprived of replenishment by *not* placing runoff back in the soil. Where possible, new roof drains should discharge into a drywell, where it can soak into the ground.

If the soil remains wet or soggy long after a rainstorm, the soil is probably saturated and cannot accommodate additional roof rainwater. To determine the ability of soil to soak up roof water, dig a narrow hole 4 ft deep where you intend to construct the drywell. Fill the hole with water and allow it to remain full for 4 hours (add water to maintain the level). Refill the hole the next day, and measure the rate at which the water level goes down. If the level drops *faster* than $\frac{1}{2}$ in. per hour, the site is okay for rainwater discharge. If the water surfaces nearby, or the level drops more slowly than $\frac{1}{2}$ in. per hour, the soil may not be able to safely accommodate roof water.

An abandoned septic system drain field can be used for roof drains, as can a rain barrel, which may be used to water the garden between storms.

DRYWELL FOR DOWNSPOUTS

Make sure the soil can safely accommodate rainwater from the roof (see previous paragraph) and that local building ordinances are in agreement. Dig a square hole 3 ft wide by $4\frac{1}{2}$ ft deep for each roof downspout. Fill the hole to within 1 ft of the surface with washed gravel. Extra rocks from the garden can be used or gravel from $\frac{3}{8}$- to $1\frac{1}{2}$-in. size range. Place a sheet of heavy plastic over the gravel to prevent soil from clogging the gravel, and fill the last foot with soil.

Dig a trench from the drywell sloping up to the roof drain outlet. Place a 4-in.-diameter plastic pipe in the trench, with one end opening into the gravel of the drywell and the other connected to the downspout.

Locate the drywell at least 10 ft from the building and 5 ft inside the property. If the drywell is too close to a building, rainwater may cause damage to the foundation or seep into the basement. Don't locate the drywell in an area that slopes down into your neighbor's yard, or in a landslide-prone area, or if septic tanks are used nearby. Drywells may cause nearby septic tank drain fields to overload, and adding water to landslide-prone soils may aggravate landslide conditions.

Figure 10-28
A manhole is an opening constructed in a storm or sewer system to permit a person to enter or leave the sewer. It is used for inspections, cleanings, and removing obstructions from the pipe. Manholes are made of brick, cast concrete, concrete block, or corrugated steel, and are covered with a square or round heavy grate at least 24-in. in diameter. The bottoms are often poured concrete, although they can be filled with gravel for percolation.

LOCATING DRAINAGE STRUCTURES

Catch basins, manhole covers, and French drains are large, visible, utilitarian elements of heavy cast iron made durable to last a lifetime. They are *not* items one would feature in a livingroom, and many designers fret over how to locate utilitarian elements in their manicured landscapes (Fig. 10–28). Three approaches stand out.

Let them fall where they may is the standard operating practice the world over. It is used by most engineers and is particularly obvious in public civil works (Fig. 10–29). The guiding rule is utility, and design is of little concern. Criticism of this approach centers around "good design," with comments such as "wonder why that was located there, when it would have made so much sense to move it two feet to the left" (Fig. 10–30a).

Try to hide 'em approach is used by the "architect's architect," the designer with endless budget and a belief that all functional aspects of the world should be covered with exotic materials, or that high-priced materials automatically mean good design. This designer will meticulously design special-shaped catch basin covers to be cast in bronze or carved from granite, or will slope a courtyard so slightly that it won't drain properly. The caricature is a bit unfair, but points out that avoiding the "utilitarian" aspects of drainage is usually expensive, less functional, and noticed by very few users (see Fig. 10–30b.)

You give me the parts, I can make it work. A compromise position where the designer accepts the functional drainage requirements, knows the design standards he is seeking, but is flexible in his range of solutions. He will utilize catalogue drainage structures and design to accepted drainage slopes. Catch basins will be worked into a score pattern with all elements carefully placed yet heavy enough to complement the utilitarian aspects of cast structures. The point is that

Figure 10-29
A "let them fall where they may" solution.

(b)

(a)

Figure 10-30 (a) Poor catch basin location. With such a strong geometric paving
pattern, it would have made more sense to use a square catch basin
grate and locate it in the center of the concrete score pattern. (b) This
specially cast concrete trench drain is expensive and clogs easily — but
it does look good.

drainage structures are expensive and utilitarian, but large enough to
become obtrusive if not considered in the design. Use standard prod-
ucts, but design them into the arrangement (Fig. 10–31).

Figure 10-31
Drainage structures can be a visual part of the design if carefully designed. This paved channel surrounds the entire court, which is raised in the center for drainage toward it.

As a general rule of thumb, *private* developments (homes, apartment and some commercial complexes) *underdesign* drainage structures, while *public* developments (parks, streets, etc.) *overdesign* them. This phenomenon is caused by the ability of most public agencies to raise capital construction funds, but their inability to raise maintainance funds; while the private sector usually wants to keep construction costs down, but is willing to provide maintainance over the years. Therefore, underground pipes and catch basins are usually too small in the private sector, and too large in the public sector. Expensive manholes are frequently specified in public work, while low cost catch basins suffice in the private sector.

SOILS AS A GRADING CONSTRAINT

Soils are a product of weathering and consist of decomposed and disintegrated parent rock that has been changed over the years to the point that they support plant life. Most soils contain an amount of dark organic material called *humus,* produced by decomposition of plant and animal materials and several layers of less decomposed material. Soils usually consist of several horizontal layers—topsoils, subsurface soils, subsoils, parent material, and eventually bedrock. A cross section is called a *soil profile,* and each layer in the profile is called a *horizon.* One of the best ways to study soil is to find an exposed soil bank or dig a pit and expose the different layers of soil.

THINGS TO LOOK FOR IN SOIL

Color—indicates quantity of organic matter, drainage, biotic activity, fertility.

Texture—the feel, sandy, silty, clayey, indicates water-holding capacity, looseness, workability of the soil.

Structure—the shape, blocky, platy, granular, indicates drainage, aeration, water intake.

Depth—indicates the amount of moisture storage and availability of minerals for plants.

The upper 6 to 8 in. of soil is called *topsoil;* below this is a lighter, more compact, less fertile layer called *subsoil.* Topsoils contain large amounts of humus to support plant life and are built up over thousands of years. Subsoils have been derived from the bedrock on which they rest, or have been moved to their present location by wind, water, glacier, etc. Subsoils derived from the underlying bedrock are called *residual soils* and have predictable characteristics; those moved in are called *transported soils* and contain rock types different from the underlying bedrock. Transported soils vary more than residual soils and are less predictable as a grading determinant.

The generalized soil profile in the following table indicates the typical different layers:

A horizon	Surface	Dark gray colored, high organic matter high biotic activity, abundant roots, commonly leached
	Subsurface	Moderately dark, many roots, moderate organic matter, commonly leached
B horizon	Subsoil	Below plow depth, brown or reddish colored, more clay than surface, fewer roots
	Lower subsoil	More yellowish and less clay, fewer roots than subsoil, less aeration than above
C horizon	Parent material	Unconsolidated, slightly weathered rocky mass from which soil develops; no biotic activity, few roots
	Bedrock	Consolidated rock

SOIL CLASSIFICATION SYSTEMS

Understanding soils as design determinants is relatively easy; applying that knowledge to specific situations becomes very difficult. There are three major soil classification systems, each based on the textural composition of soil interpreted for a specific need. The textural composition includes gravel, sand, silt, clay, and organic soils.

The most widely used engineering system of soil classification was devised by the U.S. Bureau of Public Roads and is used in AASHO standards. It groups soils into seven groups, A-1 to A-7. Classification is based on load bearing, with A-1 being the highest and best-graded nonplastic particles:

The Unified Soil Classification System has been used by the Corps of Engineers and Bureau of Reclamation. It also identifies soils according to their textural and plasticity characteristics, dividing soils into course-grained soils, fine-grained soils, and organic soils. (See page 263.)

The U.S. Department of Agriculture has combined several soil classification systems into a simple triad that places sand, silt, and clay on each side, and describes various soils as composed of percentages of the three (Fig. 10–32).

Knowledge of soil types and their characteristics interpreted for land-use decisions forms an important input to grading. In many metropolitan areas, the U.S. Department of Agriculture has reinterpreted agricultural soils information for use in making urban land-use decisions. Their soil scientists analyzed what land-related activities occurred during urbanization, such as *long-term problems* (landslides, flooding, erosion, water pollution, etc.), *what had to be constructed* (foundations, septic drain fields, utility systems, roads, drainage, etc.) and *broad land-use categories* (industrial, residential, recreation, woodland, ecological, etc.). They then looked at soil characteristics that might affect these activities, such as drainage, depth to bedrock, soil type, etc., and mapped soils according to the following limitations.

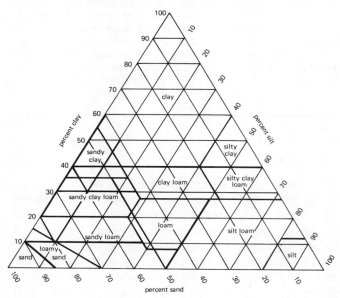

Figure 10-32   Guide for textural classification.

UNIFIED SOIL CLASSIFICATION SYSTEM

		NAME	FOUNDATION	VALUE AS BASE UNDER PAVEMENT	COMPRESSIBILITY & EXPANSION	DRAINAGE CHARACTERISTICS
COARSE GRAINED SOILS	Gravel and Gravelly Soils	GW – well-graded gravels or gravel-sands mixture; little or no fines	excellent	good	almost none	excellent
		GP – poorly graded gravels or gravel-sands mixtures, little or no fines	good to excellent	poor to fair	almost none	excellent
		GM – silty gravels, gravel-sand, silt mixtures	good to excellent	fair to good	very slight	fair to poor
		CC – clayey gravels, gravel-sand-clay mixtures	good	poor	slight	poor
	Sand and Sandy Soils	SW – well-graded sands or gravelly sands, little or no fines	good	poor	almost none	excellent
		SP – poorly graded sands or gravelly sands, little or no fines	fair to good	poor to not suitable	almost none	excellent
		SM – silty sands, sand-silt mixtures	fair to good	poor	very slight	fair to poor
		CC – clayey sands, sand clay mixtures	poor to fair	not suitable	slight to medium	poor
FINE GRAINED SOILS	Silts and Clays	ML – inorganic silts and very fine sands, rock, flour, silts or clays, fine sands or clayey silts with slight plasticity.	fair to poor	not suitable	slight to medium	fair to poor
		CL – inorganic clays of low to medium elasticity, gravelly clays, sandy clays, silty clays, clays	fair to poor	not suitable	medium	practically impervious
		OL – organic silts and organic silt-clays or nonplasticity	poor	not suitable	medium to high	poor
	Silts and Clays	MN – inorganic silts, micaceous, or diatomaceous fine sandy or silty soils, elastic silts	poor	not suitable	high	poor to fair
		CH – inorganic clays of high elasticity, fat clays	poor to very poor	not suitable	high	practically impervious
		CH – organic clays of high plasticity, organic silts	poor to very poor	not suitable	high	practically impervious
Highly Organic Soils		PT – peat and other highly organic soils	not suitable	not suitable	very high	fair to poor

LIMITING SOIL FEATURES (U.S. DEPARTMENT OF AGRICULTURE)

Texture too fine; too coarse.

Gravelly or stony.

Less than optimum bearing capacity.

Drainage class unfavorable; depth to seasonal water table too shallow; drainage may be needed; flooding or ponding hazard.

Slope or topography unfavorable; imposes use or construction hazard; slippage potential.

Depth to bedrock or impervious material is limiting.

Frost action potential is moderate or high.

Shrink–swell potential is moderate or high.

Permeability (percolation rate) is restricted.

Accessibility by equipment is restricted.

Excavation difficult owing to consolidated materials, or clay or silty clay soil texture.

Piping hazard.

Thickness of suitable material is limited.

Erosion hazard is moderate, severe, or very severe.

Shear strength is moderate or low; slope stability is fair or poor.

Compaction characteristics are fair or poor.

Permeability rate is too rapid.

Low water-holding capacity.

Organic soil.

Possible pollution of groundwater even though site is at least well drained.

Soil textures permit ready sloughing of sidewalls.

Compressibility is medium, high, or very high.

Moist consistency is loose, firm, very firm, or extremely firm.

Excessive fines or limited supply.

ESTIMATED SOIL PROPERTIES

Depth to seasonal high water table refers to the highest level at which the groundwater stands for a significant period of time.

Depth from surface indicates the thickness of significant layers of a typical profile. The thickness of the horizons differs somewhat among mapping units of the small soil series.

Percentage passing sieve refers to the percentage of dry soil material that will pass sieves of the indicated sizes.

Permeability refers to the rate at which water moves downward through undisturbed soil. It depends largely on the texture, structure, porosity, and density of the soil.

Available water capacity represents the maximum amount of water that plants can obtain from the soil.

Reaction refers to the acidity or alkalinity of the soil, expressed in terms of pH. A pH of 7.0 is neutral. Values less than 7.0 indicate acidity, and values more than 7.0 indicate alkalinity.

Shrink–swell potential is an indication of the volume change that can be expected with a change in moisture content. It depends largely on the amount and type of clay in the soil. In general, soils classified as CH or A-7 have a high shrink–swell potential; soils classified as SP, GW, or A-1 have a low shrink–swell potential.

Corrosivity refers to the deterioration of concrete or untreated steel pipelines as a result of exposure to oxygen and moisture and to chemical and electrolytic reactions.

On a large grading project or one involving difficult terrain, soil types should be mapped and understood to minimize problems during the grading. The principal soil characteristics that affect grading are as follows:

Angle of repose
Permeability
Erosion hazard
Slippage potential

ANGLE OF REPOSE—Each soil has an equilibrium angle at which it will stand naturally. If this angle is exceeded, the soil will slump or slip off. This angle varies with the soil grain size and shape, the character of the material, and the proportion of water present. Any cut or fill cannot exceed this natural angle of repose if stability is expected. Generally, sandy and gravelly soils have a fairly steep angle of repose, whereas clay, silt, or loams do not. Constantly wet or completely dry soils have a shallower angle of repose than well-drained but moist soils. Typical angles of repose are as follows:

Firm earth in place, 1.1
Loose earth or humus soil, 1.5:1
Firm clay, 1.5:1
Wet clay, 3:1
Dry sand, 1.75:1
Wet sand, 1.25:1

Figure 10-33
Fine sand can stand at an almost perpendicular angle of repose. However,
there will be continual sluffage at the
bottom, as is evidenced by grassy protion
near right corner of photo. A major
slump is always a possibility.

These ratios vary with rainfall, moisture content, subsurface geology, plant cover, etc. (Fig. 10–33).

PERMEABILITY – This is particularly important when designing the drainage plan (Fig. 10–34 and 10–35). Runoff can be disposed of in a closed system, or it can infiltrate into permeable soils as if it were a sponge. Disposing of runoff through permeable soils is good practice as it reduces cost and raises the water table. Generally, sandy and gravelly soils are more permeable than clay and loamy soils. However, many sandy soils are underlain with impermeable clay layers that reduce infiltration and may flood following severe rain. Additionally,

- Paving permeable soils prevents water from percolating into the soil. This is unecological in principle, and should be done only where the situation is extreme. Build on impermeable soil and drain to permeable soils.
- Planting exposed banks with thick, matty, and deep-rooted plants helps stabilize the soil. Planting can reduce minor slippage, but is of little effect against a major slide.
- Terrace with cross ditches to prevent excessive water from crossing the bank. Drain ditches should be placed above the bank, with terraces at intermediate intervals to reduce the quantity of water.

Figure 10-34
Standing water in this tree pit will eventually kill it. If the soil isn't permeable, install a subsurface drain line or culvert, as shown in Figure 10-33.

Figure 10-35
A small-diameter plastic pipe can sometimes be used to drain a tree pit; it needs maintenance to prevent clogging and the walk may crack.

- Subsurface drains may be drilled into the bank to relieve groundwater. This method is expensive, and it is difficult to predict the results.

Soil permeability is the important factor in locating any septic system. Obviously, gravel or sandy soils will ensure proper operation of a septic system; however, topography and underlying impermeable soils are almost more important. An impermeable subsurface or steep topography may cause effluent to flow laterally and surface at a lower elevation raising health hazards (Fig. 10-36).

In pervious soils, grading below the water table usually requires dewatering or drainage of the site during construction. Drainage is accomplished by constructing a sump, well point, or deep well at the lowest level and pumping out the water.

EROSION HAZARD—All grading causes erosion. All soils erode, although some more than others. There are two principal concerns: first, topsoil, which is the lifeblood of our plant community, should *not* be allowed to erode. The process of building this top layer of soil is time

Figure 10-36
A septic tank is a watertight concrete box into which sewage is flushed and detained for about a day. Most of the solids settle into the bottom of the tank where biological action decomposes them further. The remaining liquid flows into an underground drain system, which distributes the effluent to be further decomposed and purified within the soil. Grading for a septic system includes a large hole for the tank and a series of lateral subdrains for discharging the effluent through subsurface drainage.

consuming and cannot be easily duplicated by man. Generally, the top layer of organic soil should be stripped carefully and stockpiled for redistribution and use following grading. The second concern is to be careful with soils subject to erosion. Erosion occurs following the steepest terrain. It begins as rivulets and eventually becomes gullies, with sedimentation somewhere below (Figs. 10–37.) Erosion is part of

Figure 10-37
Erosion of an unplanted 1:2 bank caused by one rainstorm.

the natural river-forming process and is quite normal as long as the time table is slow and long; however, man tends to hasten the process to the point of causing problems.

Grading for Erosion Control. On large projects where erosion is likely, it is becoming acceptable practice to prepare the grading plan, *anticipate* where erosion will occur, and devise a pregrading plan to stop erosion. Pregrading utilizes small check dams or holding basins below the area of major grading. The pregrading work must be carefully carried out using small equipment (possibly a backhoe or by hand) and should be immediately seeded or planted so it will stabilize. Pregrading adds to the overall grading costs, and benefits are not immediately realized, so there is some resistance to its use. However, grading permits are becoming more difficult to obtain, and the addition of an erosion-control plan may help, perhaps proving an immediate benefit from a client's point of view.

Grading during the *dry season* followed immediately by planting may reduce erosion damage. Scheduling sensitive projects should ensure that difficult grading operations are performed during the dry season. Small, rubber-tired equipment or hand grading is economical in sensitive grading situations to minimize disturbance.

SLIPPAGE POTENTIAL—Slippage occurs when shear stress between layers of soil exceeds the shear strength of those soils. This can occur by increasing the stress or by decreasing the shear strength. The increased stress must be over a large area, and the slope must be relatively high and quite steep before the slip is likely to occur.

Increased soil stress is caused by removing the bottom (toe) of the bank or by increasing weight at the top of the bank. An excavation at the bottom of the bank for a building or a swimming pool is likely to cause increased stress. Steepening the slope beyond its normal angle of repose also causes stress. The addition of a building at the top of a slope with more drainage water increases the weight or pressure on the soil and is likely to cause slippage (Fig. 10–38).

Reduction of shear strength is caused by a change in the soil property. Clay can be softened by the addition of water. As the surface dries, it can crack, allowing water to penetrate into the soil. Finally, water entering the soil can create friction between layers of noncohesive soil, which may result in a buoyancy that causes the upper layers of soil to float free of the soils below. Noncohesive soils such as sands and gravels are held together purely by friction between particles, which is easily dislodged.

Figure 10–38
Bent or bowed trees on steep land are usually a good indicator of slippage.

Prevention of slippage requires study of the geology and soil types, with careful design to solve any uncovered problems. Possible solutions include the following:

Avoiding all impossible sites.

Reducing the proposed gradient by extending the bank. This uses more land and exposes more soil to erosion, but sometimes can reduce the slippage potential (Fig. 10–39).

Underdraining the bank to allow groundwater to flow out, rather than be trapped within the bank. Underdraining is expensive and not always successful, but may help (Fig. 10–40).

Building on pile or pole foundation to avoid disturbing the ground.

Removing an amount of soil equivalent to the weight of the proposed structure. This balances the pre and post condition, by adding no weight.

Installing concrete retaining walls with deep footings can produce satisfactory results, but is expensive.

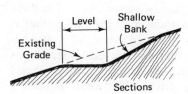

Figure 10–39

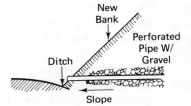

Figure 10–40

This is not a detailed analysis of all the soil problems one might encounter in grading. It is merely a warning to check for conditions that may cause trouble over the long run.

DATA SOURCES

Climatology
N.O.A.A. (National Oceanographic and Aeronautic Agency) (U.S. Department of Commerce): tables of climatic data for states and cities
State Water Resource Boards: precipitation data
Theses and dissertations: in climatology, meteorology, and geography

Geology/Hydrology
Geological Survey (U.S. Department of Interior): maps of bedrock geology, water resource bulletins, and supply papers; engineering geology for some areas
State Departments of Geology (and often Mines and Water Resources): maps of bedrock geology, surficial geology, groundwater resources; sometimes engineering geology
Corps of Engineers (U.S. Army): reports data on flooding potential, floodplains
Flood-Control Districts
Aerial Photographs: surficial geology where not obscured by vegetation

Soils
Soil Conservation Service (U.S. Department of Agriculture): soils surveys and interpretations
Theses and dissertations: in geology, soils, physical geography, forest resources

---

CLEAN-OUTS

All runoff carries some silt particles, which settle out when the speed of runoff flow is reduced. Like a streambed, heavy particles settle first, followed by finer and finer particles. If unattended, this siltation process may finally clog a pipe, catch basin or streambed. To prevent this, clean-out facilities are installed wherever siltation is likely to occur.

WHAT IS A CLEAN-OUT? — A clean-out is an access hole for either man or machinery to remove trapped silt. If a person is to remove the silt, the opening must be at least 30 in. for easy access, while access for a shovel, vacuum or plumbers snake can be 15 in. (See Fig. 10–41.)

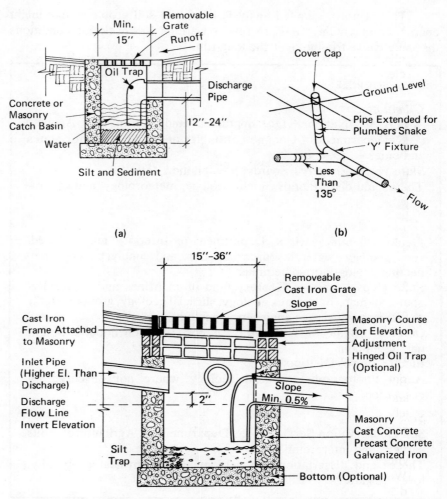

Figure 10-41 (a) Section: catch basin with silt trap. (b) Cutaway: pipe extended to ground level for clean-out.

WHERE ARE THEY LOCATED?—Wherever reduction in speed of runoff occurs. The three most likely locations are:

1. The first collection point where overland runoff enters the underground system. Typically a catch basin is used, with a sediment and oil trap and removable grate to allow vacuum or shovel cleaning.

2. Whenever a pipe turns an angle *less* than 135°, unless the bend is a large radius. The clean-out can be a catch basin, manhole (for

access) or pipe extended to ground surface for insertion of a
plumbers snake.

3. Wherever the slope of an underground pipe is decreased. This
change will reduce the rate of flows and cause siltations. The
clean-out can be via a catch basin, manhole or extended pipe.

Figure 10–41(c)
Combination catch basin and manhole.
This catch basin is constructed of a large
diameter galvanized pipe, which can be
accessed for cleaning. You can also see
the removable cast iron grate, the enclosed cast iron frame and the cast concrete top. (See diagram.)

SUBSURFACE DRAINAGE

Surface drainage has the lowest maintenance and construction
cost and should be used wherever possible. Some areas cannot be effectively drained on the surface and require a system of underground
perforated pipes to collect and dispose of water. These areas include playfields, poorly drained soils, planting areas requiring dry conditions, and
low-lying flatlands and farms to increase productivity.

Water enters the pipe through a series of perforations, which
should be placed facing down to minimize clogging. An exception occurs in extremely pervious soil, where it is likely that water in the pipe
would percolate into the surrounding soil; lightweight plastic pipe is
preferred from 5 to 10 in. in size. Short sections of clay or concrete tile
can also be used, although they can be easily misaligned and are heavy
and slow to install. Typically, perforated pipe is laid in trenches that
are wider and deeper than the pipe. The trenches are backfilled with
gravel or crushed stone, which is carried to about 1 ft from the surface
and sealed with tar paper. The remaining 1 ft is backfilled with earth
and can be planted.

The starting point for laying out any system is always the disposal
location, as it has to be in the *lowest* point. Disposal can be into a
storm drain system, a holding basin, swale, or stream depending on
conditions. It should not cause flooding on adjacent property. Drain

lines should be at least 2 ft deep unless potential frost damage requires them to be deeper. Pipe slope can vary from 0.1 to 1 percent and should be at a constant grade so that silt will not deposit at any depression.

Pipe spacing depends on soil texture, land configuration, and whether complete or partial drainage is necessary. A typical system will have several laterals connecting to a main line (Fig. 10—42). Pipes may be spaced further apart in sandy or gravelly soil; however, if lines are spaced too far, the center portion will not drain. Main lines are often tapered from 5 in. to larger as they collect laterals.

Excavations for subdrains should be at least 6 in. deeper than the flow line and at least 8 in. wider on each side of the pipe. A layer of gravel or crushed stone should be placed on the bottom of the trench to prevent pipe settlement and eliminate silt from clogging the holes.

Figure 10–42
A subsurface drainage system under construction showing the laterals connecting to submains, which finally connect to the main (running horizontally across the lower edge of the photo). The ditches were dug with a Ditch Witch following rough grading, and hand grading will finish off this small golf tee.

Decrease the amount of gravel toward the outlet to prevent seepage within the gravel. The outlet section of pipe is usually not perforated and is laid directly on the trench bottom. Backfill material should be compacted gravel or crushed stone that varies in depth according to the soil type. Backfill material should be relatively fine and just slightly more pervious than the soil to be drained. The finer the backfill, the less infiltration of silt. As water will flow through the backfill faster than through the natural soil, the system never backs up.

If the area is to be planted, the gravel should be sealed with building paper to reduce silting, and topsoil and planting added. If the area is to remove surface as well as subsurface water, the gravel is carried to ground surface, with course stones at the top.

The perforations should usually be laid facing *down;* infiltration efficiency is thus highest and silting is reduced. The upper end of all subdrain pipes should be capped, and the outlet should have a screen or flap to eliminate rodents. Clean-out risers should be installed at the upper end of all main lines to occasionally flush out silt, and manholes are required at change in alignments as in storm sewers.

DRAINING PLAYFIELDS — A typical subdrainage system consists of main lines spaced 100 to 200 ft apart, to which laterals are connected. Laterals are spaced from 15 to 25 ft apart, depending on soil, slope, and use conditions. Mains vary in size from 6 to 10 in. as more laterals feed them. Laterals are 4 to 6 in. in diameter and are perforated to allow groundwater to infiltrate. Laterals slope slightly toward the main, which in turn slopes toward the outlet. All pipes are buried at least 24 in. deep, and the ditch backfilled with pea gravel or granular fill. To reduce siltation, pipes must be carefully installed and wrapped with fiberglass strands or covered with asphalt paper (Fig. 10–43a and b). Fig. 10–43b shows how a typical playfield is drained.

Subsurface drainage for agricultural fields is usually spaced farther apart, as shown in the following table:

SOIL TEXTURE	PIPE SPACING	PIPE DEPTH IN FEET
Clay	35–70	2.5–3.0
Silt loam	65–100	3.0–4.0
Sandy loam	100–300	3.5–4.5
Organic soils	80–200	3.5–4.5

Figure 10–43(a)
A main line showing lateral connections. These laterals are spaced about 20 ft apart and run out in length approximately 100 ft. Each lateral is 4 in. in diameter; the main is 8 in. The pipe used here is corrugated plastic and the concrete box can be used for clean-out purposes. Each ditch will be backfilled with crushed gravel and covered with tar paper and the final soil preparation.

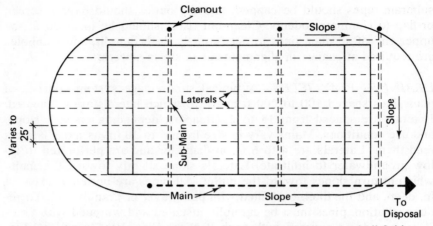

Figure 10-43(b) **Diagrammatic subsurface drainage layout for a football field.**

EXERCISE
GRADING A SMALL APARTMENT COMPLEX

This final exercise should combine all the factors of grading and drainage covered in this book.

Prepare a grading and drainage plan for the apartment project; include the following:

1. Pad elevation where appropriate.
2. Finish floor elevation (9 in. above pad elevation).
3. Necessary drainage structures with diagrammatic connection.
4. Spot elevations where required.
5. Design Sections A, B, and C on the sheet where indicated.
6. Retaining walls, curbs, steps, ramps where necessary.
7. Save all trees.

MISCELLANEOUS NOTES CONCERNING THE PROBLEM — There is parking under the two buildings. Conclude grading within property lines. Show retaining walls and curbs as double lines. Show underground drainage lines as double dashed lines. Include a legend on the sheet if you use symbols. Draw the three sections indicated on plan (show existing and proposed ground line but don't exaggerate the vertical scale). Assume your own slope criteria according to recommended slope standards. Give top of wall elevations if you use retaining walls.

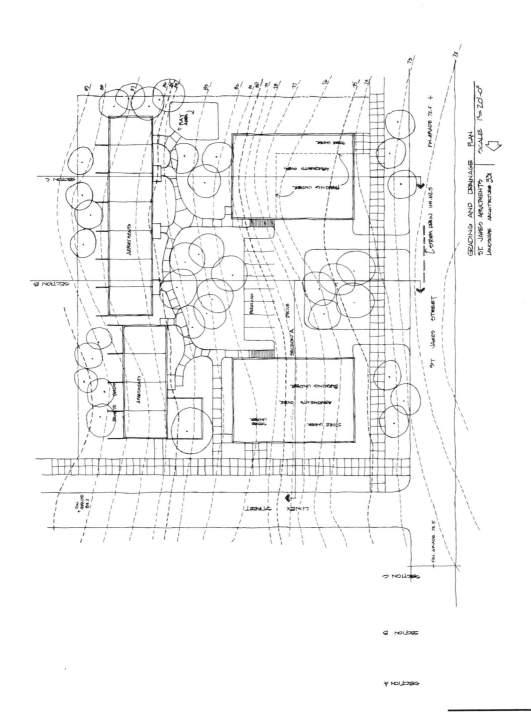

GRADING AND DRAINAGE PLAN
ST. JAMES APARTMENTS
LANDSCAPE ARCHITECTURE 331   SCALE 1"=20'-0"

277

SUGGESTED PROCEDURES

Grading: 1. Outline *all* areas to be saved (ungraded), that is, buildings, tree clusters, etc. Indicate the approximate limits around items you would like to maintain.
2. Block grade the entire site.
3. Identify those areas that could present grading problems. Roughly grade these trouble areas.
4. Indicate approximate location of all stairs and/or retaining walls.

Drainage: 1. Indicate with arrows and H.P.'s (high points) all drainage swales that may be necessary to adequately drain the site. (Make sure that these drainage ways correspond with your rough grading ideas.)
2. Indicate the approximate locations of all drainage structures (catch basins, area drains, etc.) that you anticipate.
3. Indicate drainage options around all buildings.

Design: 1. Be prepared to explain your overall drainage concept; that is, will it handle all water on surface? Will it use mostly subsurface drainage structures? And so on.
2. Be prepared to discuss your conceptual grading scheme. Enlarge this drawing three times.

AASHO—American Association of State Highway Officials, an organization that has developed standards for roadway construction.

Aquifer—an underground geological formation of sand, gravel, and fractured rock that transmits large amounts of water.

Area drain—a drain used to collect water from a specific area and connected directly to an underground pipe.

Barrier-free access—a continuous, unobstructed path of travel 32-in. wide by 80-in. high and not exceeding 8 percent throughout the site and building connecting all designated accessible facilities.

Bench marks—accurately determined points of elevation that usually are marked by a monument.

Berm—a large, shaped bank of earth.

Block grading—a rough grading method to establish basic ground form using every fifth contour line.

Catch basin—a drainage structure used to collect water from a specific area with a deep pit to catch sediment.

Circumference—the outside edge or perimeter of a circle. The formula for determining the length of a circumference is $2\pi r$. ($\pi = 3.14$.)

Coefficient of runoff—a fixed ratio of runoff to rainfall used in the Rational Method of computing storm-water runoff.

Compaction—reduction in soil volume by pressure from rollers or tampers.

Contour—a line drawn on a plan that connects all points to equal elevation above or below a known or assumed reference point.

Contour interval—the vertical distance between adjacent contour lines.

Culvert—an underground conduit used to carry water by gravity flow.

Daylight—term used to indicate the meeting at grade of a drain line and slope.

Detention pond—a depression designed to detain storm runoff for a short period of time, usually until the storm passes.

Drywell—a large pit filled with gravel and reaching into lower sandy or gravelly soil to discharge water.

Ecology—a study dealing with the interactions between organisms and their environment.

Elevation—the elevation of a point is the vertical distance above or below another, the elevation of which is known or assumed. Elevations are generally based on mean sea level datum, which is the average of a series of observations of the levels of high and low tides of the ocean taken at convenient points over a long period of time.

Erosion—the wearing away of land surface by detachment and transport of soils by water or wind.

Evapotranspiration—the moisture that escapes into the atmosphere by evaporation and transpiration from living plants.

Fall line—the direction of drainage or a line perpendicular to the contours.

Finish grade elevation—usually refers to the surface level of the ground after completion of all work.

Floodplain—areas adjacent to streams or rivers subject to regular flooding.

Floor elevation—the *finish grade* of existing or proposed buildings; usually given for the first floor, unless another floor meets grade.

Footing—the widened base of a foundation used to spread the weight over the ground.

Form line—an approximate contour (i.e., hachure, shading).

French drain—a linear drain consisting of a trench filled with loose stones, which discharges runoff back into the soil.

Frost-free fill—material such as clean sands and gravels for subgrade preparation of roads.

Gabion—a large, heavy-gauge wire basket filled with stones used for retaining walls or erosion control. Gabions require no foundation, and can be easily installed in sensitive landscapes.

Grade—the given or proposed elevation at any spot. Grade also means the height of the ground level somewhere (synonymous with elevation); and indicates a slope or gradient.

Gradient—the rate of slope between two points. Expressed by angle percentage of slope, or ratio of horizontal distance to vertical change in elevation.

Grading—the movement of earth by cuts and fills to create landforms.

Groundwater level—the depth below finish grade at which the soil is saturated with water.

Hachure — a technique to depict landform using shading.

Horizontal curve — a road curve in plan view.

Hydrograph water — a graph showing variation in stream-water depth or the volume of water flowing past a point in a stream over a period of time.

Impervious soil — relatively waterproof soil.

Invert elevation — the *flow line* elevation of a pipe, culvert, channel, etc., given at all changes of alignment, and at each point of entry and departure of all structures.

Kilometer — 1000 meters or about 0.6 mile.

Large scale — detail plan scale enabling exact descriptions to be made (such as $\frac{1}{8}$, $\frac{1}{4}$, $\frac{3}{16}$, etc., scale).

Manhole — an access hole and chamber in a drainage system to allow inspection, cleaning, and repair.

Meter — a unit length equal to 39.37 inches, 1000 millimeters, or 100 centimeters.

Open flow drainage — removal of rainwater via surface drainage.

Percolation — movement of water through pore spaces in the ground.

Permeability — capacity of a soil to transmit water through it. Sand and gravels are highly permeable; clay and silt are not.

Piezometer — an instrument for measuring pressure or compressibility in soil compaction and surcharging.

Plateau — a large, relatively level land area that is raised above the adjacent land; the flattened top of a hill or mountain.

Plumb — vertical or 90° to the horizontal. Term used to indicate that a wall, fence, post, etc., is straight (vertical).

Point of curvature (P.C.) — is the point at which the curve departs from the tangent as one proceeds around the curve in the direction of change.

Point of intersection (P.I.) — the point at which the two tangents intersect.

Point of tangency (P.T.) — the end of the curve and the beginning of the tangent to which the curve is connected.

Profile — the trace of the intersection of an imaginary vertical plane with the ground surface; normally used in road design.

Rational Method — a method for computing approximate storm-water-runoff volumes using a formula relating rainfall intensity, a coefficient of runoff, and watershed acreage.

Residual soils — soils developed from the parent rock over which they now lie.

Retention pond — a permanent pond holding or retaining storm water.

Runoff—the surface flow of water from an area or the total volume of surface flow during a specific time.

Sections or cross sections—sections are profile slices through the earth; cross sections are profiles taken at right angles to center line of a project or road.

Sedimentation—the deposition or accumulation of sediment.

Sheeting or shoring—vertical piles driven around a deep excavation to prevent the sides from collapsing. Also refers to a thin layer of water moving across a surface.

Slope (or gradient)—the inclination of a surface expressed in percentage or as a proportion.

Soil permeability—the quality of a soil that enables water or air to move through it. Sand and gravel are permeable; clays and silts are not.

Soil profile—a vertical section showing the layers of soil at a site; usually three layers, called A, B, and C horizons, and varying from topsoil to bedrock.

Soil texture—the relative proportions of sand, silt, and clay.

Soil water-holding capacity—the capacity of a soil to hold water; useful in determining runoff rate.

Spot elevations—used to supplement the contour lines, to show variations from the normal gradient between the contour lines. Gradients between spot elevations are considered uniform unless vertical curves are indicated.

Standard Proctor Test—a laboratory test used to determine soil compaction. The test uses a metal cylinder with a weighted ram to compact soil samples. Most compacted fills are specified to meet 95 percent of the Standard Proctor Test, which is sometimes referred to as the Standard AASHO compaction.

Storm sewer—a drain used for conveying rainwater, but *not* sewage or industrial wastes, to a point of disposal.

Subgrade—the upper surface of the native soil on which is placed the road, foundations, topsoil, or other final materials.

Subsoil—the B horizon of soils, or the soil below which roots normally grow.

Superelevation—a horizontal curve with the outside radius higher than the inside to counter the pull of gravity while traveling at high speeds.

Surcharge—a temporary loading of soil to induce settlement. Following settlement, the extra soil will be removed as the permanent structure replaces it.

Swale—a wide, shallow, slightly sloping ditch that collects and transports runoff as open flow drainage.

Trench drain—(sometimes called strip drain)—a linear drain with a concrete channel beneath used to collect water along a linear space.

Water-holding capacity—the ability of soil to hold water against gravity. Clay soils have a high capacity; sandy soils low.

Watershed—the total catchment area above a given point on a stream that contributes water to the stream or river. Watersheds are separated by a summit or ridge.

Water table—the upper limit of the soil that is wholly saturated with water.

Weir—an adjustable dam across a stream to control the water level or measure flow.

Zero percent increase—an approach to drainage that restricts the amount of storm water that can leave the project to the amount of runoff *prior* to construction.

1. A _____ percent grade would be a minimum for lawn areas requiring surface drainage.
   (a) 1 (b) 2 (c) 3 (d) 4 (e) 6

2. A _____ percent grade should be considered a maximum for paved pedestrian walks, especially where freezing conditions occur.
   (a) 2 (b) 5 (c) 10 (d) 15 (e) 20

3. A _____ percent grade should be considered maximum for a highway with large truck traffic.
   (a) 2 (b) 5 (c) 10 (d) 15

4. A _____ percent grade is the maximum slope that may appear visually level.
   (a) 1 (b) 3 (c) 10 (d) 15

5. Where drainage pipes change direction, a _____ should be used.
   (a) area drain (b) French drain (c) drywell (d) clean-out

6. A _____ slope would be maximum for a lawn requiring mowing.
   (a) 1:1 (b) 2:1 (c) ¾:1 (d) 4:1

7. A cut slope is generally capable of being _____ than a fill slope.
   (a) steeper (b) same as (c) more gentle

8. A 22½ degree slope is equivalent to a _____ ratio.
   (a) 2:1 (b) 1:2 (c) 1:4 (d) 1:3

9. To determine the percentage of any slope divide the _____ distance by the _____ .
   (a) horizontal (b) vertical

10. Give the main advantage of grading by cut.

11. Grading a circulation route _____ to the contours minimizes grading but results in a steeper route.
    (a) parallel (b) diagonal (c) perpendicular (d) combination

12. An 8 percent ramp is equivalent to _____ slope.
    (a) 1:10 (b) 1:12.5 (c) 1:12 (d) 1:16.5

13. In describing slope as a ratio, the _____ dimension is listed first.
    (a) diagonal (b) horizontal (c) vertical (d) none

14. The recommended maximum gradient discussed for handicapped is _____ percent.
    (a) 6 (b) 12 (c) 8 (d) 10

15. Describe a *contour line*.

16. A proposed contour that moves in the direction of a lower contour is _____ .
    (a) cutting (b) filling (c) removing earth (d) combination

17. A contour that closes on itself is _____ .
    (a) an error (b) a summit (c) a depression (d) filling

18. Equally spaced contours indicate _____ .
    (a) a swale (b) a walkway (c) a level area (d) a uniform slope

19. A valley is indicated by contours _____ .
    (a) at evenly spaced intervals (b) pointing toward lower contours (c) pointing toward higher contours (d) spaced at increasing interval

20. Contour lines cross each other at _____ .
    (a) a ridge (b) a filled depression (c) an overhanging cliff (c) no point

21. Contours that are close together indicate _____ .
    (a) a valley (b) a ridge (c) a steep slope (d) a gentle slope

22. Coordinates are used to locate _____ .
    (a) datum (b) a point (c) axes of reference (d) lines

23. A Township, the basic unit for U.S. mapping, consists of _____ square miles of land.
    (a) 36 (b) 6 (c) 25 (d) 20 (e) 100

24. List the four ways that rainfall is removed from where it falls.

25. Which way accounts for most removal?

26. The primary vehicle for removing runoff is _____ .
    (a) catch basin (b) gravity (c) area drain (d) culvert

27. A 2 percent slope is equivalent to _____ inch(es) per foot.
    (a) $\frac{1}{4}$ (b) 2 (c) $\frac{1}{8}$ (d) 3

28. A 25 percent slope is equivalent to 1 foot vertical to every _____ feet horizontal.
    (a) 25 (b) 2.5 (c) 4 (d) 5

29. Most grading computations should be carried to _____ decimal place(s).
    (a) 1 (b) 3 (c) 2 (d) 0

30. Stairs should be grouped with a minimum of _____ risers to avoid stumbling.
    (a) 1 (b) 2 (c) 3 (d) 4 (e) 5

31. List six site factors that provide guiding constraints in developing a grading plan.

32. List the two main reasons why an open runoff system is superior to a closed system.

33. List five factors that a designer must consider in designing a drainage plan.

34. An invert elevation is the elevation of _____ .
    (a) the lowest point of an area drain (b) the center line of a culvert (c) the bottom of the pipe leading out of an area drain (d) the top of the pipe leading out of an area drain

35. Curbs are indicated by a break in the contour line that begins again _____ .
    (a) downhill (b) uphill (c) adjacent to it

36. Generally, the high or low point of a vertical curve should _____ the midpoint of a horizontal curve.
    (a) precede (b) follow (c) coincide with (d) bear no relation with

37. Roadways should have a _____-foot-high clearance for trucks.
    (a) 15 (b) 20 (c) 18 (d) 12

38. The basic formula for determining gradients mathematically is _____ .

$$\text{(a) } 6 = \frac{L}{D} \quad \text{(b) } 6 = \frac{D}{L} \quad \text{(c) } 1 = \frac{6}{D} \quad \text{(d) } D = \frac{L}{6}$$

39. The safe *minimum* grade for most paved areas is _____ percent.
    (a) 1 (b) 1.5 (c) 2 (d) 3

40. The standard formula for determining volume of cut or fill is _____ times _____ times _____ .

41. Most soils will _____ after placement.
    (a) shrink (b) expand (c) remain the same

42. List five factors that can reduce the cost of grading.

43. What is the most popular kind of street for families to live on?

44. List five conditions when grading should be avoided or special care exercised.

45. List four methods to substitute for a mechanical grading solution.

46. Draw a sketch plan of a retaining wall showing how contour lines meet the wall.

47. Most western cities are laid out in a _____ road pattern.
    (a) radial (b) ring (c) grid (d) linear (e) radial–ring
48. Public roadways occupy approximately _____ percent of our urbanized land.
    (a) 25–35 (b) 10–15 (c) 15–25 (d) 35–45
49. Draw a diagram of a hammerhead cul-de-sac.
50. Draw a diagram of a street diverter.
51. Draw a diagram of a pedestrian safe-cross.

REQUIRED DRAFTING EQUIPMENT

This drafting equipment is necessary and useful for most courses in design. We do not recommend purchasing a complete outfit immediately, but rather obtain the minimum equipment and add as you need to.

One of each:

36-in. plastic-edged T-square
30° 10-in. plastic triangle
45° 10-in. plastic triangle
Mechanical drawing pencil
Pencil pointer (for above)
Metal erasing shield
Pink pearl eraser

Roll of ½-in. drafting tape
10-yard roll 36-in. clear print, 1000H
50-yard roll 24-in. wide buff or white
 flimsy tracing paper
Architectural scale
Engineering scale

Two of each:
2h, h, and f leads

Additional Equipment (desirable, but not necessary)
10-in. adjustable triangle
3- by 6-ft piece of drafting table linoleum
One No. 1 or 2 rapidograph pen
Circle template
Compass
Felt-tipped pens
Soft drawing pencils (No. 2)
Fishing tackle box for storage

ADDITIONAL READING

Reading material in landscape construction is scattered and broken into small and special categories. You will find additional references in each of these books, and should search out the information when the specific case demands it.

Charter, S. P. R. *Man on Earth,* Contact Editions, Sausalito, Calif., 1962.

Eckbo, Garrett. *Landscape for Living,* McGraw Hill, Inc., New York, 1950.

Farb, Peter, and Life Magazine. *Ecology; The Forest; The Sea; The Desert;* Time, Inc., New York, 1963.

Hyams, Edward. *Soil and Civilization,* Thaimes and Hundson, London, 1952.

Lynch, Kevin. *Site Planning,* 2nd ed., M.I.T. Press, Cambridge, Mass., 1972.

Parker, H., and J. MacGuire. *Simplified Site Engineering for Architects and Builders,* John Wiley & Sons, Inc., New York, 1954.

Peattie, Donald C. *The Flowering Earth,* Viking Press, New York, 1939.

Scott, J. S. *Dictionary of Civil Engineering,* Penguin Books, Baltimore, Md., 1965.

Simonds, John O. *Landscape Architecture,* McGraw Hill, Inc., New York, 1961.

Storer, John. *The Web of Life.* NAL, New York, 1972.

Straub, Hans. *A History of Civil Engineering,* M.I.T. Press, Cambridge, Mass., 1952.

INDEX